WHERE THE ROAD ENDS

ALSO BY BINKA LE BRETON

The Greatest Gift:
The Courageous Life and Martyrdom
of Sister Dorothy Stang

Trapped: Modern-day Slavery in the
Brazilian Amazon Rainforest

A Land to Die For

Voices from the Amazon

WHERE THE ROAD ENDS

A Home in the Brazilian Rainforest

A MEMOIR BY
BINKA LE BRETON

THOMAS DUNNE BOOKS
St. Martin's Press ⚞ New York

THOMAS DUNNE BOOKS.
An imprint of St. Martin's Press.

WHERE THE ROAD ENDS. Copyright © 2010 by Binka Le Breton. All
rights reserved. Printed in the United States of America. For information,
address St. Martin's Press, 175 Fifth Avenue, New York, N.Y. 10010.

www.thomasdunnebooks.com
www.stmartins.com

Book design by William Ruoto

LIBRARY OF CONGRESS CATALOGING-IN-PUBLICATION DATA

Le Breton, Binka.
    Where the road ends : a home in the Brazilian rainforest / Binka Le
Breton.—1st ed.
        p. cm.
    Includes bibliographical references and index.
    ISBN 978-0-312-57405-5 (alk. paper)
    1. Nature—Effect of human beings on—Amazon River
Region. 2. Rural development—Environmental aspects—Amazon
River Region. 3. Le Breton, Binka. 4. Le Breton, Robin.
5. Conservationists—Biography. 6. Amazon River Region—Social
conditions. 7. Amazon River Region—Economic conditions. I. Title.
    GF532.A4.L434 2010
    981.06'40922—dc22

                                                    2009047616

First Edition: May 2010

10 9 8 7 6 5 4 3 2 1

For Robin,
who dreamed of the Big Rock Candy Mountain
and found the Land of Milk and Honey in Brazil.
The road was long and rocky, but the view from the top
is glorious.

CONTENTS

ACKNOWLEDGMENTS

Thanks are due to a special group of people who are involved, in one way or another, in the Iracambi adventure. First to Gus and Juliet (and later to their families), who were, and are, unfailing in their support for their crazy parents. To our mothers, who smiled indulgently when we told them we were off to seek our fortunes in South America. To Jeannie, Jim, Martin, and Sarah, who launched us on our adventure and are always there for our returns. To Luiza, mentor, defender, and much-loved member of our extended family. To Rosana, who shared her passion for cattle, and Gabetto, who planted the first trees in the forest. To Linda, who helped shape the book, to Ed, who is the best author's agent ever, and to the staff at St. Martin's Press, who did such a wonderful job. And, of course, to all the characters who appear in the book and continue to enrich our lives.

It's a sparkling afternoon and after the morning rain everything smells fresh and green. Halfway up the hill and across the broad green valley I can see the house. It looks as if it's been there forever. As if it belongs there. The house that Robin built.

My horse is sweating after the slippery trail around the high forest, but he senses the homeward stretch and breaks into the smooth easy gait of the Tennessee walking horse—five thousand miles south of Tennessee. We clatter over the wooden bridge, through the gate, and onto the rutted road that leads to Iracambi. Albertinho's house has been freshly color-washed and the water is running strongly over the bridge into his maize field. The pasture is dotted with cows and horses on grassy islands as the river carves new channels, and the water lilies are flowering the palest purple. A graceful white heron takes wing and I know he has been fishing in the ponds, but somehow I can't bring myself to begrudge him his supper.

Turning up the hill, I pass the dairy with its humming machinery. Horses are tethered to the railings, two or three dogs are curled up asleep, the calves are skipping around on the grass, and six-year-old Romária, all curly hair and honey-colored skin, is frowning in concentration as she fills their feeding bottles. A small black puppy of indeterminate breed takes a run at the guinea hens, which flap away, emitting the most satisfying squawks.

The rutted stretch of road between the dairy and the house is so steep that even the youngest and fittest arrive panting. The bougainvillea is flowering riotously, hot pink and lilac. The house hides behind a wealth of greenery, the steps half overgrown with morning glory, scarlet and orange zinnias, deep blue hydrangeas, and wild pineapples. I tie my horse in the shade of a sixty-foot eucalyptus, slip off my boots on the back veranda, and walk into the kitchen, breathing in the familiar scents of coffee and woodsmoke. Marinha has left the place scrubbed and sparkling, with a large vase of flowers on the big old table and on the tiled counter some fresh bread covered with an embroidered cloth. The two Boxers bound out to greet me and the sound of a Mozart symphony alerts me to the fact that Robin is in the study.

The front door is propped open, beckoning me out onto the veranda to admire, once again, the long view over the mountains. It's a view that changes from hour to hour: from a smiling tropical landscape painted in infinite shades of green to massive granite peaks etched starkly against a sky so blue it hurts your eyes. Some days the mist streams over the mountains like water, curtains of rain sweep across the valley, thunder rolls around the peaks, and lightning stabs the sky. Sometimes in the evening we sit in the swing seat and watch the night steal softly in, waiting for the barn owls to swoop silently out from their home above the front door. On moonlit nights we can see each fold of the hills as clearly as if it were day, and watch the fireflies mimicking the stars wheeling overhead. As darkness falls, the chorus of night sounds starts up—frogs croaking, crickets chirping, a cow calling to her calf, the river running strongly down the valley, the screech of the owls, the songs of the night birds.

I turn back into the house, catching the piercingly sweet scent of jasmine that drifts in from the secret garden outside our bedroom window. I'm tired and hungry, and as the last bars of the Mozart symphony draw to a close, I head toward the study in search of Robin. It's good to be home.

WHERE THE ROAD ENDS

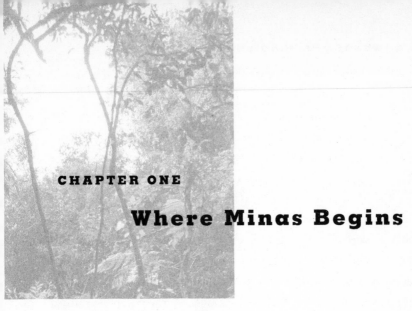

CHAPTER ONE

Where Minas Begins

Minas begins where the road ends.
—São Paulo saying

July 1989

It wasn't easy to find. Promised lands never are. Ours was a seven-hour drive from Rio de Janeiro on a twisty potholed road through exuberant jungle, past towering granite mountains toward an empty land that stretched into the blue distance. It was a major highway that ran from Buenos Aires on the distant windy pampas to the Amazon river in the north, winding up and down through patches of forest and steep grassy hillsides, past sleepy towns and broad muddy rivers, on and on into the mountains of Minas Gerais.

Five hours into the journey, past the town of Muriaé, we pulled off the asphalt and onto a steep rutted road that led sharply up into the mountains. The elderly Land Rover that had brought us thousands of miles groaned as it picked up speed. Swerving to avoid a horse-drawn cart on a particularly nasty bend, Robin pumped the brakes but the car refused to slow. "Shit!" he muttered as he shot around a blind corner. "The fucking brakes have gone. Just as well we're here, really. . . ."

Here? I thought to myself. That depends on where here is.

Since piling our stuff into the back of the car six months earlier in Washington, D.C., my husband and I had headed west and south to West Virginia, Tennessee, Arkansas, and Texas, and then turned south to Mexico and beyond, on a journey to a new life. It had been a time out of time—to leave behind our past and ready ourselves for what lay ahead. There had been lots of adventures. Hiking up a volcano in Guatemala, we had watched in awe as the mountainside suddenly split open like a ripe tomato, sending streams of molten lava pouring toward us. We'd been stranded for weeks in Costa Rica waiting for a spare engine part to arrive from Europe, and we'd watched, entranced, the magical green quetzal birds flying dream-like through cloud forests. We'd shivered as iron gates clanged shut behind us ("for your safety, señores") inside a filthy hotel in Panama City, we'd sunbathed on pink sandy beaches beside dark brown rivers in the empty spaces of the Grand Savanna in Venezuela, we'd dug the car out of bottomless mud in the northern Amazon, we'd been bitten to distraction by small *pium* flies and enormous man-eating mosquitoes, and we'd toasted the sunset with the local moonshine while floating down the Rio Negro on a barge after the road ran out.

But it hadn't been just another tourist trip. For us there would be no safe return to the family home, no more fighting the traffic en route to the office, no more comfortable evenings telling travelers' tales to our friends. No more weekends off. This was the beginning of the rest of our lives.

I guess you could call it a midlife crisis. When I stopped to think rationally, I knew it was madness. But to Robin it was the fulfillment of a lifelong ambition. Ever since he was a child living on a farm halfway up a mountain in Kenya, he had dreamed of getting his own patch of land and making something of it. "I've done enough parachuting in and out of other people's lives," he told me. "I want to stop talking and start doing."

For years he'd worked in international development, jetting from continent to continent helping hungry people feed themselves. Green from graduate school, he'd started working with an agency of the British government. At the job interview they asked where he played on the cricket field, whereas in an interview for a student visa to the United States he'd been asked if he'd ever been a communist.

Agricultural economists were a rare breed in the early seventies, and the Commonwealth Development Corporation decided to send him to an area of Ethiopia so remote that there was no written language. They hoped his wife was a "good trooper," and felt sure that household goods could be taken in by oxcart. When, for some reason, that idea fell through, they sent us to Jakarta, where the economy was in ruins and we never did have a car that ran properly. Robin worked with a colleague from the International Monetary Fund who recommended a move to Washington, but when it was time to leave Jakarta, Robin was offered a posting in Zaire. He spoke good French, he had tropical experience, and the call of Africa was strong. He bought a Range Rover, duty free, and made plans to drive it across the Sahara—until the coup d'état in Zaire, when he was told to stay in London. But he couldn't keep his car without paying duty, so he got a cheap flight to Washington and found a position with the World Bank. It was a grand way for us to see the world and raise our two kids, and they'd quickly become accustomed to moving from one language and one capital city to another. I once overheard our daughter Juliet, at age three, telling a friend, "My daddy goes round in taxis visiting governments."

While Robin had been visiting governments I had been playing concerts—classical music on whatever grand piano I could find. It didn't pay much but I loved it and did it well.

We'd moved from London to Nairobi, to Jakarta to Washington to New Delhi. But Robin never lost sight of his dream. Like recurring malaria it kept surfacing and shifting—in New Delhi it was a palace in Rajasthan, in Nairobi a game ranch in the desert, in Washington a cattle ranch in the Rockies. We'd done a spell in Brazil, too, and that was when things had finally come to a head. We'd educated our children, paid our mortgage, and found a country where it never snowed. Still in our forties, we had time and energy on our side. It was now or never.

Our new home was in the state of Minas Gerais in southeastern Brazil. Somewhat larger than France, extending from the borders of Rio de Janeiro all the way to Brasília on the high savanna, Minas was settled in the eighteenth century when the first gold strikes were made. Intrepid adventurers streamed across the mountains from Rio and São Paulo to make and lose their fortunes, leaving a legacy of elegant little colonial towns adorned with baroque churches richly ornamented with gold leaf. Minas became an important state, and remains so to this day, long after the gold has been mined out.

A few years earlier, when we'd been living in the decaying port city of Recife, we'd been attracted by the sound of Minas. Forest; mountains; tough, feisty people; hearty farmhouse cooking. Minas seemed a good place to chase a dream.

We packed our teenage kids into the car and drove south for three days to see for ourselves. It was a ten-hour drive from the state border to Muriaé, the town where we'd chosen to set up our base camp. (It took me several tries before I learned to pronounce it properly: Moo-ree-aye-eh, with an accent on the last vowel.) We stayed in an old farmhouse belonging to a local landowner whose name, improbably, was Lenin. He received us with traditional Minas hospitality, fed us enormous meals, and introduced us to the county farm agent who took us up into the backcountry to look at some properties. The first was hidden deep in the forest, where there wasn't an acre of flat land, and the caretaker looked like a *bandido*. The second was an attractive little coffee farm, not far from Muriaé. The third was high in the mountains, isolated, wild, and absolutely magnificent.

Back at Lenin's we held a family conference. Seventeen-year-old Juliet was already thinking horses. Always the practical one of the family, she was in favor of the coffee farm. "It's convenient for the town and it doesn't require a huge investment," she announced. "The house is fine and it's got some good pasture. Plus you know all about growing coffee, Dad, at least that's what you've always told us." Her elder brother disagreed strongly. "I think we should go for the one in the mountains," he declared. "I mean, if you have to choose between a nice little coffee farm and a piece of land that is magnificent, romantic, and totally impractical, why hesitate?"

"For crying out loud, Gus," said Juliet. "It may be magnificent and romantic and all that. But just think a minute. There's nothing there. It's been abandoned. How can anyone possibly make a living out of it?"

"That's my point," said Gus. "There's nothing there. Mountains, forest, rivers, but no working farm. So Dad can set it up just the way he wants. The stuff of dreams."

We held a secret ballot, and it came out tied. We sat up half the night arguing and then we took a second vote. This time the decision was unanimous: in favor of the isolated farm in the mountains.

The price was right; we could trade it for our family house in Washington and still have something left over. The farm came with resident cowboy Albertinho, who had been squatting there for several years in the absence of the owner, and scraped a living by planting and hunting, occasionally getting a day's work at coffee harvest. He suggested we buy a few cows and offered to look after them. We closed the deal, told him we'd be back within the year, and flew to the States to spend our last year in Washington, settle Juliet into college, and say goodbye to our past.

For six months Robin and I had been living outside time— traveling between two worlds as we made our way south. Now, suddenly, our journey was almost over, and our destination lay ahead of us in the misty mountains. We'd named it Iracambi, the Tupi Indian name for Land of Milk and Honey. Like Muriaé, the accent was on the last vowel, Ee-ra-cam-bee, as Robin patiently explained to our friends who couldn't get their tongues around the name.

The narrow track headed abruptly off up a rocky pass. Bone-shakingly corrugated and dusty in the dry season, at the first drop of rain it would become a morass of thick red mud. An occasional ancient truck ground its way up the mountain, coating us in fine red dust, but most of the traffic was horse powered—with the exception of the occasional oxcart, groaning and swaying on solid wooden wheels. Twisting and turning crazily, the road to Iracambi ran between steep slopes planted with coffee, past small, square homesteads painted white and blue, and through patches of dark forest clinging to the hilltops and eroded, overgrazed cattle pastures until it came finally to the next village: two cobbled streets of low buildings, an impressive church on a hill, a bar, and a bus stop. The village was called Rosário da Limeira, which means the Rosary of Lime Trees, but you wouldn't have known it since there were no signs anywhere, and no lime trees, either. After the village the road wandered off toward the peaks, dropping finally down into a broad green valley flanked by forested mountains. A lazy brown river meandered through the grassy fields where a small herd of cattle were grazing placidly. This was our new home, and suddenly our new life was beginning. Caught between excitement and panic, I gave Robin a small smile, and he squeezed my hand.

Around the next bend the road was barred by a sagging wooden gate, and there, sitting on a gray horse, was a bandy-legged man with a drooping mustache and a battered straw hat. It was Albertinho.

He opened the gate with a flourish. "I heard a car," he said matter-of-factly, "So I figured it must be you." Wheeling on his horse, he galloped ahead of us, past a patch of sugarcane and a few straggling coffee bushes to the dilapidated mud house that he shared with his wife, Maria, their three children, a skinny dog, a caged canary, and a small spotted pig.

Albertinho looked about thirty. Like most of the inhabitants of these mountains he was of mixed blood: European, African, and South American Indian. Short and slender but tough as a whiplash, he habitually wore a fierce expression—occasionally lightened by a smile of rare sweetness. Maria was several years younger. Dressed in a faded T-shirt, knee-length skirt, and flip-flops, she had pulled her wavy brown hair into a knot and was standing at the window, cradling a baby. She leaned out, smiling a welcome, and I noticed that her front teeth were missing. Albertinho muttered something, and Maria disappeared into the house, returning with a flask of strong sweet coffee. We climbed stiffly out of the car and stood in the sunshine while two small girls gazed at us from a safe distance, and the skinny dog scratched itself vigorously on the front step. I took a grateful sip of the coffee. It was hot and black and tasted wonderful.

Everything looked clean and well cared for. Flowering plants in rusting cans were hanging on the veranda, and an old-fashioned rose bush was planted outside the front door. The family's washing was draped over a barbed-wire fence. The pig was rooting in a mud wallow, a couple of scrawny hens were perched in a basket in an orange tree, and Albertinho's gray horse was tied to a hitching post outside the front door.

"*Obrigado,*" said Robin, accepting another glass of coffee from Maria. "Thank you." He turned to Albertinho. "I think, Albertinho, we'd better get over to the house and get settled in before dark."

"*Ah eh,*" said Albertinho. "That's right."

Albertinho and Maria led the way across a decrepit wooden bridge, alongside a swamp, and up a small overgrown path to the farmhouse. Like all the local houses it was tucked into a fold in the hills, near a spring and half hidden from view. Crouched in an abandoned cane field, it had been empty for several months and looked forlorn. It needed chickens and a pig and a collection of small children playing outside; it needed washing on the line and a horse tethered to the fence.

Its cracking plaster was covered with several layers of white-wash, tinted blue, but the paint on its wooden shutters had long since baked off in the sun. The house was built up on solid stone supports to keep the termites at bay, and four concrete steps led to the front door, held shut by a piece of wire twisted around a nail. Maria unwound the wire and pushed the door open. We trooped in behind her, hesitating a minute to let our eyes get accustomed to the gloom, and then blinking as she unlatched the wooden shutters to let the light stream in. The house was bare and dusty, but it felt friendly enough, and the floorboards were solid. Still, the rafters were festooned with spiderwebs, there were no ceilings, and the underside of the roof tiles was encrusted with years' worth of accumulated soot from the wood fire. Maria saw my face and flashed me a brief smile. "Don't worry," she said, "I'll have it cleaned up in no time."

"That's right," added Albertinho, stepping through the doorway. "Maria will sweep the place out, and you don't need to trouble yourself about the vampire bats. I've already cleared them out."

"Thank you, Albertinho," I said, repressing a shudder, and braced myself to inspect the rest of the house.

It didn't take long. There wasn't much to see—six little rooms, and the smoke-stained kitchen, painted in faded pink. The kitchen door led to a small veranda with a large concrete sink into which water flowed directly from the spring, through an ancient hose. A precarious mud structure in the back had once been used as a grain store and chicken house, and outside the front door there was a gnarled gourd tree half choked with flowering vines. I walked into the late afternoon sunshine to join Robin outside.

Iridescent hummingbirds flashed past the scarlet hibiscus flowers, and a flock of green parrots flew overhead, chattering noisily. The banana leaves rustled in the breeze, and I jumped as a cricket started up right beside me, sounding exactly like a ringing phone. I leaned against the tree and studied the house. The paintwork was faded, and some of the roof tiles were cracked, but it was solidly built, and it would do fine for now. Robin already had great plans for the house he would build, although he'd warned me it might be several months before we could get started. "Need to lick the farm into shape first," he told me. "Shouldn't take long." I closed my eyes and thought back to our house in Washington, with its antique furniture, polished floors, modern kitchen, and shady backyard, and I laughed aloud.

Maria thrust the baby into the arms of one of her very small daughters, cut a bunch of twigs, tied them together with grass, and made a broom. Soon clouds of dust were flying around the house and cinders were rattling onto the wooden floor. Maria's little girl gazed at us shyly, cradling the baby, and the skinny dog settled itself on the front doorstep with a proprietorial air.

"Better start unloading," said Robin briskly, diving into the back of the car. "We'll just get out the bedding for now, and something for supper." With the ease of long practice he unearthed hammocks and sleeping bags, a small gas cooker, and the box of food that we'd picked up in Muriaé. An accomplished traveler, Robin was famous for living for weeks out of the contents of his overnight bag, from which he would produce all sorts of useful stuff: 100 watt light bulbs, mosquito coils, Swiss Army knife, soap for fixing a leaky fuel tank, chewing gum for a leaking radiator, and a set of liar's dice to pass the time at the airport.

We'd met on a boat traveling to Africa, and Robin had held me spellbound with stories of lions and elephants. In those days he wore shorts, knee-length stockings, and ankle boots. Later he switched to long pants, but he stuck to his safari boots through thick and thin, and only with the greatest reluctance and on very special occasions—such as his own wedding—does he wear polished black shoes. Which may explain why he never got promoted to the highest echelons of the World Bank. Around five foot ten, he is a shade taller than me, with a slender build, a generous mouth, unruly brown hair, brown eyes, and such a deep tan that when they saw the wedding photographs several of my English friends thought ours was a mixed-race marriage.

Robin rearranged the contents of the car, leaving tent, spare wheels, tool case, cans of fuel, boxes of books and maps, and our backpacks until needed. Albertinho cheerfully heaved the bedding bags through the front door and put them on the newly swept floor, I stacked the food in the kitchen, and Robin strung the hammocks in the front bedroom.

"Well, if that's all, I'll be going on home," said Maria, propping the broom outside the back door as she took possession of the baby.

"*Tchau, Maria, obrigada*. Bye Maria, thanks." I smiled as she set off down the path, trailed by her two small daughters and the dog. Albertinho delved into the pocket of his ancient jacket, extracted a corn-leaf cigarette, lit it, dragged deeply, and exhaled with great satisfaction. Muttering good night, he walked jauntily off toward his house.

The sun was sinking behind the mountain, the temperature was dropping fast, and it was time to find some warm clothes. Robin rummaged for the dregs of our bottle of Scotch, and we sat together on the front steps watching the light fade as the mist crept up the valley. At three thousand feet above sea level there was a chill in the air that quickly drove us into the house. We lit a candle, set up the cooker, opened a can of soup, and heated it up. A nasty little wind was whipping up through the floorboards, and the flickering candlelight did little to disperse the shadows. I thought of vampire bats and shivered. With no friendly campfire, no book to read together, and no Scotch left in the bottle, there was little to do but get ready for bed. We pulled on our long johns, climbed into our hammocks, and settled ourselves for the night. It wasn't yet nine o'clock, but we were tired and our down sleeping bags were the warmest option available. Robin insisted on opening the wooden shutters, despite the cold. "It won't be any warmer with the shutters closed," he pointed out. "It's not as if there are any ceilings. Besides, I want to see the stars." I looked up at the roof tiles, noticing a chink of light through the cracks as I wriggled down into the comfort of my sleeping bag. My feelings were decidedly mixed.

Sometime before dawn a sudden rainstorm awoke me from deep sleep, and as I struggled back to consciousness I realized that water was dripping steadily through the roof onto my feet. Shifting my position, I huddled down into my sleeping bag, but I couldn't get back to sleep. Dark night thoughts assailed me on every side. Now what? whispered my demons. What in the world are you doing here, Binka? How are you going to make out, stuck at the end of a long muddy road with no electricity, no plumbing, no telephone, and nobody to talk to? You know nothing about farming. It wasn't even your idea. Remember those friends who insisted that you were too old and too soft to become farmers? Didn't it ever occur to you that they might be right? Tossing restlessly, I suddenly felt a sharp pang of yearning for bluebell woods and London buses, for crisp winter days in Virginia and classical music on the radio. I glanced across at Robin. He was lying on his back, snoring gently.

But joy comes in the morning. The early sun was lighting the dense green forest on the hillside when I awoke again. The house was rich with the smell of coffee. Robin swept through the door, mug in hand. Clad in a faded green shirt and pants with his favorite safari boots, he looked like a farmer already. "Come on, lazybones," he said, shaking my hammock vigorously. "Time to go exploring."

The farm wasn't large by Brazilian standards, where some properties are larger than small countries in Europe; it was supposed to be somewhere around five hundred acres, though it hadn't ever been properly surveyed. The land didn't currently produce anything, but Robin was convinced it had potential, largely because of its abundant water. In front of the blue house lay a broad green valley, where the river made a series of large and lazy loops. A second river ran down from behind Albertinho's house, and a small stream flowed into the valley from a secret little forest to the west of the blue house. A narrow track ran steeply up the hill toward the mountains, and a sagging wire fence marked the boundary with the adjoining piece of land, which belonged to an absentee landowner and was lying unused. There were three houses on the property: ours, Albertinho's, and a little empty house across the valley known as the Casa Sozinha—the Lonely House. Our house was built from soft local brick, the others were made of mud and wattle, and all three were roofed with handmade curved tiles.

We made our way down the overgrown path and turned left up the steep hill into the forest. Last night's rain had left a layer of mud on the road, and the vegetation smelled fresh and green. I could hear the sound of a waterfall somewhere in the valley, and ahead of us the Graminha peak was silhouetted sharply against the blue sky.

"See up there?" Robin pointed to the granite rock face. "There used to be a logging settlement halfway up the mountain, but now it's all gone back to jungle, and Albertinho says there are wild cats in the forest. I think he must be talking about ocelots."

As we were to discover, there were four varieties of wild cats in our forests—all nocturnal and not easy to spot. Pumas and jaguars lived up on the mountaintops, but the smaller spotted ocelots and even smaller margays would sometimes come down from the forest and steal chickens. As far as Albertinho was concerned they were all wild cats.

I pictured myself sitting silent on a rock, watching a sleek spotted ocelot with her cubs. A flock of toucans landed in the bananas and started feasting. Monkeys were chattering in the forest, and brilliant blue butterflies drifted through the undergrowth. "Yes, Albertinho," I would say casually next time we met, "I saw the ocelot again today."

We paused at the top of the hill to admire the green valley spread beneath. The river was running strong and brown and the water was over the rickety wooden bridge by Albertinho's house. We looked out over our kingdom: the black and white cattle, the wooden corral, our blue home half hidden among the banana trees, the little empty house beside the river. Down in the valley we could see Albertinho emerging from his house and heading toward us. After a few minutes he noticed us and waved. We waved back and headed down the hill.

W e found him standing on the muddy bridge, puffing serenely on a cigarette.

"That was a good rain last night," he informed us.

"Does the water often go over the bridge like this?" Robin asked.

"*Ah eh.*" Albertinho nodded. "That's what happens when it rains. Floods over the bridge, floods right down the valley. When the river rises there's days we can't get out. The grader hasn't been near the place in two years. They have to bring it all the way from Muriaé, see? And when the roads are bad it can't get here."

We digested this information in silence.

"This road can be underwater for days on end," Albertinho continued, "and every once in a while the bridge gets washed away. In fact," he kicked the timbers with the toe of his boot, "if you ask me, it won't last much longer. Half the planks are rotten."

"We'll soon get that fixed," said Robin.

"Well," Albertinho frowned, "like I said, it's supposed to be the county that does it." He paused. "Except they don't."

If you lived in our mountains, we later learned, you became accustomed to wading through the mud. The horses were shod with special nonskid horseshoes, but most people went barefoot. No sense in ruining a good pair of boots.

B ehind Albertinho's house the farm's previous owner had constructed a small but serviceable hydroelectric plant that operated with a beat-up generator salvaged from a Volkswagen Beetle. Albertinho took us on a tour.

We scrambled up the hillside to the water channel. Albertinho raised the water gate and the water gushed into the down pipe that led to the generator house. I could hear the creaking of the water-wheel as it began to turn, and the steady splash of the water. "I've kept this system running for six years now," he informed us, lead-ing the way down to the little whitewashed building that housed the machinery. "That's the generator, and here's where we grind the corn and sharpen our knives. See that lightbulb? That shows me how much power I've got, so that I can control the water intake." He grinned. "It's nice to have electric light. Most people around here don't have it."

We don't have it, either, I thought to myself. But that could be fixed. Besides, we had been camping in the wild for so long that we'd become accustomed to candles.

As we wandered back to the house for lunch, I looked at our property—for the first time—as a place where we would have to make a living. The farm was spectacularly beautiful. It had good stands of forest, and it was well watered. But it wasn't really good farming country. There was hardly an acre of flat land anywhere, and forest soils were notoriously poor. If we were going to make it work, we'd need to be creative.

Almost on the crest of a range of mountains that ran from the state of São Paulo in the south to Bahia in the north, ours was an area that had remained inaccessible for years, had been opened up after World War II for logging, and was gradually settled by sub-sistence farmers. They grew rice, beans, corn, manioc, and peanuts and had neatly fenced small gardens for vegetables and medicinal herbs. They knew which plants to use in case of snakebite and in-fection, and the women knew how to ease a difficult birth and prescribe charms to attract unwilling lovers.

Our new neighbors were a hardworking people. Men rose be-fore dawn, milked their cows, saddled their horses, and went off to the fields, leaving the women to embark on the never-ending round of caring for the children, collecting and chopping firewood, sorting the beans, pounding the rice in large wooden mortars, roasting and grinding the coffee, and preparing the lunch. Only when this was done would they turn their attention to sweeping the house, scouring the cooking pots, washing the clothes, and tending the chickens, pigs, and vegetables. The cash crop was coffee, and when prices were good they made a little money. There had been one golden era in the fifties and sixties when some of them had been able to enlarge their houses and replace dirt floors with cement. One or two had even installed generators. But prices had fallen, inflation was rampant, and people were barely hanging on. It was an area of bare-bones subsistence farming, and we were coming here to make something out of the land. I couldn't decide whether we were being hopelessly naive or just plain crazy.

Before we set up the farm, we needed to fix up the house. I dug out the last of our pickled onions, cut thick slabs of bread and cheese, and sat down with Robin to review the situation. The first thing to tackle was the plumbing. The only running water was in the concrete sink on the back veranda, and we had no functioning toilet. There was a battered privy out back, but it didn't look inviting, and it didn't even look safe. Most of the flooring was rotting, and I was convinced there were snakes in the long grass. There was, however, an alternative—a small cubicle that someone had cobbled together just off the back veranda. Albertinho referred to it as the bathroom, but it contained nothing beyond a couple of sawn-off water pipes and a lavatory. Robin figured he could make it work with some hose and a bucket. "Best not to think about the drains," he told me. "Not yet, anyway. I'm pretty sure they go straight into the river."

Another priority was the kitchen. Years of cooking on a smoky woodstove had left a thick, sticky layer of soot on the rafters and on the underside of the tiles, and despite Maria's best efforts the previous night's rain had dislodged a large quantity of black cinders. And, as we had already learned, the roof was far from watertight. If we could keep the rain out, fix up the plumbing, resuscitate the wood-burning stove, and install the electricity, we'd be off to a good start. There'd be plenty of time to worry about refinements like hot water and a telephone. And furniture, of course.

Before leaving Recife for our final year in Washington we had bought some of the local furniture and had taken up a friend's kind offer to store it on his farm. But it proved to be a false economy. The furniture was cheaply made, and after we'd found a truck to bring it down, we discovered that most of it had been severely damaged by termites and was crumbling to nothing. The few pieces that we loved, including my grand piano, were still in Washington awaiting shipment, and we could only hope that they hadn't suffered a similar fate.

B y the way, I forgot to tell you we're invited to a party," Robin remarked a couple of days later.

"Can't be," I said, "we don't know anyone."

"Don't be ridiculous, of course we do. It's Albertinho's eldest daughter. She's going to be six and they've invited us round. At seven o'clock. Do you think you can find a little something to take her?"

"It's not as if there's a drugstore on the corner," I told him irritably. "But I do have some balloons, as it happens. Never travel without them, you know that."

As we set off through the black night, the air was full of unfamiliar sounds: the croaking of frogs, the chirping of crickets, a nightjar hooting, a cow mooing, the splashing sound of the river. I had wondered how we were going to sustain the conversation, since Albertinho wasn't one for idle chitchat, and Maria's Portuguese was so heavily accented that I had the greatest difficulty in understanding her. She couldn't understand me, either, and sometimes resorted to shouting—which made things even worse.

But I needn't have worried. Albertinho's small kitchen was cozy with its brightly burning fire, and smelled of wood smoke and coffee. Maria was standing by the woodstove with the baby in her arms, stirring a bubbling pot of sweet rice. Grandfather Olavo was comfortably ensconced on a wooden bench in the warmest corner of the room, and the two little girls, scrubbed and silent, were sitting beside him swinging their legs. A single 40-watt bulb, dangling from a sooty strand of barbed wire, produced an erratic light. Albertinho's ancient muzzle loader was propped up in the rafters, next to a fine Western saddle suspended from a length of rawhide. A birdcage covered by a dishtowel contained a yellow canary. Albertinho was sitting on a sack of rice playing Brazilian country music on his accordion.

I tossed a balloon to Robin several times so that everyone could see how to play, and then sent it over to Sandra, the birthday girl. She gave me a shy smile and tossed it back, and soon everyone had joined in, including Grandfather Olavo, who was enjoying himself enormously, grinning broadly to reveal a fine set of gold teeth. Sandra accidentally popped one of the balloons. As her face crumpled, I jumped up, ran around the corner, pulled another one from my pocket, blew it up, and presented it to her. She flashed a timid smile and lobbed it to her grandfather.

Maria served us bowls of sweet milky rice, explaining that it was a special birthday treat, and Sandra brought us glasses of black coffee heavy with molasses. Albertinho played a selection of tunes while Grandfather Olavo tapped his foot in time with the music. At the end of the evening he took his balloon, very carefully let all the air out of it, and put it in his pocket. It looked like a used condom.

Robin and I said our good-byes and walked cautiously out into the inky night, waiting for our eyes to adjust to the darkness. The air was soft and warm, and smelled of orange blossom. An owl swooped overhead, and the moon slipped out from behind a cloud, lighting our path. We crossed the bridge, admired the fireflies flitting over the swamp, and turned up the grassy path that led to the blue house—our new home in the land of milk and honey.

CHAPTER TWO

Home on the Range

"Today," announced Robin a few days later, as we sat side by side on the front steps drinking our coffee in the sunshine, "we're going to brand the cows. And we're going to fit them with ear tags."

"Sounds good." I nodded. "Tell me more."

"Nothing to it; you'll see for yourself. Albertinho will give us a hand."

"He's something else, that one." I drained my coffee mug. "Have you seen him catch his horse? Runs up behind it, vaults on its back, and gallops off, without a rope or a bridle or anything."

"Oh yes, he's quite the cowboy," said Robin. "But he shouldn't go chasing after the cows at top speed like that. Cows don't like it. It upsets them."

It was a glorious morning, the mist was rising from the fields, and the spiderwebs on the fence were beaded with dew. We walked down the overgrown path, past the swamp, and through the gate into the big pasture, arriving just in time to see Albertinho herding the cows at full gallop. They streamed into the corral in a cloud of dust, and he slammed the gate behind them.

Robin raised an eyebrow expressively but said nothing. Albertinho jumped off his horse, tied it to the corral fence, squatted down, and made a little fire to heat the branding iron, while Robin sorted out the ear tags—yellow for the in-calf cows and white for the heifers.

"Bom dia," said a voice behind us. "Good morning." I started in surprise, and turned to see a wiry middle-aged man with a toothbrush mustache and an ancient straw hat seated on a white mule with a carefully knotted tail. It was our neighbor Jair, who lived in the neatly painted house past our main gate. Together with his three sons he ran a small farm where they planted coffee, cane, corn, and beans. Every morning he loaded up his pony cart with the milk from his thirteen cows and set off for the village, dispensing milk and gossip in equal proportions to his customers along the way. His daily round afforded him the perfect opportunity to gather and exchange the latest news, providing a valuable public service to complement the birth, marriage, and death announcements on the local radio. Not only did Jair know everything about everybody, he knew the price of everything, could figure out the toughest problem, and was never fazed. Many smallholders in our mountains had been driven off their land by the sheer difficulty of making a living from these unforgiving soils, but Jair was canny and resilient enough to hang on.

Good morning, Jair," said Robin. "How are you doing?"

"Not so bad," said Jair carefully. "How about yourself?"

"Just taking a look at the cattle. Branding, ear tagging, giving them a dose of tick medicine. Routine stuff."

Jair nodded. "It's a bad year for ticks. Don't remember when it was so bad. But it'll be better when the moon changes." He dismounted briskly, tied his mule to the railings, and pounced on the ear-tag applicator. "Ear tags?" he inquired. "What do you want those for?"

"For our records," explained Robin, "so we can tell which cow is which."

"I never have any trouble telling my cows apart." Jair looked at him sideways. "But then I was born to it, wasn't I?"

Robin smiled.

"Well," Jair continued, "now that I'm here I might as well give you a hand. Show you how it's done."

"Thanks very much." Robin winked at me. "Albertinho, you drive the cows into the crush, I'll put in the ear tags, and maybe you could do the branding, Jair?"

Jair nodded.

"Fine. Binka, you're in charge of the tick medicine—it's a measured dose. Pour it on the shoulder and back along the spine for about six inches. Make sure you stand on the railings and work from the top. Never ever put your hand between the railings or you could break your arm."

"Okay." I was on full alert.

Albertinho climbed into the corral and herded the nearest cow into the crush. She was a pretty little Jersey cross, and Robin had immediately christened her Buttercup. Jair expertly pinned her into place by slipping a stout plank behind her, and Albertinho seized her horns, holding her steady. "Okay, Binka," Robin told me. "All set?"

I shinned up onto the second rail, leaned over Buttercup, who was stamping restlessly, and poured a trickle of medicine along her backbone.

"That's it," said Robin. "Now stand clear."

Buttercup started violently as Robin snapped the applicator

into her ear, throwing her head up so hard that Albertinho lost his footing. She catapulted herself violently backward just as Jair whipped the red-hot iron out of the fire and stamped her flank with a perfect brand.

"Good work." Robin gave a big grin. "One down and twenty-five to go."

An hour later it was all done. Amid a smell of burning hair and dust Albertinho herded the cows back into the field while Jair climbed onto his mule and trotted off home.

"I feel like a real cowpuncher," I said happily to Robin. "Let's go find something to eat."

Later that day Albertinho dropped by. Robin was chopping wood and I was scrubbing my jeans in the concrete sink. Albertinho watched us for a moment, then leaned against the wall and took out a corn-leaf cigarette.

"You know something," he began, "now that the cattle have got ear tags, they won't be so easy to steal." He struck a match, lit up, and inhaled deeply. "You can always alter a brand mark but you can't hide a hole in the ear."

"Hmm," said Robin. "That's right."

"*Ah eh.*" Albertinho nodded and took a deep drag on his cigarette.

There was a companionable silence.

"It was kind of Jair to help," Robin commented, splitting a log cleanly down the middle.

"Wanted to see what was going on," muttered Albertinho. "Can't stand to miss out on anything, that man."

"I bet he doesn't miss much!" I laughed, scrubbing vigorously. "Not with all the gossip he picks up on his milk round. Keeps a little store, too, doesn't he?"

"Not what you'd call a proper store," Albertinho sniffed. "Cooking oil, soap, candles, tobacco, the odd bottle of liquor, that sort of thing. Charges a lot, so people don't buy from him if they can possibly avoid it. And he won't give credit, the tightfisted old bastard."

Scarcely had Albertinho wandered off down the track when I distinctly heard the sound of a car. "Hey, Robin, there's a car coming."

"Can't be. There aren't any cars round here. Except for Jair's. Bought it a few years ago, but apparently he never learned to drive."

"Maybe it's one of his sons driving."

"Oh no, that car never gets used. Jair doesn't like to spend good money on fuel, so Albertinho says."

"Well, it must be someone," I remarked as the distinctive *putt putt* of a Volkswagen Beetle grew steadily louder. We put down our tools and walked to the front of the house, just in time to see an elderly yellow vehicle nosing its way up the path and coming to a halt in the shade of the gourd tree. It was piloted by a beefy man in a straw hat, and perched next to him on the front seat was Jair. There was another figure wedged in the back, but I couldn't make out who it was.

"*Boa tarde,*" said Jair, jumping out of the car. "Good afternoon. I've brought you a bottle of milk." He held out a brown glass bottle with a corncob stopper.

"How very kind." I smiled at him. "Thank you."

I stowed the bottle inside the house and when I turned back I saw that Jair's wife had emerged from the car. Small, dark-haired, she was possessed of insatiable curiosity about everything, and reminded me of a mouse with a whiffly nose. Her name was Cassilda, but it should have been Cassandra, as we were soon to discover. If ever anyone's glass was half empty, it was Cassilda's. If the sun was shining, it was too hot; if it wasn't, it was too cold. It was either so wet that everything mildewed or so dry that all her plants died. She worked her fingers to the bone for her family but nobody appreciated her, and she was a martyr to her migraines. Giving me a perfunctory nod, she set off to inspect the premises.

In the meantime the driver was slowly extricating himself from the car. He mopped his brow, which was an alarming shade of red, and ambled over, extending a large, hamlike hand.

"Good afternoon," he said, breathing heavily. "My name is João Larino."

"Boa tarde," I answered formally.

Portuguese is a difficult language, and even educated Brazilians don't always speak it properly. But I was an accomplished linguist and prided myself on my grasp of the language. When I'd first arrived in Brazil five years earlier, one of my friends had told me my Portuguese was *"muito esquisito."* Accustomed to Spanish, I took it as a compliment; I'd thought it was good, if not exactly exquisite. It was only later, by chance, that I heard the word *"esquisito"* in a different context and looked it up. It meant weird.

Somewhat chastened, I plunged back into the study of Portuguese, and by the time we left Recife I could hold my own in the highest literary circles. But not at Iracambi. I soon discovered that if I wanted to be understood I had better speak slowly, hold back on the subjunctives, and simplify my vocabulary. Even so, I wasn't always understood. Our neighbors spoke with heavy accents, often swallowed the final syllable of their words, and introduced us to several rustic expressions that later made us the butt of many a joke among our more educated friends.

"I'm Binka."

He looked at me doubtfully and I hastily corrected myself. "Bianca, I mean." Nobody could ever get my name, so they called me Bianca after a popular character in a soap opera.

There was a pause.

"I came about the cow," said João Red Face.

Which cow? I wondered.

João turned to Robin. This was man talk. "Jair told me you were looking for a good cow. So I thought maybe you'd like to buy mine. She's a beauty. Gives a lot of milk."

João's cow was the first of many to be offered to us by our neighbors. Any time they needed a bit of cash they would come around proposing to sell us, at great personal sacrifice, their very best cow, their pride and joy and the mother of all milkers. With bland smiles they demanded outrageous prices for cows that proved to be ancient and bony, sickly, barren, lame, blind, minus one or more teats, or just plain hard to handle.

"How kind, Senhor João," said Robin. "We're not looking for any cows right now. But we'll certainly bear it in mind."

João sighed and lowered himself onto the rickety bench under the tree.

Jair was examining the dusty Land Rover. "Never seen a car like this before," he remarked. "Did you get it in São Paulo?"

"No," said Robin. "We got it in London."

Jair was not impressed. He'd never heard of London. "Hmm," he continued, "must have cost a lot."

Cassilda emerged from her rapid tour of the house. "I've known this house for years," she informed us. "This farm used to belong to my uncle. A nice place it was then, a proper farm. Used to carry six hundred head of cattle."

"What happened?" I asked, looking up at the hillside with its exuberant growth of weeds.

"He sold up and left. Went north to Bahia. Said it was better cattle country up there." She settled down on the bench and turned her attention to Robin. "You'll be installing the electricity, I take it?"

"Oh yes," he answered. "Just as soon as we've got the wiring."

"Wonderful thing, the electricity," she continued. "It was my uncle who installed it on this farm. I always say, once you've got it you can't imagine how you ever did without it."

Robin nodded.

"In fact," she remarked, "we're thinking of getting a television. You'll be getting one yourselves, maybe?"

"Oh, I don't think so."

"You really should have one," said Cassilda. "Then you can watch the soap operas." I could see Robin flinch.

"Got a gas cooker, I see," Cassilda persisted.

"That's right," I affirmed.

"I never liked gas," she announced.

"Very expensive," Jair chimed in.

"Everything's expensive these days," sniffed Cassilda. "Just look at the price of land."

"Yes, well, you paid a lot for this farm, didn't you?" Jair looked at us slyly. "And the whole place gone to rack and ruin."

"Used to be a nice little place," said Cassilda defensively. "In my uncle's day." She turned to Robin. "You oughtn't to have left that Albertinho in charge. He's a funny one. Runs off and hides in the forest sometimes. It's his Indian blood."

Hmm," said Albertinho later. "That Cassilda. Always on about her uncle. I could tell you a thing or two about him."

I looked up inquiringly, but he refused to be drawn out.

"As for João," he added darkly. "He's all right most of the time. But he goes very odd when the moon is full."

Later that evening the conversation returned to the question of plumbing. "We need to get a showerhead," said Robin.

"We need to get a hot shower," I retorted.

"I entirely agree. A hot shower would be wonderful. Especially on these cold evenings. But first we'll have to connect up the electricity. And for that we need, let me see, wire, poles, fittings, plugs, and switches."

"Does that mean a trip to town? I don't suppose you can get that sort of stuff in Limeira."

"That's where you're wrong," Robin informed me. "Albertinho was telling me there's a shop in Limeira that sells everything."

"What do you suppose he means by 'everything'?"

"There's only one way to find out," said Robin. "We'll go there tomorrow."

M y expectations of Rosário da Limeira were based on the novels of Jorge Amado, with their colorful characters ranging from white-haired patriarchs in linen suits to ragged gunmen loyal unto death, bright-eyed *mulatas* with swinging hips, stout black matrons selling coconut candy, dashing horsemen in leather hats, mustachioed Lebanese traders, heavy-drinking *bandidos,* and perhaps the occasional rabid dog to add a spice of danger.

Five miles away along rutted mountain roads, the village boasted a well kept square where horses were tethered in the shade and old men sat on wooden benches watching the world go by. A miscellaneous collection of little stores sold rice, beans, coils of tarry tobacco, enamel plates, plastic buckets, sticky blocks of brown sugar, notebooks, thread, bars of virulently colored orange and green soap, hats, spurs, girths, horseshoes, and patent remedies. A two-story building housed a butcher's and above it the meeting place for the Assembly of God. A dusty *farmácia* stocked medicines that were long past their sell-by date and exorbitantly expensive. Farther down the street, the bakery sold hard white rolls, and just opposite was a gloomy warehouse full of ancient machinery belonging to Armir Toko, the

Coffee Baron. He was a rich man, but you wouldn't have thought it to look at him. Small and wizened, he wore thick glasses and drove a battered VW Beetle, the only car that stood up to the rutted dirt roads of the backcountry.

Tucked away in backyards were small sawmills, rice-hulling machines, a blacksmith, and a carpenter's shop. The square was dominated by Armir's house—a proper city house that boasted iron railings, glass windows, and a balcony. Three doors to the right was the farmers' store, belonging to João Bosco, a skinny young man with a sweet smile and a severe squint. His shop was a treasure trove of rope, wire, sacks of lime, chain, yokes for oxen, saddles and halters, stirrups, harnesses, seeds, fertilizer, and veterinary medicines. He even carried basic electrical supplies. Just across the road was the post office, open twice a day when the bus arrived. Law and order were maintained by the fat policeman, who was sometimes to be found in his dank office tapping away lethargically on a battered typewriter. There was a public telephone in the bar, but it didn't work very well. There were thirty subscribers in Rosário da Limeira, and only one telephone line. To call out you had to raise the operator in Juiz de Fora, over a hundred miles away. If you wanted to call overseas, you had to wait for her to call you back. She never did.

The social center of the village was Murilo's bar, presided over by the one-eyed barman. Here the men congregated to watch *futebol* on a flickering television screen, regaling themselves with shots of *cachaça* and fried cheese pasties, and sometimes on a Saturday night there'd be a shootout.

But things were quiet enough that morning, and everyone was going peaceably about their business. The place reminded me of a frontier town in the Old West, complete with cowboys. A mob of steers went clattering across the cobblestones, driven by a dashing young man in a straw Stetson. Behind them trotted the garbage collector, shovel in hand. Women sat at their doors crocheting. Children played in the dust. Half the population of the village was hanging out of their windows to stare at us. I waved at them. There was no response.

"Not very friendly, are they?" I remarked to Robin.

"People in this state are famous for being cautious," he laughed. "Give them time—they'll get used to us."

B ack on the farm the plumbing project progressed steadily. Albertinho laid the drains, cobbled together the hose, and installed a showerhead. I chose a hot afternoon for my first shower, but even then the water was so cold it took my breath away. I shot out of the bathroom clutching my towel around me and collided with Robin, who was standing at the sink drinking a glass of water.

"What's the matter?" he demanded.

"It's the frigging water. It's freezing!"

"What's all the fuss about? I thought you were English."

"We have hot water in England."

"Oh, really?" he said. "I never noticed. But we'll soon have hot water here. Anyway, cold showers are good for you."

Years earlier Robin had taken a course on farm electrification, as an easy option in graduate school. "It was a lot more fun than statistics," he once told me, "and I always knew it would come in useful one day."

"So how do I get a hot shower?" I asked, toweling myself briskly.

"It's very simple. All we have to do is run a line from the generator, wire up the house, and install an electric shower. Shouldn't take long. Albertinho can do the outside wiring, I'll do the inside, and we'll soon have the place livable."

*   *   *

I n our part of the mountains it wasn't the custom to live in villages. Each family built its house in a fold of the valley where the water was good and kept itself to itself. Extended families stuck together, and there was a great deal of intermarriage. It was hard to marry outside the family in any case, since your circle of acquaintances was normally restricted to those you could reach on horseback. In the late 1960s the Catholic Church had made an attempt to create communities, encouraging farmers to donate some land for chapels and sometimes little one-room schoolhouses. There were three such communities near Iracambi, the most flourishing of which was called São Pedro. It had been settled by a large family whose ancestors had come from Italy. Hard workers, they had built up their community into a prosperous little hamlet with several houses, a chapel, a football pitch, and a school.

São Geraldo, the community nearest to Iracambi, had been less successful. It consisted of three brothers and their families who all lived within shouting distance of one another. The brothers' names were Jair (who helped us brand the cattle), Sebastião, and Geraldinho. Years earlier there had been a violent family quarrel, and although nobody would say what it was all about, the brothers had refused to speak to one another ever since. Not surprisingly, the community had withered and died, the school had closed, and the chapel was falling into ruins.

Farther up the mountain was a small community called Graminha, which consisted of a few scattered homesteads, a chapel, and a school. The former attracted more customers than the latter since it was difficult to find teachers prepared to face conditions in the isolated communities—they either spent the week camping in the schoolhouse or commuted from Muriaé by a combination of bus, truck, and footslogging. The salary was miserably low and often months in arrears, and they had no educational materials to speak of; they also had to deal with up to twenty children aged seven to fifteen in four different grades all sharing one room. The school day ran for a total of four hours, and although the teachers did their best, they weren't very well educated themselves. In any case, school was not considered a priority, and the children only came to school when they weren't needed at home. Girls were required to help around the house, look after the younger children, and take hot food to the men in the fields. Boys were enlisted to do the heavier work, and during harvest season everyone was drafted to lend a hand. Hardly any of the adults could read, and few saw the need for it.

Albertinho couldn't read, either. But he was proving to be a man of parts. He was a born fixer, and it didn't take him long to dig the postholes and string the wire for the electricity connection. Robin installed lightbulbs and switches in every room, and even put a light fixture over the front door. Jair pointed out that it was an unnecessary extravagance since you needed the light inside the house and not outside, but Robin just laughed and said he wanted to be able to see how to open the door. After several days and a last-minute trip to Limeira in search of lightbulbs, the interior wiring was complete.

"Terrific," I told Robin as he screwed in the last bulb. "So are we ready to roll?"

"Not quite," he said. "It's the outside wiring. The posts aren't in place yet."

"I thought Albertinho was going to do them last week. What happened?"

"He says he's waiting."

"Waiting? What for?"

"For the moon to change. He says," explained Robin carefully, "you can't cut posts on the waxing moon. They rot."

*   *   *

O*i*," came a hoarse croaking from outside the door. Albertinho was standing there with the corpse of a large snake dangling off the end of a bamboo pole. Measuring a good four feet, it had mottled brown markings on its back and a livid yellow belly.

"What kind of snake is that?" I asked him, keeping a safe distance.

"A yellow belly," he told me.

I consulted my book. It was a fer-de-lance, member of the pit viper family, so named because of its V-shaped head that resembled the tip of a spear. It was extremely poisonous.

"Hey, listen to this," I told Robin. "Fer-de-lance, *Bothrops* species. Even the juveniles are highly venomous, and up to fifty are born at a time. Venom is fast acting and very painful. It rapidly destroys blood cells and vessels and produces extensive necrosis of tissue around the bite. The fer-de-lance is abundant in overgrown tangle." I looked apprehensively at the thick growth of bush around the house.

"Don't worry," said Robin. "I told you before. Snakes are much more frightened of you than you are of them."

But I took to keeping a machete on the back veranda, just in case.

T he farm, or *fazenda* as we learned to call it, was vibrant with wildlife. My favorites were the hummingbirds. Several varieties lived in the hibiscus, glittering blue, green, purple, and elegant tan. Robin placed feeders at the windows and soon the hummingbirds had adopted the house as their own. They came whirring through at high speed, lingering under the tiles to catch tiny insects. They hovered around the feeders, dive-bombing one another and squabbling over the sugar water. Wrens nested in the rafters and a family of sparrows waited expectantly for us to open the shutters in the morning so they could hop inside to investigate the contents of the cooking pots. A dazzling scarlet tanager discovered Robin's shaving mirror and spent hours admiring itself in front of it. A small black grassquit jumped tirelessly up and down on the fence wire whistling its mating song. A pair of ovenbirds took up residence in the avocado tree and painstakingly constructed their neat mud house, with its entrance facing away from the prevailing wind.

We had large numbers of animal visitors. Field mice would scamper around at night, occasionally knocking food off the shelves. A small whiskery opossum made its home underneath the linen chest in the kitchen. One of its larger relatives, almost the size of a cat, took to walking boldly along the beams and raiding the bunches of bananas that we hung there. The swamp in front of the house was alive with a thousand frogs that would start their evening performance with the precision of a well-directed orchestra. Occasionally a large toad would hop onto the back veranda. Big black spiders with yellow spots would weave intricate and beautiful webs in the rafters and under the eaves, and we learned to leave them be, since they were harmless to humans and did a good job of keeping the house free from flies and mosquitoes. I didn't mind those spiders so much, but I had no hesitation in killing the tarantulas that sometimes lurked in dark corners.

Rhinoceros beetles blundered about, crashing into things and falling onto their backs, where they lay aimlessly waving their legs. June bugs attached themselves to our clothes like scarabs. Green moths masqueraded as leaves, brown moths as pieces of bark. Yellow butterflies hovered near the corral in clouds, small red ones with lacy wings and intricate jewel-like patterns fluttered around the flowers, and big blue morpho butterflies floated through the forest, iridescent against the dark foliage. Large gray lizards scurried heavy-footedly across the tiled roof, while their handsome cousins the monitors, green as the grass, lay on the rocks by the river.

As the rains drew near, we admired the sound and light show of the tropical evening. Fireflies danced over the pastures. The frogs were joined by a chorus of crickets. On stormy nights lightning would pierce the darkness, thunder would roll around the mountains, and the rain would rattle on the roof. The rains were coming but we were all prepared. Dry firewood was stacked on the veranda, the chimney had been swept, and we'd bought a bed. The moon had changed, the posts had been erected, and the electricity supply was connected up. We were settling into life in the rainforest, and it was good.

CHAPTER THREE

Lords of the Land

S o tell me," said our host, gazing at us innocently with his big blue eyes, "have you heard about the murder?"

A couple of months into the adventure, we'd been invited to spend the day with Lenin and his wife, and were seated once again on the upstairs veranda of the large, comfortable farmhouse where our family had voted to buy Iracambi.

Lenin lived in comparative civilization, less than fifteen miles from Muriaé, and just off the paved road. From our thickly padded cane chairs we could see out over his garden, with its vermilion flowering hibiscus and stately royal palm trees. He was speaking a courtly, classic Portuguese, a pleasure to hear after the heavy accents of our rural neighbors.

"Murder?" I asked.

"I knew it!" exclaimed Lenin. "Nobody's told you."

"Told us what?"

"Now, Lenin, behave yourself." His wife, Ircema, a striking woman with olive skin and green eyes, looked at him sternly. "Just get on and tell them."

"All right, all right," said Lenin good-humoredly. "Let's start at the beginning. You know that little place on your southern boundary? Belongs to a man called Adão Polla?"

We both nodded.

"And you know the dam that supplies the water for your generator? Your land is on one side of the river and his is on the other. Well, there's a saying in Brazil that more murders are committed because of water rights than because of women. And that's how it was."

He poured himself a cup of dark, sweet coffee, and urged us to help ourselves. I shifted in my seat impatiently and he smiled.

"Remember when you bought the place it had been abandoned? And someone must have told you that once upon a time they used to run six hundred head of cattle on it? Well," he paused dramatically, "the owner's name was Aurélio, and one fine day he took it into his head to install a little hydropowered generator. The one you're using now. So he built a dam on his land and made a deal with his neighbors, the Polla family, because they owned some of the valley bottom and their land was due to be flooded."

He paused and gazed at us benignly. "But old Polla didn't realize he was going to lose the best part of his rice field in the flood, and by the time he figured it out it was too late. So he did something unheard of. He found a lawyer and took Aurélio to court."

"He won, too," added Ircema, pulling out a silver cigarette case and lighting up.

"Got himself a good settlement—"

"Went and bought a Volkswagen Beetle—although he didn't know how to drive."

"He should have left it at that," said Lenin. "But he didn't. He did a very stupid thing. Started telling everybody that he'd screwed his rich neighbor and got a car out of him. The story went around like wildfire, and Aurélio was furious. So—"

"He hired a gunman—," Ircema chimed in.

"Who was known as One Legged Joe—," added Lenin.

"Because he'd been injured in a shootout."

"Had two legs, but he used to limp—"

"They called him the fastest gun in Limeira." Ircema smiled.

"One afternoon he rode up to old Polla's house and asked for a glass of water. Mrs. Polla went in to get it, and old Polla came out for a chat. He didn't often get a visitor and he liked to hear the news. And then," Lenin paused dramatically, "the *pistoleiro* shot him dead."

Robin and I looked at one another, aghast.

"His wife came out," Ircema continued, "And the *pistoleiro* shot her, too."

"But she didn't die," Lenin completed. "She's alive and well and living in Limeira."

There was a moment's silence.

"And what happened to Aurélio?" Robin recovered himself.

"Nothing, of course," laughed Ircema. "Well, that's to say, nothing happened to *him*. The *pistoleiro* was picked up by the police. They beat him up, but then they let him go."

"Lack of proof," added Lenin.

"How much proof do you *need*?" I raised an eyebrow.

"Brazilian law says the police have to catch him *in flagrante*," said Lenin. "So all he'd have to do would be run off and hide in the forest for twenty-four hours, and then he'd be safe."

"But surely they'd go after Aurélio?" I asked. "After all, he was the author of the crime."

"No proof there, either," said Ircema. "And even if there were, the police would be sure not to find it."

"They'd never arrest a landowner," added Lenin.

"That's true enough," said Ircema. "But here's an interesting fact. The neighbors ganged up on Aurélio. Cut his fence wire, set fire to his pastures, stole his cattle, that sort of thing. Made his life so difficult that he took off. Sold up and went to Bahia."

"Lost all his money and died," Lenin completed. "And everyone thought it served him right."

"So it did," Ircema said. "And now, after hearing all that, I expect you're feeling hungry?"

L enin had already told us he was delighted that we had bought a *fazenda* in the area and that we were to count on him for anything we needed. His advice to us was to steer clear of local politics, but, if we did need anything, his background in law and his position as long-standing town councilor would always be available to us. And, if ever our road was impassable, which did happen sometimes during the rains, we'd be welcome to stay with him. Over lunch, as we tucked into platefuls of black beans with pork and shredded greens, he told us about his family. His grandfather had arrived in the area in 1883, when Muriaé had been nothing more than a settlement, and the road a dirt track leading north. It was an untamed country in those days, with land for the taking. Lenin's grandfather was a surveyor, and his work led him to travel the length and breadth of the state, but he never found anywhere else that pleased him so well. So he brought his young wife into the backcountry, and together they started a farm and raised a family of eight, naming each child after a famous historical figure. One of his sons was called Vivaldi, and he in turn named his sons for the two men he most admired: Lenin and Roosevelt. Roosevelt became a businessman, but Lenin's heart was in the land. After a varied career spent working in an airline, studying law, and becoming a surveyor, he found a wife, returned to the family farm, and settled happily into the life of an old-style patriarchal landowner. He was a popular figure in the county, with a taste for poetry and music, and a love for fine food and good conversation.

After coffee prices collapsed in the late 1970s, Ircema turned the house into a hotel, catering to city folks who enjoyed the peace and quiet of the countryside—seasoned with the comforts of ample home cooking, a well-stocked bar, a freshwater pool, and pony rides for the children. An avuncular figure in his late sixties, Lenin relished his position as head of his extended family, which he ruled with benevolent and total control.

"So your family were pioneers," remarked Robin, helping himself to another spoonful of beans. "It must have been pretty wild back then. And even wilder up there in Limeira, from what you say."

Ircema passed him a dish of pork crackling and smiled. Limeira had always had a reputation for violence, she explained. It was to do with being up in the mountains, and bordering the neighboring county. County lines were traditionally good spots for outlaws who could move backward and forward to avoid the local police, and Limeira was particularly well placed with its rugged mountains and dense forest. Not to mention the road—if you could call it a road. More like a cattle trail, really, only passable for traffic within the previous four or five years, and even so, only during the dry season. The place was known as a hideout for bandits, and in the days of the mule trains the drivers were always armed. There'd been some fierce skirmishes, and several deaths.

"Sounds like the Wild West," I reflected. "And what was it like round here?" I turned to Lenin. "Was it so different?"

"Well, I suppose not," he said thoughtfully. "Everyone carried a gun, of course. A lot of people still do."

It had been a wonderful childhood, he told us. Always so much going on. His parents planted coffee, raised cattle, and grew all their own food. As kids they ran wild and never wore shoes. They used to swim in the river, hunt in the forest, ride bareback, and steal the cream from the dairy. Every Christmas their cousins came to visit them from Rio. It was quite a journey—they would take the train to Leopoldina and change onto the branch line to Muriaé. The train left Rio at six in the morning and got to Muriaé in the late afternoon. The road didn't come through until the 1970s.

"What did you do about school?" I inquired. "Was there a school in Muriaé?"

"Oh, Lord no!" Lenin smiled. "We had a governess."

She came from Rio, but she'd once been to Europe and taught them a bit of French. In those days French was considered the language of civilized people, and few people learned English. When Lenin was thirteen he was sent off to Petrópolis, near Rio, to a school run by the Holy Ghost Fathers. It was a good education but extremely strict: The boys were marched off to Mass every day, and he swore that when he left school he'd never go again.

Ircema, on the other hand, had been raised in Muriaé. She described it as the classic small town where nothing ever happened. Even the streets weren't cobbled, for the most part, and they kept a pair of draft horses in the main square to pull the cars out of the mud.

"That sounds familiar." Robin smiled. "I was raised in Kenya, so I've spent a lot of my time digging cars out of the mud."

Ircema passed around a selection of sweet, sticky desserts made from different fruits, and *doce de leite,* which tasted like smoky fudge. I took a small spoonful of coconut candy. It was excruciatingly sweet and absolutely delicious.

I asked how she and Lenin had met, and whether they'd known each other as children. Never in her wildest dreams had she imagined marrying Lenin, she confided. He came from a well-established family of landowners, whereas her parents were Spiritualists, and her mother used to tell her repeatedly that she'd better get herself an education because she'd never find a husband: Nobody would marry a Spiritualist.

Lenin smiled at her affectionately. "I warned Ircema that if she married me she'd have to go and live in the backwoods, over on the borders of Espírito Santo, and she never hesitated for a minute."

"You were the only chance I had." Ircema winked at me. "I couldn't afford to lose you. Now then, how about some coffee?"

"Thank you," I said as she poured the strong, sweet liquid into a tiny cup. "It's delicious."

"Homegrown," Lenin assured me. "Best Minas coffee. A hundred years ago this was one of the largest coffee-producing areas in Brazil; in fact, there were something like sixty coffee factories scattered around."

The local coffee had been called Rio-Zona, he told us, because it came from the Zona da Mata forest region on the borders of Rio state. Originally the coffee had been planted farther south in the mountains near São Paulo, but occasionally a frost there would wipe out the entire crop. So people started moving north into the mountains of Minas, where they discovered the ideal climate for coffee. When the forest was first cleared there was some residual fertility in the soil and the crops were good, so the price went up. When the price went up, people rushed to plant more, so the market was glutted and the price fell. It was the classic Brazilian cycle of boom and bust.

One of the boom cycles had been in the 1950s, and it was around then that the population of Limeira began to expand. The original settlement was founded in the mid 1800s near a waterhole on the main cattle trail across the mountains. Someone built a bar and a trading post, a handful of loggers moved in and made a few clearings in the forest, and pretty soon there was a small community. They built a chapel by the lime trees and dedicated it to Our Lady, and that's how it came to be called Rosário da Limeira.

There had been Indians in the forest in those days, an isolated group called the Puri that had moved up from the coast to escape from the settlers.

"You know that mountain you can see from your place, Itajuru?" Lenin asked. "I don't suppose you know what the name means?"

"Someone told me it means the Place of Sorrows," I said.

"That's right."

Nobody knew where the name came from. People talked of human sacrifice, but Lenin's opinion was that there may have been a massacre there. Still, nobody knew for sure, and now they never would, since there weren't any full-blood Puris left. Even when Lenin was a child they were fast disappearing. They'd been captured by the whites and made to work. They got sick and died, or lost their lands and died of broken hearts. The whites called themselves Christians but didn't behave like Christians, and they referred to the Indians as savages. Treated them like wild animals. It was a terrible chapter in Brazilian history.

"Tell me something." Robin stirred in his chair. "How was the land settled round here? Was it homesteaded?"

"Yes, it was. Starting around the mid-nineteenth century. And they were good-size landholdings—hundreds of acres and sometimes thousands. Of course, most of the big landowners didn't do much with the land. It was more a symbol of their wealth and prestige. Everyone called them the colonels."

I remembered reading about the colonels. It was an honorary title, and they had no connection to the military. But if there was any local trouble they were expected to provide a few hands to help out.

"The Brazilian version of the Kentucky colonels," Lenin continued. "They had a lot of land, and a lot of political power, and some of them were very wealthy. They started with cattle and sugarcane, and later got into coffee. Then the smaller farmers followed suit. But the price collapsed and they ripped out the coffee and put the land under pasture."

The Brazilian economy had always been that way, he explained, ever since the early days of Portuguese settlement. Unlike the settlers in North America, the Portuguese hadn't come to stay. They had come to seek their fortunes, and they stayed because the living was easy and the rules of hospitality among the indigenous tribes included sharing their women. The Portuguese took out the trees for timber, planted sugar on the cleared land, and imported African slaves to do the work. There was plenty of sunshine, plenty of rain, and plenty of space, and concepts like conservation and sustainability hadn't yet been invented.

It was a land that had everything—huge territory and immense mineral and biological resources; a place that liked to call itself the Land of Tomorrow and yet, somehow, tomorrow never came. It hadn't come to the other Latin American countries, either. The southern Europeans had figured that the New World was the pot of gold at the end of the rainbow. They plundered the continent and stayed on because there was no reason to leave.

"I can see that," I said contentedly as I gazed out over the garden where the shadows were lengthening. "I can't see any reason to leave, either. Except that if we stay much longer it'll be dark and we'll never get back up the mountain."

"Come back soon," said Lenin, as Ircema pressed a packet of homegrown coffee into my hand. "We're always here if you need us."

"Thank you both, we will."

* * *

H ow come nobody told us about the murder?" I asked Robin as we headed onto the dirt road home. "And you do realize who Aurélio was, don't you?"

"Of course." Robin swerved to avoid a pothole. "Cassilda's uncle who went to Bahia—"

"Because it was good cattle country—"

"Lost all his money and died—"

"And serve him right." We smiled at each other.

"The question is," I continued, "is the vendetta still in force?"

"I reckon if anything was going to happen it would have happened by now," Robin assured me. "But there's still a vendetta going on between the Tokos and the Freitas."

"Freitas?"

"The family that owns the store where we get our building supplies. It's a long story, Albertinho told me once. Seems there was an illicit romance, somebody got murdered, there was a vengeance killing, and then it turned into a vendetta. The two families have been enemies ever since."

"Oh, I know what you're talking about. You mean Armir's father who was playing dice on his front veranda when a horseman rode up and shot him dead?"

"Seems to be a bit of a tradition round these parts," Robin confirmed.

M any of the families in our area were descended from the Italian immigrants who had come to Brazil at the turn of the century as indentured laborers. After slavery had been declared illegal, there was a sudden shortage of labor to work on the sugar estates and coffee plantations of São Paulo. Shiploads of Italian immigrants had arrived, fleeing the Old Country for the New World. They worked hard and did well, and many of them managed to pay off their passages and buy small farms in the states of São Paulo, Rio, and Minas. In some areas they kept their language, though not in ours. But a few of the old customs lingered on. They ate pasta and polenta and lots of tomato paste. And they kept alive the ancient tradition of the vendetta.

The town councilor for Rosário da Limeira was descended from a family of Sicilians. His name was Bertoni. A wiry figure, he was a hard worker with an instinctive feel for the land. Despite the fact that he'd never learned to read, he'd built up a successful coffee business and made a lot of money. His blond wife kept the books and spent his money on shelves full of china ornaments and white satin sofas piled high with lacy cushions. She once invited me in for coffee, and she and I made polite conversation while her husband perched awkwardly on the edge of the sofa, itching for an excuse to get back to work.

Bertoni was a distant relative of the Tokos, a connection he had taken advantage of when he ran for the Muriaé town council. He was popular with the local community, particularly around election time, when he would go around the houses handing out powdered milk for the children, bags of cement for the young marrieds, and patent medicines for the old people. He'd make all sorts of promises about fixing the roads, helping out with the marketing of their coffee and ensuring that medical attention was available to the needy. The night before the election he would organize a barbecue and rodeo for his constituents. In return they would line up to vote for him, he would thank them effusively, and the following day everything would be back to normal.

*   *   *

T his business of vendettas," I remarked to Robin as we sat down by the woodstove that evening. "Let me just get this straight. Jair doesn't speak to his brother Sebastião. The other brother, Geraldinho, doesn't speak to either of them, Adão's father was murdered by Cassilda's uncle, and the Tokos and the Freitas are at one another's throats. What would you say were our chances of catching a stray bullet?"

"Fair to moderate," laughed Robin. "No, seriously, we'll be fine if we just keep quiet and keep out of it."

"Bunch of ignorant rednecks." I made a face. I had read as much as I could before coming to live in Minas, and I had been struck by an article by a Brazilian anthropologist about the early settlement of the state that explained why *mineiros* were renowned for being canny and suspicious. The first settlers had crossed the mountains from the coast on a perilous journey through the backcountry in search of gold. As wildcat miners they were staunch individualists and lived by the local saying *"Cada um por si e Deus por todos,"* which translates to "Every man for himself and God for every man"—an interesting variation of the northern expression "Every man for himself and the Devil take the hindermost."

It was dense forest, full of Indians and bandits; since settlers never knew who was who, they didn't run out to welcome strangers but waited for them to declare themselves. They didn't know whom they could trust, so they didn't trust anyone. Shoot first, ask questions later.

I reflected that it must take years to change that way of thinking. In an isolated place like Iracambi, how did people learn new things? Not in school, since most of them had never been. Not by reading books, because hardly anyone could read.

There was always the radio. That was where people got the news of births, marriages, and deaths. The radio acted as a commu-

nity mailbox passing on messages from family members, announcements of local events like baptisms and weddings, cattle prices,
weather forecasts, even selected items of national and regional news.

"But how can people learn new things?" I was thinking aloud.

"Good point." Robin looked up. "I've been thinking about that
myself. Could be where we come in."

"Say again?"

"Can't see how anything is going to change unless we get
started."

"Started on *what*?"

"Finding some opportunities for people here."

"Do you mean business opportunities? Some sort of skills training? Dressmaking, cheese making, carpentry, that sort of thing?"

"Anything that opens new horizons. Literacy, for example."

"That's not a bad idea. But who would teach it?"

"As it happens, I was talking last week to the people from the
rural extension service in Muriaé," Robin told me. "They can set up
mini–training courses if we can get enough people together."

"He's serious," I muttered to myself as I bolted out onto the back
veranda for a glass of water. I leaned against the concrete sink and
looked out at the sky. It was very dark and there was a faint ring
around the moon.

Wait a minute, though. This wasn't supposed to be the deal. I
mean, this was an adventure, right? Robin's dream. Not a crusade.
I guess I'd never really thought it through. I hadn't imagined we'd
be here forever. I was enjoying the adventure—so far. But this talk
of changing the world sounded suspiciously like a mission. What
made Robin think he could change the world, anyway? What
made him think this particular corner of the world wanted to be
changed?

I thought of Maria, leaning out of her window the day we arrived, or stirring the sweet rice on the woodstove on the evening of the birthday party. Did she want something different? If so, did she know what it was? I thought of Washington. I thought of my kids—both of them grown and studying. I thought of my mother and wished, suddenly and passionately, that she was there to talk to. She had felt that the whole Iracambi adventure was a bad idea as far as I was concerned, and that I'd be wasting my talents in the backwoods. Several years later her curiosity was to get the better of her and she would come visit, at which point she would become a staunch supporter. But that was in the future.

Our children were 100 percent behind our move to Iracambi, pointing out that Robin and I had given them a wonderful childhood and launched them safely into the world, and therefore Robin had every right to follow his dream. But they had dreams of their own. Like his father, Gus had been born in Africa and was already looking south. His plans varied from game ranching to mine clearing, and he was applying to work with Mozambican refugees. Juliet was altogether more Latin, and had developed a passion for Costa Rica, where she had worked in rainforest conservation. She might see her future in Brazil further down the line. But then again, she might fall in love with someone from the city. Or move to Australia. There were no guarantees. When I expressed such misgivings to Robin he told me not to be negative.

I discovered, too, that I was missing my music. I'd been ready for a change of career, since the life of a soloist had been both demanding and lonely. But even when my piano finally arrived I found I couldn't play without an audience, and it was only later that I settled into my new career as a writer.

I thought of my friends, so far away, and all of a sudden a wave of self-pity washed over me. What exactly had I let myself in for? What was my role going to be? What would happen to me if Robin fell under a bus? We'd staked our all on Iracambi, and if things went wrong there would be no easy way out.

"Hey, Binka!" Robin called from inside. "Are you okay?"

"I'm fine," I lied, running back into the warmth of the kitchen. "Just fine."

CHAPTER FOUR

Busting the Broncs in
Belisário

Hey, Robin!" I dug him vigorously in the ribs.

"What's the matter?" came the sleepy reply.

"There's somebody out there!"

Robin sat up in bed. "What's that again?"

I padded over to the window and opened the wooden shutter. The night was full of noises: the whistling of crickets, the croaking of frogs, the screech of an owl.

"*I* can't hear anything." Robin snuggled down under the blanket.

I pulled on a sweater and opened the front door. There was a bright moon, and I could clearly see the gourd tree silhouetted against the starry sky. I paused, straining my ears, and then I heard it again. Voices.

"Robin! Binka! Anyone home?" It took me a few seconds to register. Somebody was speaking English. I didn't often hear my own language except when I was talking to Robin, or listening to the BBC on the shortwave radio.

I hurried out into the moonlight and then I recognized our

visitor. "Oh my God!" I exclaimed. "I can't believe it! This is wonderful!"

It was Dorothee, a young woman we'd met months earlier on an icy mountaintop in Venezuela. We'd been coming from Washington; she and her partner, Alain, had been coming from Munich, and they'd watched from their camper bus as a freak storm blew our tent over and soaked us to the skin. We were struggling to disentangle ourselves from the wreckage when we heard a voice asking, in German, if we were all right. Emerging into the friendly beam of a flashlight, we were shepherded into the warmth and comfort of their little bus to be given clean towels, thick slices of fruitcake, and mugs of coffee laced with brandy. We'd exchanged travelers' tales and they'd promised to visit us if they ever got as far as Brazil.

Dorothee came running up and kissed me on both cheeks, Latin style. She was bundled up in a fleece, but its hood couldn't hide her big smile. "So sorry for arriving unexpectedly," she said breathlessly. "But we couldn't find your phone number anywhere."

"I'm not surprised," I laughed. "We don't have a phone."

"Well, look who's here!" Robin bounded down the steps and gave Dorothee a big hug. "Where's Alain? And what's happened to your car?"

"Left it on the road," Dorothee told him. "Alain's looking after it. He's mortally scared of dogs, so he sent me on ahead. Hey, Alain! You can come down now. It's quite safe."

Tall, blond Alain came loping up, dressed in a sweatshirt and jeans. "Hi, guys," he exclaimed. "You told us your place was off the beaten track. But I didn't quite imagine how far off!"

"How did you manage to track us down?" I demanded, linking arms with Dorothee and leading her toward the house.

"It wasn't so hard!" She smiled. "We got as far as Ouro Preto, and I looked at the map and found Muriaé. I remember you told us it was your nearest town. So we checked out your address and the guy in the gas station told us how to get to Rosário da Limeira. We stopped at the bar, and Alain asked directions. Everyone knew you, but they all told us different things, and finally one man volunteered to come with us. Said he lived round here and he'd be glad of the ride. We dropped him off at your gate. Just as well we had him along, otherwise we'd have been driving round all night."

"That's impressive," I exclaimed. "Now come on in and tell us about your adventures."

"That'll have to wait till tomorrow." Dorothee yawned. "It's been a long day and we're ready for bed. Is it okay if we park under this tree?"

Alain carefully maneuvered the camper bus along the track, and fifteen minutes later we were all in bed and asleep.

I n the morning I woke to the smell of freshly brewed coffee and looked out the window to see Dorothee and Alain serenely eating their breakfast at a little table set up under the gourd tree.

"*Grüss Gott!*" said Dorothee. "What a beautiful place you have— we can't wait to see everything! And do you know what? We really need a break from traveling. So if it's okay with you and if you can use us, we're here to help out. We've got plenty of supplies and a whole crate of wine."

Within a few days our visitors had become part of the farm family. They made friends with Albertinho's little girls, learned how to drive cattle, and walked all the way up the river to its source. As Alain and Robin worked on the cars, Dorothee helped me whitewash the kitchen and cooked delicious dinners on the woodstove; together we shared bottles of wine under the gourd tree and talked into the night. They told us of their plan to see South America before returning to work in Germany, and maybe starting a family. "It's the trip of a lifetime," Dorothee confided as she stirred a large pot of fragrant curry. "It was now or never. So we drew out all our savings and here we are. But we want to hear about *you*—after all the places you've lived and the adventures you've had, you suddenly take off and start a completely new life. You've been here how long now? Two months?"

Robin nodded.

"Must be a good campsite!" Dorothee grinned mischievously. "Do you reckon you'll be able to settle down here?"

Settle down? Her words hit me in the solar plexus.

In the excitement of the adventure I hadn't really registered that I might actually be settling down. Subconsciously I had thought of it as yet another overseas posting, even though this was a posting with a difference—with no support structure and nobody to answer to. Except each other. But it wasn't as though we were irrevocably committed. We could sell up, pack up, and move on any time. The secret of happiness, traveling light. Robin, on the other hand, had always yearned for his own place. And he had big plans. Plans that maybe didn't fit into a three- or four-year time span. He wanted to get the *fazenda* up and running, and he was growing increasingly concerned about the destruction of the forest. "People round here are cutting the forest because they can't see it has any value," he would say. "But there's got to be a way to make money out of the standing forest without cutting it down. And that's what I want to figure out."

"Let me put it this way." Dorothee spooned some mango chutney onto my plate. "This place is magic, really magic. And I'm sure that you guys will make it into something special. But it is a bit off the map, isn't it? Don't you ever miss the big world?"

Robin and I exchanged glances, and there was a moment's silence. "You want to know something?" he declared. "I really don't. Miss the big world, I mean. That's because there's so much to do here. All these years I've been telling people about tropical farming and now I'm finally getting to do it for myself. Now that *is* magic."

"What about you, Binka?" Alain turned to me.

Myriad images flashed through my brain. I remembered the thrill of walking onto the stage, the moment of recollection before I started to play, the joy of making music for one particular audience at one particular moment. Evenings at the theater or the opera, smoked salmon and raspberries with chilled white wine. Driving across the Sahara, riding on elephants in Madhya Pradesh, trekking in Ladakh.

I took a deep breath. "Do I miss the big world? Sure I do! I miss a lot of things. Seeing friends and family, knowing what's going on, listening to music, lying around reading the Sunday papers. And I do get lonely sometimes."

"Well, that's understandable." Dorothee smiled warmly at me. "But let me tell you something. You won't be lonely for long. Once people hear about this place they'll be beating a path to your door. You'll see."

It was kindly meant, but I couldn't imagine it. Not for a second.

I have an important announcement," said Robin as we sat over breakfast one morning. "We've been invited to exhibit at the Belisário agricultural show."

"Belisário?" asked Dorothee.

"It's a little village over there." Robin gestured across the valley. "Hardly any bigger than Limeira."

"I love agricultural shows," said Alain. "When I was a kid in France I used to go to the show every year. I won my first prize when I was six."

"What did you win it for?" I asked.

"For the biggest zucchini," said Alain modestly, and I hid a smile.

"We haven't got any of those," Robin laughed, "but there are all sorts of classes we could enter—if we *had* anything to enter. Livestock, vegetables, fruit, all the usual things. Best milk cow, best pig, best calf, and best bull. Western saddle horses, bronco busting, and much more. So Albertinho tells me."

"Sounds great," said Dorothee. "How about I make a cake?"

"Sacher torte?" I brightened.

"I'm not sure I could do that on a wood-burning stove. But I could do something a little bit special. Something from Germany."

"You bet," Robin told her. "So long as I get to eat some of it. Oh, and," he turned to me innocently, "I forgot. They sent a special message to ask if you'd care to enter some handwork. Crochet, preferably."

"Very funny," I snapped. Robin knew perfectly well that I didn't know one end of a crochet hook from the other, and could care less.

"It's a reasonable request." Alain grinned at me. "After all, most farm wives do crochet and make jam and that sort of thing."

"Well, I'm not exactly a farm wife," I pointed out.

"No," agreed Alain, "But people here don't know that."

He had a point, and in that respect I certainly didn't measure up very well. Farm wives looked after the pigs and chickens, grew wonderful vegetables, cooked hearty meals, made jams and preserves, bottle-fed orphan calves, helped in the coffee fields, raised large families, and still found time to crochet dishcloths. And what about me? I hated chickens. I forgot to water the vegetables, burned the jam, was a distracted cook, and doubted if I could even lay hands on a needle and thread. And I had absolutely no ambitions in the field of crochet dishcloths. No, as a farm wife I wasn't up to par.

This unprofitable train of thought was interrupted by Robin.

"Never mind," he said loyally, "I didn't marry you for your crochet dishcloths."

"Just as well," I shot back, somewhat mollified.

T he day of the show dawned fine and clear, and somehow we all managed to squeeze into the car, together with Albertinho, his two little girls, and a large box containing Dorothee's chocolate cake.

The road to Belisário looked more like a donkey trail than anything else. We started by turning left out of the main gate, crossing the bridge by Jair's house, and heading up the hill past Sebastião's place. Sebastião had a face crisscrossed with wrinkles, bright brown eyes, a wonderful smile, and a perfect set of false teeth. He was a dab hand with herbal remedies and a great talker; he loved to tell the story of Noah's Ark and the Great Flood. He was also keenly interested in flying saucers, and was convinced there was gold in "them thar hills." On certain moonlit nights he'd look across the valley to the hill behind our house and see a mysterious phosphorescence that he called the Mother of Gold.

After Sebastião's, the road curled away across the mountains until it reached the next farm, which boasted a house with glass windows that belonged to Jair's brother Geraldinho. I wondered if the road was going to end in his muddy farmyard, but Albertinho shooed the cows out of the way and urged us on. Through the rickety gate, up the hill, and past another little chapel, the road wound on through dark green coffee bushes and emerald green rice fields, steeply down into a patch of thick forest that opened out to reveal the rock face of Itajuru looming above. I remembered the Place of Sorrows and shivered.

We rounded a corner and suddenly caught sight of the Belisário church tower, silhouetted against a granite bluff. On our left was a quarry with large slabs of gleaming granite stacked by the road. "Do you see that?" Robin pointed. "Albertinho says they export it to Italy."

There was, indeed, a hint of Italy in Belisário, with its fine church and its backdrop of blue peaks. The village was looking its best, with multicolored flags and bunting draped across the street, and many of the houses freshly whitewashed for the occasion. Horsemen trotted importantly over the cobbles, a long line of pony traps was waiting to enter the show ground, and a large crowd was making its way down to join in the fun.

Jair had told us that the villages of Belisário and Limeira were bitter rivals. Both had been talking for years about becoming proper towns with proper prefects and councils, but they weren't prepared to go in together, and neither of them was big enough to go it alone. So they remained forgotten in the mountains, neglected by the county government and resentful of one another.

Limeira was the richer of the two, because of the Toko's thriving coffee business. But Belisário had a primary school funded by foreign money in some forgotten aid project designed to bring about economic development. Somehow it hadn't happened and the handsome school buildings were half empty. But the soccer field was in daily use and once a year it was converted into an impromptu showground.

We parked in the main street and joined the throng heading for the show. A large banner had been strung across the road thanking the local state deputy for his patronage—although he hadn't put in an appearance. But nobody minded; they were in high spirits and all set to have a good time.

The livestock section was housed in a line of neatly thatched pens, where pride of place was given to a fine selection of hairy spotted pigs. Next to them a dozen mixed-breed cows languidly chewed the cud while their liquid-eyed calves nuzzled at their teats. The last pen was devoted to horses—each one groomed until it shone—and one pretty little mare sporting an elaborately beaded mane.

Behind the livestock was a row of stalls doing a lively trade in plastic combs, hair ornaments, cheap jewelry, and violently colored lipsticks for the girls; and cigarettes, felt hats, suede boots, and fancy girths for the men. There was barbecued meat and corn on the cob for the hungry; soft drinks, beer, and *cachaça* for the thirsty. Children were running around everywhere, their faces covered in sticky pink cotton candy

"I need to find someplace to leave the cake," Dorothee announced. "I'm guessing it'll be inside the school."

Leaving the men to admire the cattle, she and I made our way through a wrought-iron gate and into the school building. The main hall was set with tables covered with immaculate white cloths, upon which someone had carefully stacked blocks of dark raw sugar, jars of multicolored fruit conserve, *doce de leite,* coconut candy, corn bread, powdery pastries made of manioc flour, soft white cheeses, and bottles of cane spirit steeped in herbs. The crafts table had a display of embroidered baby clothes and crochet dishcloths, wooden bowls and chopping boards, neatly woven baskets, bunches of dried flowers, grass brooms, rag rugs, and painted wooden stools. Hanging from the beams were ox yokes, finely tooled leather saddles, brightly colored horse blankets, rawhide lassos, and ornamented bridles.

"I can't see any cakes," said Dorothee anxiously. "Let's ask."

A buxom woman in a short skirt was hovering around the exhibits. "Excuse me," Dorothee tackled her in a mixture of Spanish and Portuguese, "I've brought an entry for the cake class. Where should I put it?"

"Cake class?" she said. "I'm sorry, we don't have one. But if you have a cake we'd be happy to put it on display."

Dorothee cautiously opened the box to reveal a large, ornately decorated chocolate cake, which she placed carefully on the table. Immediately a crowd of small children materialized from nowhere and stood gazing at it longingly.

"Wow!" came a chorus of voices, and Dorothee smiled.

We emerged from the school building just as the sound system burst into life and a male voice announced: "Testing, testing, one two three, testing, testing."

I looked toward the ring. Half a dozen smartly turned-out cowboys were getting ready for the bronco-busting competition. They wore tight-fitting jeans with leather chaps and checked shirts, and were passing cigarettes from hand to hand to soothe their nerves. Meanwhile, the local dandies, in clean white shirts, sharply creased jeans, and ankle boots with pointed toes were huddled together eyeing the girls. Couples were strolling arm in arm, young mothers showing off their babies to one another, grannies sitting in the shade and chatting, old men smoking corn-leaf cigarettes, and small children swarming in all directions.

The loudspeaker crackled violently. "And now, ladies and gentlemen," a voice came through on full volume, "for the event we've all been waiting for—the Fourth Annual Bronco-Busting Competition! And this year we have six contenders for the title. First, Belisário's very own Antonio Cerqueira."

A burst of applause came from the Belisário supporters.

"And next," from the loudspeaker, "from Limeira, João Larino!"

A stout figure marched into the ring and took a deep bow. I recognized João Red Face.

"Isn't he the one that goes very odd when the moon is full?" I whispered to Robin.

"Hush!"

"From Muriaé, Pedro de Oliveira!" A little old man with bandy legs rolled into the arena.

"Now *he* looks the part," commented Alain. "A real cowboy."

"From Ervália, José Maria!"

"From Itajuru, Vanderlei!"

Renewed applause.

"And now," the voice rose half an octave, "we have last year's champion—Roberto da Silva dos *Santos*!"

In swept the champion, tight jeaned, ten gallon hatted, flourishing a whip. The crowd went wild.

The cowboys marched around the ring, waving and smiling while the crowd applauded noisily. At a signal from the master of ceremonies they filed out to wait their turn, and a hush fell upon the spectators. One by one the cowboys swaggered over to the wooden rail, climbed up, and lowered themselves onto the wildly gyrating broncos. None of them lasted longer than a few seconds before being thrown, but fortunately there were no broken bones.

There was a short pause while the judges conferred and then the crackling loudspeaker burst into life. "This year's Belisário Champion Bronco Buster," the announcer informed us, "is Pedro de *Oliveira*! A big hand, please, ladies and gentlemen, for the winner."

The crowd exploded into a cacophony of shouts and whistles.

"And now, ladies and gentlemen," continued the voice, after several vain attempts to make itself heard, "we shall have a short break, followed by the *lambada* competition."

Lambada was the craze that was sweeping Latin America: an extravagantly sensuous dance where the couples wiggled their way across the floor, glued at the hip. A series of young girls in skintight jeans and the briefest of shiny tops sashayed their way around the ring, clinging to their partners, eliciting wolf whistles and ribald comments from the crowd. I glanced across at Alain. His eyes were popping out of his head.

*   *   *

T hat *lambada* is quite something," said Alain dreamily that evening, as we settled ourselves under the gourd tree for a slice of Dorothee's mouthwatering chocolate cake. "You can see why the Vatican doesn't approve of it. Is it true they tried to ban it?"

"That's right." Robin nodded. "But nobody in Brazil paid any attention."

"The trouble is," said Dorothee, "that you can't dance it properly unless you've got Latin blood. We Germans are too uptight. Can't bend in the right places."

"It's not just a case of being physically flexible," I added. "It's our whole way of thinking and approaching things. We're not as creative as the Latins. Not so adaptable. Take the *jeito,* for example."

"*Jeito?*" Alain raised an eyebrow.

"Brazil's greatest contribution to getting by," Robin told him. "It's all about finding a creative solution to an impossible problem. In Brazil there's always a way."

"That's as may be," Alain sniffed. "But you can take flexibility too far. Brazilians have no idea of time. They're always late for everything. Drives me crazy."

"You know something, Alain?" said Dorothee tranquilly. "For a Frenchman you're more German than the Germans."

"Too right," Alain agreed. "Why do you think I went to live in Munich?"

"But seriously," Dorothee continued, filling up our glasses. "Let's go back to the *lambada* for a moment. Talking about flexibility and being adaptable, do you think that you'll ever be accepted in a place like this? Or will you always be outsiders?"

That was something I preferred not to think about. I didn't want to be a perpetual outsider. But I knew I'd never be an insider, either. And deep down I never really expected to be here long enough for it to matter.

"If we stick around for a few years I guess they'll get used to us," Robin answered. "It's not like they think of us as foreigners; they reckon we come from São Paulo, which is about the wildest place they can imagine. But, having said that, you have to remember that this is a very conservative rural society and Minas is probably the most traditional state in Brazil."

"That's right," I said. "*Mineiros* are known to be cautious; in fact they say *mineiro* sleeps on the floor so he won't fall out of bed!"

"There's all sorts of *mineiro* jokes," Robin added. "*Mineiro* never talks with strangers, never steps where it's wet, and only bets on a certainty."

We all laughed. "What about the large farmers?" Dorothee asked. "Are they equally canny?"

"I shouldn't be surprised," Robin told her. "But in any case we don't see much of them because they live in town. It's not the custom in Latin countries for landowners to live on the land. They reckon the countryside is for peasants; that's why it's so neglected."

"Neglected and badly farmed." Alain added. "I can see the people round here are hard workers. But they don't understand how to care for the land. Planting the coffee on steep slopes like these. It's a recipe for erosion."

I agreed with Alain, but I pointed out that the area had only been settled within living memory and people still did slash-and-burn agriculture. Which was okay if they moved their field every couple of years, but exhausted the soil if they kept planting in the same place.

There was more to it than that, Robin added. It was hard to get credit in Brazil and small farmers didn't have the money to make improvements.

"They don't have the choice, either," I said. "Most of them can barely read and write. Schools in the countryside only go to fourth grade and most of the kids don't even make it that far."

"Things will start changing now you two are here." Dorothee smiled. "And, speaking of that, tell us your plans for Iracambi. What will we see next time we come visit?"

"Depends when you come." Robin pushed his chair back and started to outline his plan. Phase One included building up a good dairy herd, improving the pastures, and planting lots of sugarcane. Phase Two would focus on reforestation, with both native species and some variety of timber trees, pine or eucalyptus. He'd been thinking of putting in fish ponds to take advantage of the water. We'd need a vegetable garden, an orchard, some proper housing for the staff. And a house for ourselves.

"Sounds like you'll have your work cut out." Dorothee smiled. "And what do you suppose Albertinho will think of all this? And Jair and the neighbors?"

"Can't be sure," said Robin. "Albertinho isn't a great one for sharing his inmost thoughts."

"A man of few words," I added. "But he did tell me something interesting. He said that ten years ago a bunch of people showed up prospecting for minerals. So when we arrived they decided we must have found gold."

"Maybe you have," said Dorothee seriously. There was a moment's silence, and then we all burst out laughing.

CHAPTER FIVE

Friends and Neighbors

Several weeks passed before we reluctantly said good-bye to Dorothee and Alain. They had already become so much a part of the family that it was hard to imagine life without them. "I can hardly bear to leave so soon," Dorothee had confided as we shared the last bottle of wine. "But we do have to get down to Patagonia while the weather holds."

"Wasn't it great to have them?" I reflected to Robin as their VW bus disappeared down the muddy road. "It's so good to be able to touch base with the big world."

"I'll miss Dorothee's cooking." Robin gave me a hug. "But we'll be able to see the big world when we go to Rio next week."

We were off to collect the family dog, who had been staying with friends in the States until we settled in. A handsome black-and-white spotted Dalmatian, he had come to live with us in New Delhi, and Robin had christened him Split in memory of a happy holiday we'd spent in Split on the Dalmatian coast. He'd followed us back to Washington, moved with us to Recife, returned to

Washington, and now he would have the run of the *fazenda* and could chase the horses to his heart's content.

Most local families had a dog or two: skinny animals of indeterminate breed that lived off kitchen scraps, barked ferociously when anyone approached, and usually stayed close to home. The exceptions were the hunting dogs that accompanied their owners into the forest at night, and one enormous mastiff that belonged to Jair's brother Geraldinho. But *mineiro* dogs didn't have names: They were referred to as "the dog" just as horses were called "the horse" or "the mare" and people were often referred to as "the man" or "the woman." Splittie quickly became a favorite with Albertinho's children, who begged their father for a puppy of their very own, and kept up the pressure until Albertinho relented. He returned one day from a visit to his father, carrying a tiny spotted puppy. The children called him Doggie, and he followed Albertinho everywhere like a small shadow. Doggie was the first dog in the area to be given a name and a personality, but the fashion quickly caught on, and soon everyone was walking around with a dog at heel, and Doggie became the name of choice.

Another major event was the arrival of the second farm family. We needed someone to help with the cows, and were looking around for a suitable candidate when Albertinho announced that he'd offered the job to his brother Antonio. People said he was an excellent cowman, so Robin went up the mountain to move the family into the little house across the river, Casa Sozinha. Everything they owned fit into the car with room to spare—two straw mattresses, a bag of clothes, some battered cooking pots, a couple of sacks of rice and beans, and a spotted pig. They also had three small children.

Antonio was short and wiry, with tightly curled hair and a face that showed clear traces of his African ancestry. His wife was called Maria of the Sorrows, but everyone knew her as Fia, and from the moment she arrived on the *fazenda* my spirits rose.

Albertinho and Antonio may have been brothers, but they didn't resemble each other in the slightest. Albertinho suffered from occasional black moods, but Antonio was always unruffled. Whatever needed to be done, at any hour of day or night, Antonio was ready to do it. If a cow fell into the ditch, it was Antonio who got her out. If she dropped down dead, it was Antonio who buried her. The day that Buttercup's calf fell into the river, it was Antonio who jumped into the water, snatched it up, jogged over to his house, rubbed it down, and gave it milk out of the baby's bottle, saving its life.

Antonio's wife, Fia, was made from sterner stuff than Maria. Fia had three small children, but that didn't mean she was going to stay at home. She didn't wait for work to turn up—she went out and found things to do. She was always popping over with a handful of lettuce seedlings or some cabbage from her garden. She taught me how to catch a Brazilian horse, not by approaching from the front with a handful of corn but by coming up from behind and throwing a rope across its back. She showed me how to tighten the two girths on a mountain saddle, one behind the forelegs and the other behind the belly to prevent the saddle from slipping. She taught me how to stop the fire smoking, and when the roof leaked she patched it with a flattened oil can. She was brimming with ideas.

"How about we raise a few goats around here?" she suggested one day. "We can keep them on that rocky patch behind Albertinho's house. It's no good for anything else, and it seems to me it's just crying out for a family of goats."

I mentioned it to Robin. "Great idea," he said. "I'm very fond of goat meat. But they'll need to be properly tethered. We don't want goats roaming loose destroying everything."

I asked Fia if, by any chance, she knew where we could come by a goat.

"Well, let me think," she pondered. "I did hear that Zé Viricius had one. It was Adáo who told me."

Our next-door neighbor to the south, Adão was the son of old Polla who was murdered by Cassilda's uncle, and Orisa was his wife. They had a neat little farm and shared a river boundary with us—the boundary that had been the cause of the murder. If you went up the hill onto their land and followed the track around to the southwest, you could climb steeply up into Iracambi forest and make a big circle back home. Just beyond Adão's, half hidden by sugarcane, was the small ramshackle house where Zé Viricius lived, together with his twin brother and their mother, Dona Cecília. She must have been well into her eighties, and when she wasn't looking after her two sons she would sit on a stool in the sunshine weaving sturdy rush baskets. Neither of her boys had married, both wore stocking caps, and they looked so alike that I couldn't tell them apart. The highlight of their week was on Sunday, when they would take turns inserting the family's one set of false teeth and walking to Limeira to sell Dona Cecília's baskets.

"Can you go and see about it, then?" I asked Fia.

"I'll go this afternoon," she said promptly.

"That Fia," I told Robin as we sat over bread and cheese at lunchtime, "is a breath of fresh air. Maybe we should hire her. You did say we were going to need someone to help out in the fields."

"Hire a *woman*?" Robin raised an eyebrow. "Do you want to start a frigging revolution?"

"Why not?"

"Such a thing has never been done," he told me equably. "It's against the natural order of things. Women work but they don't get paid; just ask any man round here. And anyway, I've already got a candidate for the job. Remember that fellow João we took on as a temporary hand last month?"

"Not the João who goes very odd when the moon is full?"

"Not him," said Robin. "No, this João is married to one of Fia's sisters, Neusa. The one with the big nose. Turns out he's quite a character. He came down to ask me for a job, and seemed delighted when I took him on. But then I heard he's not happy with the house I'm offering. Wouldn't tell me direct, oh dear, no—he's much too *mineiro* for that. But he told someone who told someone else, and it got back to me just like it was meant to!"

"Which house did you have in mind?" I asked.

"I asked Jair if he'd rent me the spare house on his place. It doesn't have any electricity, but João told me he didn't mind that. Said he'd never lived in a house with electricity anyway."

"So what's the problem?"

"It's all to do with hot lunches. João says it's too far for his wife to bring him a hot lunch, and he can't abide a cold meal."

It was only later that we learned the significance of this. Casual laborers—who were hired only by the day—were known as *bóias frias* (cold lunches), but regular farm workers insisted on having a hot meal delivered to them in the fields.

The whole issue of meals and mealtimes was something that took a little getting used to. Robin and I had breakfast early, but Albertinho and Antonio started work at seven on an empty stomach; they stopped at nine thirty for a large meal of rice and beans with vegetables and polenta, and occasionally a piece of salt pork or an egg. We had a coffee break at eleven; they had one at twelve. We had a sandwich or a bowl of soup somewhere around one; they stopped for more rice and beans at three and then worked through till five. We lit the woodstove in the evenings and had a cooked supper; they had a coffee after work.

With such variations in our timetables it was a miracle that anything got done. But somehow it did, and when I compared things with how they had been a few months earlier, I could see clear signs of progress. Robin's plan was to get the farm running smoothly, starting with improvements to the houses. Jobs on the list included clearing the pastures, fixing the fencing, planting fodder grass and cane for the cattle, and building a better corral, barn, and later a proper dairy.

The three men had made a good start. They'd cleared the thick growth of bush on the hillside and installed hundreds of feet of straight, tight fencing. The worst of the holes in the road had been filled in, and Albertinho had dug drains on the boggy bits. The staff houses had been fixed up and painted, the cane and fodder fields had been plowed and planted, and a covered milking area was under construction as the first phase of the Iracambi Dairy. The place was beginning to look like a proper farm.

After considerable difficulty and inordinate expense, we had also succeeded in buying a locally assembled Toyota pickup to replace the trusty Land Rover, which was not legally permitted to remain in the country for more than six months. The only four-wheel drive vehicle available, the model had been designed in the 1950s, was shoddily made, handled badly, and was rapidly promoted in Robin's eyes to The Worst Car I Have Ever Owned. In its honeymoon period (which lasted less than a week), he named it the Amazon Queen, but it wasn't long before he was referring to it as That Piece of Junk. We had also bought a handsome gray horse called Floriano, who came with a brightly painted wooden cart, and were negotiating with the local cattle dealer to buy a Holstein bull.

F ia came skipping up to the house one evening, leading a large blond nanny goat with a magnificent beard and a disdainful expression. "Here she is," she announced, tethering the goat to the gourd tree. "We've got her on a week's trial."

The goat held her head slightly to one side, looked at us out of her green eyes, effortlessly broke her rope, and walked off into the tomato patch.

"Hey!" Robin shot after her and grabbed the end of her rope. The goat stood stock-still and refused to budge. "Obstinate beast," he muttered. "That's the trouble with goats. They're almost as bad as mules."

"But she is very handsome," I pointed out as she and Robin glared at one another. "What shall we call her?"

"How about Jezebel?" offered Robin.

"Not quite right," I told him. "Keep thinking."

"Something more topical, perhaps. Golda Meir? Mrs. Gandhi?"

"You're getting hotter," I said. "Oh, I know! Mrs. Thatcher."

And Mrs. Thatcher it was.

Zé Viricius dropped by with a big smile to collect his money. Fortunately it was his day to wear the family set of teeth, otherwise we would never have followed what he was saying.

"She's a fine goat," Robin told him, counting out a wad of money. "I'm not denying that. But she's a damned nuisance. Won't stay where she's put."

Zé Viricius waved his hands in protest. "You c-can leave her on the other side of the river," he said, frowning with concentration. "Goats don't like g-getting their f-feet wet."

"She'll never stay there," Robin exclaimed. "It's not properly fenced."

"Oh yes, she will," he assured us. "G-goats hate water."

Fia led her away, but in less than five minutes she came trotting up the path and made a beeline for the vegetable patch.

"This won't do," said Robin irritably. "Either we fence off the vegetables or else we tether the goat."

Mrs. Thatcher looked at me loftily as I lunged for her rope.

"We need to get a stake," said Robin. "Hang on to her and I'll find something."

I grabbed Mrs. Thatcher while he went in search of a stout stake and drove it deep into the ground. "That's better," he said complacently, and stood back to admire his efforts, just as Mrs. Thatcher uprooted the stake and trotted demurely off into the tomato patch.

"Maybe we should fence off the tomatoes." I stifled a smile.

"Okay, okay," said Robin with clenched teeth. "I'll ask Antonio."

F ia introduced us to her parents, Jerson and Maria. They had seven children and lived on a small piece of land farther up toward Graminha peak. Like most of our neighbors they were barely making ends meet. They could grow enough to eat, but there was never any money for extras. Coffee prices had declined sharply in recent years, and Jerson could no longer afford fertilizer, so his bushes produced a smaller crop every year. The only way he could put enough food on the table was by expanding his coffee field, and the only way he could do that was by chopping down more forest. It was against the law, but with all those children to feed, what else could he do?

Somewhere along the line Dona Maria had learned to read—a bit. This gave her considerable authority in the community, reinforced by an imposing pair of steel-framed glasses perched on the very end of her prominent nose. She was also a leading light in the local church group.

With a few notable exceptions, our neighbors were religious people who attended Mass when they could and celebrated the myriad saints' days with considerable gusto. None of this stopped them from hunting in our forest, fishing in our rivers, selling us defective merchandise, or attempting to take advantage of our presence in innumerable highly creative ways.

Jesus, His mother, and all His saints were considered to be living members of the community; their names were constantly called upon, and everything was dependent on their good will. Regular prayer cycles were held, in accordance with the seasons. May was the month of the Blessed Virgin Mary, and every house erected a wooden cross outside the front door, decorated with colored paper or strips of cloth. There was much visiting back and forth, and prayers would be said for nine consecutive nights and were frequently concluded by the letting off of a firework or two. Easter and patron saints' days were celebrated with particular fervor, and accompanied by serious amounts of food, liquor, and general merriment.

Not all the locals were Catholics, however. Several competing Protestant sects had attracted converts in sufficient numbers to upset the local padres, who accused the Protestants of not being proper Christians—which the Protestants rebutted by maintaining that since the Catholics hadn't been born again they were excluded from the Book of Life. In order to preserve themselves from contamination, the Protestants (who referred to themselves as Believers) protected their virtue by means of draconian rules on such matters as dos and don'ts (mostly don'ts) for women, concerned with dress, head coverings, and the dangers of tobacco, liquor, and sex. The Catholics were considerably more advanced on the question of women's liberation, while the Believers took a mournful delight in insisting that a woman's place was in the home and that no good would come of letting her out.

Albertinho had never been known to darken the door of a church, and neither had Jair and Cassilda. But Fia and her family were assiduous Catholics, and they hadn't been on the *fazenda* long before she invited us to a prayer meeting in the little house across the river that she shared with Antonio, their three children, and the pig.

On the appointed evening Robin and I made our way through the field, crossed the river on the stepping stones, added our shoes to the pile on the back veranda, and, stooping our heads, entered the kitchen.

The scene that met our eyes was in stark contrast to the Catholic church in Limeira, with its plaster saints and jam jars of wilting flowers. The little group that had assembled in the simplicity of that neatly whitewashed kitchen was expecting to meet with God, and I felt sure He would answer their prayers.

In accordance with local custom we circled the room, taking everyone by the hand and murmuring a blessing over each child. Dona Maria adjusted her glasses, picked up a well-worn service sheet, and began. She read slowly but clearly, stumbling occasionally over the difficult bits but tackling everything, including instructions such as "Now the leader will turn toward the people and say . . ." From time to time she led the company in enthusiastic but not very tuneful singing. When she got to the end of the service sheet, she laid it down, drew her glasses off her nose, snapped them shut, and settled herself on the wooden bench by the stove.

Her place was taken by a dapper figure with a fine mustache and elegant blue jacket who introduced himself as Toninho and proceeded to give us a short talk based on the Bible readings: the light of the world and the salt of the earth. He lit a candle and sent it around so each person could hold the light and pass it on. He then poured a few grains of salt into each outstretched hand and told us how salt added savor to our food as well as preserved it. He spoke as though he expected Jesus to walk through the door at any moment, and I couldn't help thinking that if He did, He would feel right at home.

I had been looking forward all week to Sunday. The weather had set in fine and hot, and Robin and I had promised each other a picnic by the river. We had discovered a wonderful hidden pool, a secret place where no one ever went.

To reach it you turned left up the river behind the corral, walked watchfully past the place where Albertinho claimed there was a boa constrictor, and headed into the forest. You scrambled alongside a chain of waterfalls till you came to the pool. It was completely surrounded by tall trees, and the scent from the swamp lilies was intoxicating. You could warm yourself on the rocks and then jump into the swirling water, swimming strongly against the current and up under the waterfall to wedge yourself in the rocks for the hydro massage of a lifetime. Best of all, it was totally private. People said it was a bottomless pool, and they were frightened to go there.

I had just finished cutting the sandwiches when I heard the sound of a horse trotting up the path. "Bother!" I muttered to myself. "Whoever it is, I hope they don't stay long."

Robin straightened up from weeding the tomatoes and looked inquiringly toward the visitor. I ducked into the kitchen out of sight and prayed fervently that my plans for a lazy afternoon were not going to be affected.

"Binka!" called Robin. "It's Fat Aparecida—you know, the wife of Pedro up by the Graminha church. She's taken sick and swears she's dying. Pedro sent to say he's sorry to bother us but could we please go up there and take a look at her?"

Aparecida lived in a pretty whitewashed house surrounded by scarlet canna lilies. A stout lady in her forties, she was much given to fits of the vapors, and Antonio told me that when she was crossed she regularly threatened to kill herself. But Fia had told me only that morning, and in the strictest confidence, that Aparecida and Toninho the catechist had been having an affair. "Ought to know better, a woman of her age," she sniffed. "And as for Toninho, you won't believe what *he* said. We called the church group together last night and told him we couldn't have him in the leadership any longer and he told us we were a bunch of hypocrites, and he'd repented of his sin and was joining the Believers. Pedro is pretending to know nothing, and Aparecida's taken to her bed."

"I'm not much inclined to go up there," I told Robin. "Everyone says she's strong as a horse."

"I know, I know," said Robin. "But apparently she does have a history of heart problems. You never know, maybe she really *is* ill."

"All right," I said reluctantly. "I'll go if you think I should. But I bet you there's nothing wrong."

"Tell you what," Robin offered, "if she really is ill I'll take her to hospital."

"It's a deal," I replied, and went in to collect my medical kit: stethoscope and manual for barefoot doctors. Designed for places like ours where there was no medical help easily available, this manual was one of my prized possessions. Written in simple language and profusely illustrated, it took the mystery out of medicine. All disease is self-limiting, it explained. People either recover or they die. The barefoot doctor needs to be able to recognize the symptoms of acute illness, and to know when the moment has come to seek expert help. The rest is common sense.

Over the preceding months we had several times been called out to look at the sick, and to take them to hospital if necessary. Since we had the only vehicle in the area we felt obliged to help out, even though frequently all that was required was a little reassurance.

It was a beautiful drive. I took the car slowly up the steep hill, careful to avoid the ruts. It was deliciously cool in the forest, and I stopped to take a deep breath of the woody smell of the trees. The road wound over the muddy river crossing and up a rocky hill. Against the backdrop of the blue peaks, a valley spread out before me, broad and wild. I drove up through the neat little farms, past the fields of dark green coffee and the miniature Alpine pastures with their cows and horses. Smoke came from the chimneys, and from time to time a figure would wave.

These people are a whole lot more friendly than the Limeira crowd, I reflected as I climbed higher and higher, past the pink-washed Graminha school and up to the little chapel among the trees.

As I pulled into the yard Pedro came running out. "Thank goodness you're here!" he cried. "Aparecida says she's dying. I've sent the boy to the *farmácia*."

I thought of the Limeira pharmacist with his dusty shelves full of outdated antibiotics. In spite of the fact that country families had been using herbal remedies for years, many people despised traditional knowledge and had developed a magical belief in the power of antibiotics. "I've got a terrible cold," they would say, "I'm going for a shot." So they would part with their hard-earned money in exchange for a shot of something that could do no good and might well do them harm. It saddened me to think of Pedro spending his money for nothing.

Aparecida had arranged herself on the sofa, surrounded by weeping children. As soon as she was sure I was within earshot she gave a loud groan.

"Well, Aparecida," I said briskly, "what's the matter with you?"

"It's my heart," she said in a stage whisper, looking around to make sure everyone had heard. "Every so often it stops beating. If I close my eyes I can see my dear dead mother coming for me. I won't be troubling you much longer."

"Aparecida," I said, "I want you to listen to my heart." I took out the stethoscope and placed the earphones over her ears. "This is what a healthy heart sounds like."

Aparecida was sufficiently curious to listen to the steady *lub dub-dub* of my heartbeat. I checked hers. It sounded every bit as good. "Now," I said, "I want you to listen to yours."

"I don't know," quavered Aparecida, "if I have the strength." And with another groan she fell back against the pillows. Pedro looked at me imploringly. The children resumed their sniffling.

Aparecida appeared to have stopped breathing. I opened her blouse and listened for a heartbeat. I could find nothing.

"Oh, *shit*!" I muttered under my breath. "Perhaps she really is dying this time!" But then I found her heartbeat, and caught her surreptitiously opening an eye.

"I think, Pedro," I said, "that we should leave Aparecida to get some rest. Is there any coffee in the kitchen?"

Aparecida shot me a venomous look as I led the whole family out of the room. "Don't worry, Pedro," I told him, "it's nothing serious."

"She says she'll die if she stays in this place," Pedro confided. "She says the people around here are wicked gossips. She says we must move right away from here if she is to get any better."

"Listen, Pedro," I told him. "Aparecida will be fine. Her heart's as good as yours or mine. Keep the children away from her and let her sleep. She'll be on her feet by tomorrow, I guarantee."

"Oh," said Pedro. "Do you really think so?"

"Yes, Pedro. I really think so."

Back on the *fazenda* I found Robin in the corral with Antonio dosing the cows. "How was Aparecida?" he asked me.

"Absolutely fine," I replied. "There's nothing the matter with her at all."

Antonio snorted. "What that woman needs," he said, "Is fifty cc of worming medicine. In the backside."

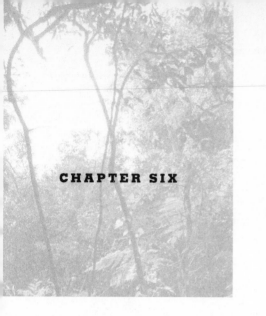

CHAPTER SIX

The Piano

D o you know what?" said Fia, sweeping the cinders vigorously off the kitchen ceiling. "Aparecida has moved her family into Limeira. Packed up lock, stock, and barrel and gone."

"Did Toninho go with her?" I steadied the stepladder as Fia leaned perilously over to hook a spiderweb off the beams.

"Oh dear me, no. That's all over. Like I told you, he's joined the Believers. Goes around quoting the Bible all the time, it's driving his family crazy."

I relayed the news to Robin that evening as we sat by the fire eating our supper.

"That *is* interesting!" he said. "She didn't run off with Toninho, did she?"

"That's the next bit of gossip. You remember Toninho was a pillar of the Graminha church? Apparently Dona Maria had words with him and he stormed out and joined the Believers."

"No kidding?" Robin spooned chili sauce onto his plate. He threw a log onto the woodstove and I pulled my chair up to the blaze. "By the way, I forgot to tell you. We got a letter from the shipping company."

"*What?*" I perked up.

"They say our stuff is due into Rio in a couple of weeks."

"Hey, that's *fabulous*!" I rushed up and gave him a hug.

"I shouldn't get too excited if I were you. It can take weeks to unload. Last I heard, the stevedores were on strike. Brazilian ports are famous for being inefficient, and things go missing all the time."

"They won't steal *our* things," I said with conviction. "There's nothing worth stealing."

"Hope they don't find the computer."

"They won't. I labeled it TYPEWRITER. And I labeled the monitor TV."

"I tell you one thing they won't steal, and that's the piano."

"They could drop it," I worried. "Remember how they managed to smash the lid when we moved to India?"

"They won't. Lightning never strikes twice. But that reminds me of something. We're going to have to demolish a wall to make room for it. Unless you want it in the kitchen."

"Don't be ridiculous."

"Albertinho will do it in a flash. He's turning into a champion builder. It's just a question of whether he can tear himself away from his current project."

Albertinho was currently working on the barn. "Can't have a proper farm without a barn," Robin had said, "although I don't know where we can find enough flat ground to build one." But Albertinho had found a spot, and had already started leveling the ground. He dropped by to borrow a hammer and announced that he'd enlisted João to help him.

"Do you reckon you can put in a road so we can get a truck up there?" asked Robin. "We'll need to deliver the bricks and cement."

"Ah eh." Albertinho shouldered his shovel and went up the hill whistling.

"Better not distract him by asking about the wall," Robin muttered. "We'll deal with that later. Now, d'you want to see the design for the barn?" He rummaged around the pile of papers on the desk and produced an old envelope covered with calculations. "It's perfectly straightforward. Three outside walls and a couple of internal ones so we can make storage rooms. The front of the barn is open so you can drive in, and this here is the inspection pit."

"The *what*?"

"The inspection pit. So we can do proper maintenance on the farm machinery. Oil and grease the cars. That sort of thing."

"Sounds very professional," I remarked. "Let's go up there and you can show me."

As we strolled up the hill I looked back at our house with a certain satisfaction. I had color-washed the walls and painted the wooden shutters, Albertinho had repaired the bench under the gourd tree, and Robin had planted flowers around the house. Hummingbirds were hovering around the feeders; the vegetable plot had been fenced off; and Mrs. Thatcher, in collar and chain, was nibbling delicately at the lower leaves of one of the banana trees.

Up at the building site João and Albertinho were sitting in a shady spot, eating thick slices of corn cake and sharing the crumbs with Doggie. The walls were marked up with posts and string, and they were halfway through digging the foundations.

"This inspection pit." Albertinho stroked his mustache. "Jair was asking me the other day why we wanted to dig a damn great hole in the ground. So we could look underneath the car, I said, and he said, why did we want to do that? To make sure the car was going all right, I said, and he told me he'd never once looked under *his* car and it was going fine. I said the hole was called an inspection pit, and you use it for doing repairs, and he said there weren't any cars to repair and anyway nobody could get up there because there wasn't a road."

Thinking about roads led us to a serious reevaluation of our business plan, such as it was. We had laid aside a special fund to get the farm up and running, and Robin's back-of-the-envelope calculations reckoned we'd soon be earning lots of money from the cows. But things weren't working out quite according to plan. The cows were starting to produce milk, but costs were high and prices were low. Fortunately for us, salaries were low, too, and since the dollar was doing well against the local currency we still had sufficient reserves to keep us going, even though inflation made it difficult to make any accurate financial predictions.

It was the first time we'd lived with inflation, and we rapidly found ourselves acquiring a whole new set of skills. The inflation rate varied from 10 to 80 percent. Per month. Most Brazilians spent their salary the day they received it—and most shopkeepers put up their prices accordingly. If you were quick off the mark you might find an item in the supermarket going at last week's price, but the supermarket staff tended to be quicker than you were. If you happened to have any spare cash you could either convert it to black-market dollars, buy gold, or put it on overnight deposit in the bank. Since we had access to neither gold nor dollars, we had to use the overnight account. The one thing you should never do was keep cash in hand, since its value would erode by the day. Prices would stay at a certain level for a certain length of time and then would double overnight. When prices were low to producers, they hoarded their produce—to the extent they could—which meant that some items would mysteriously disappear off the market and you would have to either resort to the black market or do without. Creative Brazilians had evolved a sophisticated system of barter whereby money never actually changed hands. But it did depend on having something to barter with. It was difficult for all of us to figure out what any particular item was worth at any particular time, and it was to be seven years before inflation was finally brought under control.

"Talking of building," I said, as Robin and I walked back to the house, "what's the story on taking down the partition wall so we can fit the piano in?"

"I decided we can do it ourselves," Robin told me. "In fact, I was going to suggest we do it this afternoon."

"Fine," I said. "You don't think it's a load-bearing wall, do you?"

Robin scratched his head. "Doesn't look like it. But it's better to be on the safe side, so we'll put the stepladder underneath the crossbeam and prop it up with the car jack. If it looks like it needs to be reinforced, we'll cut a tree to make a central column. Wouldn't want the house to come crumbling round our ears."

The house was a warren of small rooms, four bedrooms and two small central rooms that we were planning to knock into one. None of the rooms was larger than ten feet by ten, except the kitchen, which was thirteen by thirteen.

Fortunately we weren't overburdened with furniture. We had converted one of the bedrooms into a study, with the desk fitted along one wall. We had four single beds, and we'd bought a double mattress while we were awaiting the arrival of the antique four-poster bed that had accompanied us around the world. Our hardwood dining table and eight chairs fit neatly into the kitchen, the camping gas stove was perched on top of a steel filing cabinet that Robin had acquired from somewhere, and the front room was furnished with a couple of benches made by Albertinho. We had painted and polished the wooden floors, whitewashed the walls, and Robin had tiled the concrete sink on the back veranda.

I put a scarf over my hair and made a pot of coffee, then found a pair of work gloves and wedged the front door open. Robin inspected the beam, selected the spot to place the jack, and tapped the wall tentatively with a hammer. The plaster crumbled, revealing a layer of irregular, handmade bricks. He carefully removed one brick and then another and handed them to me. I stacked them outside the front door and piled the rubble in the corner.

It was dusty work but satisfying, and it wasn't long before we had excavated a hole big enough to put in the stepladder and the car jack. "Just as well there's nobody around," I remarked to Robin as I trudged over to the door with another load of bricks. "Wouldn't it be just our luck to have Jair turn up the very moment the house falls down?"

But Jair stayed away, and the house stayed up, and after I had swept up the dust and Robin had removed the rubble the room looked positively spacious.

"That's far better," said Robin as he folded the stepladder. "Can't think why we didn't take the wall out earlier."

I hadn't lived in such a tiny house since our days in graduate school, but Fia, who was helping out with the cleaning, kept complaining that the house was too big. I smiled to myself as I thought back to the large luxurious houses in the Washington suburbs. Houses that were empty all day long as the occupants worked to pay off their mortgages. Neighborhoods where people hardly knew one another's names. Sidewalks where nobody walked. Streets where no children played. The contrast with Iracambi could hardly be greater, not only with our little house but with all the other little houses, where there was always space for an extra person in the big bed that took up the whole room, and extra guests would be accommodated on rush mats on the floor.

Robin had been raised in an oversize log cabin on a mountain in Kenya, with a glorious garden where seven gardeners toiled under the direction of his mother. The house was full of flowers, and every afternoon his parents drank tea served on a silver tray with

scones and butter. The rooms smelled of woodsmoke and floor polish, and at night the family sat by the dim light of the generator
and were waited on by servants in long gowns. I was raised in England in a series of Georgian houses furnished with antiques
where the silver and brass were polished till they gleamed, there
was a constant stream of guests, and someone was always playing
music. Home to Robin was a place where he could keep his stuff.
He was an inveterate collector of nuts and bolts, pieces of rope, old
magazines and books. Home to me was a place to be comfortable.
I pictured the house that we would build, with whitewashed walls,
colorful hangings, and painted tiles. But we couldn't get started on
it just yet. There were more important things to be done first, and
we needed to devote our time and our money to the farm.

Albertinho and João worked like demons on the barn, and
three weeks later it was finished. The inspection pit became
the talk of the neighborhood, and Fia's brother came down to ask
if we were hiring any mechanics. No, he didn't have any experience, and yes, he was willing to learn. But Albertinho had cornered
the market for himself. He took to going around with a large
wrench sticking out of his pocket, and spent most of his weekends
in the barn—repairing a gate, making a new feed trough for the
cattle, or greasing the car. On Sunday afternoons he would dis-
creetly borrow Robin's tools and hold a bicycle clinic outside his
house. João and his family moved into Albertinho's granary, and
Albertinho built them a woodstove and ran a wire across the yard
so that they could have light in the evenings.

There were other developments. Antonio was milking a handful of cows in the makeshift shelter on the site of the new dairy,
and Fia was making soft white cheeses that tasted like Greek feta.
Every week she would wrap them carefully in a cloth, place them

in a wheelbarrow, and steer it across the tree trunk that served as a footbridge over the river. We took the cheese into Muriaé and sold it to Dona Maria at the fruit shop. She swore it was the best in town and begged us for more. "Of course it's the best," said Fia complacently. "*Our* cheese is made from pure milk. Most people water the milk down. Or worse."

"What do you mean?" I asked her.

"Well, I'm naming no names." Fia rolled her eyes. "But there are some people who dilute the milk with cow's urine."

"Yuck!" I exclaimed, feeling sick to my stomach.

M uriaé was our local town, the county capital, and the place to get anything beyond the bare basics available in Limeira. Before coming here and realizing quite how bad the roads were, I had thought I might teach English there. Do aerobics. Finally master the guitar. But the town lay one-and-a-half-hour's tedious journey from the *fazenda,* and sometimes during the rains you couldn't get there at all. There were three roads that led to it, and none of them was easy. You could go to Limeira, turn left through the square, and make your way over a dirt road through a couple of hamlets until you joined the main road and wound down the mountain to the hot little valley where Muriaé sweltered in perpetual heat. Alternatively, you could go through Belisário and head down the precarious mountain road until you met the main Rio-Bahia highway, with ten glorious miles of paving. A third option led through the community of São Domingos, past the hydro-powered generator that supplied electricity to the surrounding area, and down onto the Rio-Bahia at a point farther toward Muriaé.

The roads were all bad, either dusty and rutted or muddy and potholed, and Muriaé turned out to be a disappointment when we did get there. It was a sprawling town on a junction of two major roads, but it hadn't quite decided what to do with itself. Although large enough to be a proper town, it still behaved like an overgrown village. Loudspeakers were mounted on lampposts on street corners, so that people could listen to news items from the local radio station, just as they did in small towns in the interior where no one could read. Shopkeepers couldn't decide whether to keep country hours for lunch (nine thirty to ten thirty), city hours (one to two), or something in between (eleven to one,) which made it hard to plan a shopping expedition.

The cobbled streets and shady squares housed a miscellaneous collection of unprepossessing supermarkets with unhygienic-looking meat counters and wilting vegetables. Because of inflation everything had to be paid for in cash, and we sometimes found at the checkout counter that we didn't have enough, and would have to decide between peanut butter and floor polish. The banks were cramped and understaffed, with long lines of people waiting impatiently in the heat, which remained unaffected by the groaning of the ancient air conditioners. There wasn't much of a service culture, either; if the item you wanted wasn't available, most shopkeepers wouldn't trouble themselves to find it for you. It was too hot to bother.

But there were compensations, which we discovered over time. A mechanic named Carlinho performed miracles to keep our car running, and we found a nice young doctor at the hospital. The bus station was a textbook example of ugly architecture, but there was a good bus service to Rio, and three daily buses to Limeira. And in the backstreets there were all manner of craftsmen: boot makers, saddlers, dressmakers, a good bakery, an ice cream shop, and fixers of every imaginable kind. Muriaé wasn't much of a town, but it would do.

Fortunately we were able to live to an increasingly large extent off the land. We drank our own milk, ate our own cheese, and bought eggs from Maria. Sometimes our neighbors would drop by with a bag of beans, a sack of unhulled rice, a handful of manioc roots, or green leaves for a salad. The surrounding families were getting accustomed to our presence, and we were slowly being accepted by the community. Robin shifted a load of corn for Jerson, and Maria gave him a cloth bag of peanuts. Old Olavo brought a letter down for me to read to him, and dug in his saddlebags to produce a root vegetable that looked like sweet potatoes and tasted like artichokes. Adão from next door traded some hard brown sugar for bamboo to fence his vegetable garden, and one evening Zé Viricius dropped by. He was wearing a neatly pressed shirt and the family set of teeth.

"I expect he's come to ask after Mrs. Thatcher," Robin whispered.

But Zé Viricius had come on another errand entirely. "It's about the b-b-bees," he began, panting with the effort.

Robin sprang to the rescue. "Zé Viricius and I have been talking about putting a hive or two in our forest," he explained.

"Great idea," I said.

Zé Viricius beamed.

"But wait a minute." A sudden thought had struck me. "You're not talking killer bees, are you?"

"Well, yes," Robin replied carefully. "Brazil *is* where the killer bees come from—in fact, they've almost driven out the native bees. But they're not really aggressive. And they make wonderful honey."

"What if they attack?" I persisted.

"They only attack if you upset them. And all you have to do is jump into the nearest river."

"Hmm!" I grunted, wondering what a normal husband would have said.

The secret, Zé Viricius taught us, was to locate the hives in the thick forest, at least a kilometer away from the dairy. Otherwise the bees were attracted to the molasses in the cattle feed, and swarmed around the troughs. He taught us to treat the bees with respect, and we were never attacked. He also insisted we should only visit the hives when the moon was in the right phase.

Everything on the farm was governed by the moon, as Maria explained one day when we met over the milking.

"Plants that grow above the ground have to be planted on the waxing moon," she told me.

"Why's that?"

Antonio had his head buried in the flank of a cow and was skillfully directing the stream of milk into a bucket.

"Because of the sap," he told me in a muffled voice. "The waxing moon draws the sap up so the plant grows stronger. Root vegetables, on the other hand, they get planted on the waning moon. Because the sap goes down into the roots, see?"

"Is that why you cut fence posts on the waning moon?"

"That's it," he confirmed. "The wood's drier so it doesn't rot."

Once we had grasped the principle, we did our best to put it into practice. Robin decided to clean out the hill above the house to make more pasture for the cows. It was a large area and much of it had reverted to bush. He figured it would take about twelve mandays, and put Albertinho and João on the job on the first day of the waning moon.

They made a good start, and Albertinho assured us they'd be done by the week's end. But early the next morning Antonio announced that a section of the fence was down, and five of the heifers were missing. He'd go after them, but could Albertinho please fix the fence? By the time Albertinho had cut the posts, dug the holes, rounded up the wire and staples, and repaired the fence, the day was half gone, and although João worked away doggedly it didn't look as though he had made much progress.

The following day was a public holiday and the day after that it rained nonstop. By Friday of the first week less than a quarter of the field had been cleared, but Albertinho was convinced they'd finish on time.

Albertinho was wrong. João's wife went off to visit her mother and wasn't there when one of their children cut herself very badly and João had to take her to the *farmácia* in Limeira. It was supposed to be the dry season but it drizzled for two days and the bush was too wet to cut properly. Albertinho developed a hacking cough, and before we knew it the moon had changed and the field was less than half cleared. The whole business would have to wait for another couple of weeks.

It would have been funny if it hadn't been so exasperating. Nothing seemed to work according to plan. We bought an expensive bag of grass seed for one of the pastures but it didn't germinate, and when Robin complained to the store in Muriaé they said we must have planted it wrong. We tried again and the birds ate it all. We spread fertilizer on the hillside and a heavy rain washed it all away in the night. We summoned all hands to build a new fence and then somebody's cousin died and everyone had to put down tools and go to the funeral. I grumbled to Robin, and he told me that's how it was with farming.

But I did wonder whether his optimistic predictions of farm income were exaggerated. Leaving the comfort of Washington was all very well, and I'd never been extravagant, but I didn't want to see everything eroding away because "that's how it is with farming." And if that was how it was, why were we here at all? We'd have done better to stick to what we knew.

W eeks passed, and there was no news of the ship bringing our things. But I started dreaming of them and planning where I would put them. Albertinho made me a bookcase for the study and some shelves for the kitchen, and Fia polished the floor in the newly opened space for the piano. I started waking up in the morning with a pleasant feeling of anticipation. Maybe today would be the day? But days came and went and Robin told me to stop worrying about it. "It'll come when it'll come," he said, annoyingly.

"Well, I just hope everyone's around when it does," I retorted.

Of course they weren't. Albertinho was in Limeira having a tooth pulled. João had run a nail into his foot and was off for a couple of days. Antonio reported that one of the cows had fallen into the ditch and could we please let him have a rope and another pair of hands, so Fia had run over to enlist the help of one of Jair's sons. Robin had wandered off to look for a rope, and I had gone to the vegetable patch to pick some lettuce for lunch.

Somehow Mrs. Thatcher had managed to break through the fence and was chewing on the young lettuce with every sign of enjoyment. I yelled at her—she paid no attention. I whacked her on the rump—she ignored me. I grabbed her by the horns and she shook me off as if I were a fly. I lost my balance and fell into the compost heap. Mrs. Thatcher looked at me sardonically and headed back to the lettuces. I was just dusting myself down and thinking black thoughts when Fia came panting up.

"There's a truck on the road," she announced, "and it's stuck in that big hole outside Albertinho's. The driver's swearing blue murder and saying that if someone doesn't get him out of there he'll never get back to Rio."

"*Rio?*"

"That's what he said. And he's got a big wooden box."

"Big wooden box? Oh my God! It must be our stuff! I must tell Robin! Fia, get this damned goat out of here before I kill her."

"No problem." Fia picked up a stick and Mrs. Thatcher trotted out as if butter wouldn't melt in her mouth.

My thoughts flew to the piano, and I prayed fervently that I would find it in one piece. I came from a family with a long history of taking pianos to far-flung places. My great-grandmother had studied with Robert Schumann, and everyone had told her she had the makings of a professional pianist. But her father would have nothing of it, so he married her off to a colonial officer serving in India and that was the end of that. My grandmother had married an army officer and taken a piano to Persia and later to New Delhi, and my mother had been raised in a large drafty house in the north of Scotland that had two grand pianos.

I panted up to the barn, with a jumble of piano memories jostling for attention in my head. The live television broadcast in Jakarta where someone had forgotten to ensure there was a piano in the studio. Arriving in Rwanda with a nasty case of dysentery and crawling into the hotel intent on lying flat, only to be accosted by a silver-haired Frenchman who kissed my hand and assured me that he had been waiting for me since January. He dosed me with a local remedy that left me constipated for a week and bore me off to his house to play Beethoven, assuring me that his wife would be "*enchantée.*" She was not. I remembered playing the first chords at a concert one stifling night in Calcutta, just as the lights went out, leaving me at the mercy of a well-meaning usher who stood behind me with a fan in one hand and a candlestick in the other, dripping hot wax down the back of my neck.

"Take it easy," Robin told me, when I delivered the glad tidings. "You run on down there and get the truck sorted out. I'll attend to the cow."

I gave him a look of pure hatred and stomped off.

I shot over to Albertinho's house to find an elderly truck, painted in bright colors and spattered with mud, firmly bogged down in the wettest part of the road. The moving men were standing on the bank giving conflicting advice, and Maria's children were watching goggle-eyed while the driver rocked his vehicle backward and forward, digging the truck in ever deeper. Jair came trotting up on his mule, tethered it to the fence, and walked around shaking his head. "It's going to be quite a job getting that truck out of here," he announced with a sly grin.

"Albertinho can do it," I told him.

"He's not here," said Jair happily. "Gone off to the dentist. I met him on the road."

"He'll be back any time now," said Maria unexpectedly. "The bus got stuck and the dentist couldn't make it."

"Where did you hear that?" I asked incredulously.

"On the radio," she answered, and at that moment, to everyone's relief, Albertinho's gray horse came trotting up the road.

Albertinho inspected the truck from every angle, cleared his throat, spat, and turned to the irate truck driver. "Well, my friend," he grinned, "you've got yourself well and truly stuck."

"*Filho da puta!*" muttered the driver.

"We'll need the Hi-Lift jack and a shovel," said Robin, who came breezing up. The cow had been rescued and he was all smiles.

Humming under his breath, Albertinho went off to the barn, where he had stored his tools. For the next thirty minutes he and the driver dug doggedly through the glutinous mud while the moving men laid a ribbon of logs in front of the wheels. Robin fetched the Toyota and made a couple of unsuccessful attempts to dislodge the truck. On the third try, with much revving of the engine, he pulled it onto dry land.

Everyone trooped over to Albertinho's house to wash off the mud, and Maria came out with a flask of coffee just as Antonio arrived to report that the cow was safely bedded down in the dairy.

The truck driver hosed the mud off his shoes, swallowed two glasses of coffee in quick succession, and then set off to inspect the wooden bridge. He came back looking disgusted. "I'm not taking my truck over there," he told us flatly. "Half the planks are rotten. We'll have to find a place to offload everything, and the quicker the better because I don't trust the weather."

"It's not going to rain," said Robin calmly, ignoring the heavy cloud that was building up over the mountains. "You guys unpack the container and we'll load the boxes into the back of the Toyota. The best place to do that is in front of Albertinho's house."

"That won't work," said the truck driver gloomily. "The truck won't fit through the gate."

"We'll move the gate," said Robin.

Albertinho nodded and signaled to Antonio. Together they grasped the gate and lifted it smoothly off its hinges. Whistling tunefully, Albertinho took a crowbar, loosened the gatepost, put both arms around it, and heaved it out. After Maria had shooed the chickens out of the way, the driver inched his truck onto the bare earth of the yard, and his men started to unload.

In our twenty-four years of married life Robin and I had moved house twenty times, but we'd never had to unpack everything and load it into the back of a pickup.

"You've got a lot of stuff," remarked Jair as he settled himself on the front steps to oversee the proceedings. "Are you planning to stay long?" I ignored him and concentrated on checking the items on the packing list as each container was opened. The boxes were stacked in two piles: the larger one to go into storage in the barn and the smaller one for the house. All we needed for now was the furniture, the piano, the computer, books and music, extra bedding, kitchen stuff, and Robin's toolkit.

The sky was clouding over as the movers worked to open the crates and unload the boxes. Jair darted around collecting discarded packing materials, Robin made trip after trip in the Toyota with a couple of men to help, Albertinho and Antonio went off to fix the bad spot in the road, and the driver made his way into Maria's kitchen in search of something to eat.

By three thirty everything had been unpacked and stowed, and the only thing left was the piano. It was heavy and awkward and really required specialist movers, but we would have to do our best with what we had. While Albertinho produced a couple of stout planks and laid them on the tailgate of the Toyota, Robin marshaled four men to lift, and the bulky crate was carefully maneuvered aboard.

Albertinho slung the planks inside and jumped up to steady the crate as Robin eased the truck over the bridge, through the puddles, and up the hill to the blue house. The next step was to get the crate out of the truck and through the front door. We then had to remove the piano, screw in its legs, turn it right side up, and lower it very carefully into position. This was the most delicate part of the operation, and a minute's distraction could be fatal. I held my breath, but everything went off without a hitch and twenty minutes later the piano was safely installed—probably the only grand piano within a hundred miles.

Robin heaved a sigh of relief. "Okay," he said briskly. "We'd better go down and get that truck out of there." We climbed into the Toyota and headed for Albertinho's just as a curtain of cloud came streaming over the mountain and there was a sudden clap of thunder. The driver had backed out of Albertinho's yard and positioned his truck in front of the place where he had been stuck earlier. Albertinho filled the hole with stones and cut some brush to lay on either side of it. Leaning on his shovel, he lit a cigarette.

"You'll be okay now," he assured the driver. "Just take a run at it and don't stop."

The driver swung into his seat, switched on the ignition, and gunned the engine. For a heart-stopping moment his wheels spun, but he kept at it and got safely past. His crew trudged after him and clambered aboard for the long journey to Rio.

"Good work, everyone, thanks!" said Robin.

"Well, that's all right then," said Antonio. "I'd better be off now to milk the cows."

The first heavy drops of rain began to fall.

"We got that truck out of here in the nick of time," Robin told Albertinho. "Another half hour and we could have been in trouble."

"Ah eh." Albertinho nodded as a sudden wind swept down the valley, blowing leaves and twigs across the road. Taking to our heels, we ran back to the shelter of his house just as the rain set in. Robin and I jumped into the car and headed home through the storm. We rushed into the house to slam the shutters against the driving rain, and had just sunk down on the sofa in the half gloom when there was a violent crack of thunder overhead, and the rain found a new spot in the eternally leaky roof.

Robin snatched up a tarpaulin and draped it over the piano. "Can't afford to let it get wet after all that," he told me. "Now how about a tune? A little Mozart, perhaps?"

"Don't be an idiot," I replied, and burst into tears.

CHAPTER SEVEN

The Casa Grande

After the excitement of playing the first chords on the piano, setting up the computer, and rediscovering a few prized possessions, it was time to start thinking about building our house. First and foremost we had to select the site, and there were several alternatives. The first was down in the valley, with a wonderful long view across the green pasture to Itajuru. It was a sheltered, sunny spot with a clear spring bubbling up at the foot of a rock face covered with flowering bromeliads. But we came to the conclusion that it was too close to the road.

"Just imagine," said Robin, "if they paved the road."

"Are you crazy?" I laughed.

"No, I'm serious. It's a county road, after all."

"But they never maintain it."

"That's not the point. If they ever did fix the road we'd be too close to it. Plus we'd be on a corner. Might have a ten-ton truck plowing into the kitchen or something."

We discovered the second possible site quite by chance when we were scrambling up the river behind the rock pool. It was an idyllic little clearing in the forest right next to a waterfall. The dappled sunlight moved across the rocks, lighting the rainbow drops of water; parrots chattered overhead; cicadas hummed; and the river ran strong and loud. Delicate feathery palms hung over the water, and above us soared an ancient tree laden with moss and orchids. Knotted lianas as thick as a person's arm snaked upward into the green leafy canopy, and a lingering scent drifted down from some invisible flower.

It was a place from which we could admire the sunrise over the valley and the sunset behind Graminha peak, but unless we cut some of the spreading forest trees we wouldn't be able to see either. Cool and leafy on a hot day, it would be dark, damp, and buggy during the rains, and the sound of rushing water, romantic though it was, meant that we couldn't hear each other speak. Sadly, we rejected it.

Once we'd decided what we did want—light, air, a place away from the road, and a north-facing aspect with the biggest view we could find—we started to look at areas that had already been cleared. The hill behind the blue house was the obvious choice—there was plenty of water and plenty of space.

After choosing the site we had to figure out how to lay hands on the building materials—most of which would come from the farm since Robin was determined to build his house out of rammed earth.

"Okay, tell me again," I asked him. "How exactly do you build something from rammed earth?"

Robin explained that rammed earth was just what it sounded like: a mixture of earth and clay, packed inside a wooden frame and tamped down. You built the wall one meter high, let it dry out, and then built another meter. You covered the walls with plastic sheeting to keep them dry, and you did the building during the dry season. Although it was a technique that had been used in several countries, nobody had heard of it in our part of Brazil. Earth was an excellent building material, he added, it cost nothing, and it would be perfect for the design he had in mind. No, he wasn't planning to run it past an architect. People had been building houses for hundreds of years before architects even existed.

R obin had been planning his dream house for most of his adult life. Its design had changed as we'd moved around the world, from a thatched cottage in Kenya to a Rajput palace in India, a Colonial manor in Virginia, and an adobe house in New Mexico. His latest design reflected his Latin American period: a Mexican-style hacienda with thick earthen walls. But there was one feature I was doubtful about—a central tower with a portcullis.

"I don't think a tower will work," I told him, as tactfully as I could. "It would be fine in Tuscany or Scotland or somewhere, but the house has to look like it belongs here. Maybe if you took away the tower . . ."

"But it's the main feature," Robin protested.

"The courtyard is wonderful," I added hastily.

"You can't see it from outside, not like the tower. But I'm glad you like the courtyard. I was thinking of making a great gate into it. Sort of like an English coaching inn."

"Show me."

He sketched it out and it looked terrific. Like one of the old colonial houses, I told him. "White walls and blue shutters."

"Geraniums in the courtyard."

"In big tubs."

"A secret garden leading off our bedroom."

"Full of scented flowers, like gardenias."

"Or jasmine."

"Will there be a fountain in the courtyard?"

Robin considered. "Could be. Or maybe a tree."

"What kind of tree?"

"A flowering tree. Flamboyant, I think."

This project was going to be fun. But who would we find to build it? I asked Robin if Albertinho would do. "I think we're going to need a real builder," he told me. "I've been asking around and it seems there are one or two, but I think our best bet is this young guy from São Pedro: John the Baptist. You've probably seen him; he's one of the stars of their football team."

"The one who plays barefoot? With the big blue eyes?"

"Everyone in São Pedro has blue eyes—they're all from the same family. But you'll recognize him when you see him. I'm inclined to favor him because he's smart, and I think he'd be on for trying something a little different. Nobody round here has ever heard of rammed earth, and the older guys might be a little hesitant to try."

Not that Robin actually knew how to build with rammed earth. But he'd bought a book in Washington and he'd been studying it carefully. We'd start by leveling the site and digging the foundations, he explained. That was going to be a big job in itself, since the foundations would be one and a half meters deep, sixty centimeters wide, and filled with stone. It was important to make them really solid because of the weight of the walls—at four meters high and fifty centimeters wide, they'd be incredibly heavy. He calculated they'd require something like four hundred tons of earth. We'd dig the earth from the field in front of the house site, and we'd turn the hole into a swimming pool. No, not a fancy blue-tiled pool, just a pond in the grass with fresh water piped into it from the spring. It would be an all-purpose pond: The cattle could drink from it, it would act as a reservoir for the dairy, and we'd be able to swim in it.

The stone for the foundations would come from the *fazenda,* he told me. "There's granite all over the place—all we have to do is to get someone to blast it. Like my parents did when they decided to build a stone house."

"But they didn't build a stone house," I said, remembering the wooden house on a mountainside in Kenya where Robin spent his childhood.

"Details, details," said Robin airily. "And you're right, they didn't. Let me tell you why. The masons worked away for six months and dug out enough stone to make a little pile. And then they worked for another six months and made another little pile. Finally after eighteen months my mother lost her patience and decided she'd never live long enough to have her stone house."

"What happened to the stone?"

"It sat around for a long time and finally they used it to build a henhouse."

The next step was to find a tractor to level the site. There were very few around, and they usually spent more time broken down than actually working. But somebody knew somebody who knew a reliable tractor driver who was rumored to be working nearby, so Antonio got on his horse and set off to strike a deal. He returned smiling broadly. "That's all fixed," he announced. "He'll drop by this afternoon to give us an estimate, and he'll start right away if the weather is okay. Albertinho says he can stay at his place and Maria will fix his lunch."

The tractor driver was a little old man with bandy legs who looked as though he'd be happier on a horse, but he knew his job and told us exactly where to place the house on the site to allow best access both to the water and the road. Once the price was settled he agreed to start the next day. He just needed to collect his things and he'd be back before nightfall.

The evening set in with a sudden chill, and after finishing his supper Robin got to his feet and pulled on his boots. "I'm just going to run over to Albertinho's," he told me. "I've remembered something I want to tell the tractor driver. Won't be long."

I threw a log on the stove and settled back with my book. Before I had finished the chapter Robin was back. "Just as well I went over there," he reported. "The poor guy was sitting outside Albertinho's house, shivering with cold. Apparently Albertinho is out somewhere and the tractor driver can't go inside until he comes back."

"Why ever not?"

"It's not the custom. He said he'd wait another ten minutes and if Albertinho wasn't back by nine would it be okay for him to come over here?"

"Perfectly idiotic him having to sit outside," I commented. "He'll catch his death of cold."

"That's how things are. If Albertinho caught him alone with Maria he'd take after him with a shotgun. Or after her, more likely. It's perfectly legal in this country for a man to kill his wife in a crime of passion."

"Crime of passion, when the poor guy is trying to warm up at the fire?"

"Albertinho might not see it that way," said Robin.

"It's not as if Maria is a raging beauty," I pointed out.

"That's not the point. After all, Albertinho did elope with her."

"*What?*"

"Maria was underage and her father wouldn't let her marry. So the lovers stole away one dark night. . . ."

"You're kidding."

"I'm serious. Maria's father chased after them but he couldn't catch them."

"However did you find out?"

"I have my sources." Robin smiled mysteriously.

* * *

The tractor driver was finished by the end of the week, and then it was time to get started on the construction. John the Baptist pedaled over on his bike to discuss the project and Robin spread out the blueprint on the kitchen table and showed him pictures of rammed-earth walls. A skinny young man with a shock of brown hair that kept falling into his eyes and a shy smile that lit up his face, he spent a long time examining the pictures and said he'd be happy to try if Robin could show him how.

"I can't *show* you, João, because I've never actually built an earth wall," Robin told him. "But I think we can figure it out between us. Mind you, we've got to dig the foundations first."

That evening Robin and I walked up the hill to the house site.

"Do you know what I'd like?" I said. "I'd like a house tour."

"Okay." Robin gave a big grin. "Come over here. This is the front porch. Just step through the door and tell me what you see."

"You tell me—you're the architect."

"All right. I'm walking through the archway into the music room. It's a nice big room, with a whole wall of bookshelves, lots of windows, and a long view out over the valley. There are windows on the inside wall, too, overlooking the courtyard. It's very light and airy, and the ceilings are high. In fact, there aren't any proper ceilings; you look up at the underside of the tiles. We'll line them with wood."

"Sounds good. What about the floors?"

"Polished wood," Robin told me. "And terra-cotta tiles in the kitchen. I think we'll have slate floors on the verandas."

"And the courtyard?"

"Cobblestones in the courtyard. Across the courtyard you come to the guest wing. Two bedrooms and bathrooms with an extra room in between. And here, to the west," he pointed toward

Graminha, "is our bedroom, and this is the study. It's got lots of bookshelves and a big desk made of hardwood. Same as the floor. And out here," he stepped out of the study door, "is the great gate to the courtyard."

"Could you drive inside, if you wanted?"

Robin considered. "You could," he said. "But you wouldn't. We'll put the garage round the back."

I squatted down in the middle of the courtyard and looked out over the mountains. The mist was pouring like a waterfall over Graminha, and the last rays of the sun were lighting the topmost peak of Itajuru.

"How long do you think it'll take to build?" I asked.

"Well." Robin scratched his head. "Digging the foundations shouldn't take more than a few weeks. Then we have to blast the stone, fill up the trenches, and put a cement plate on top. In the meantime, John the Baptist can be getting on with the cementing."

"What cementing?"

"Reinforced concrete columns on each corner to take the weight of the roof, and an arch where the kitchen meets the music room. After that we can build the walls. If all goes well we could be roofed in by Christmas."

"That's not long!" I exclaimed.

"Hold on!" said Robin. "I didn't say *which* Christmas."

D o we have the money to do all this?" I inquired a few days later when I came across Robin seated at the kitchen table and frowning as he punched numbers into a calculator.

"All what?"

This was Robin's way of avoiding the issue, but I wouldn't let him get away with it. "Build the house, you idiot."

Robin looked me straight in the eye. "No, we don't," he told me. "Not yet, anyway. But I've figured out how to do it. I've been canvassing a few of my colleagues in Washington and there are plenty of consulting jobs to be had, especially for Portuguese speakers. So I'll go off and make money, you run the farm, and the building crew will work on the house. It's a good use of resources."

"Run the farm? *Me?*"

"Sure. Nothing to it, really. All you have to do is tell everyone what to do, keep the supplies stocked up, and pay the wages. No big deal."

I slumped down in the rocking chair with a million things running through my mind. What if the car broke down? Or one of the cows got sick? What if there was a problem with the building project and I didn't know the answer? "Well, okay," I said finally. "You'll have to leave me with clear instructions."

"No problem," he told me. "And if anything comes up you can always give me a call."

"Oh, sure," I muttered. "All I need is a frigging phone."

M y days were full enough already without running the farm. It wasn't as if the house was large, and Fia came in twice a week to do the heavy cleaning, but I still had to wage a constant battle against mud, dust, and spiderwebs. Meanwhile, Robin and I were settling into a daily routine that suited us both.

Robin got up early and made the coffee; I emerged a little later and joined him for breakfast after he had planned the day's activities with Albertinho, Antonio, and João. After breakfast Antonio would load the milk onto the pony cart for the trip to Limeira to meet the milk truck. If the horse was lame, one of us had to take the car instead and if it was my turn I had to rely on the unpredictable better nature of the truck driver to load the heavy churns onto his truck. There were regular chores to be done with the cattle:

vaccinating, spraying, dehorning, and branding. Robin had bought me a glossy bay stallion called Consolo, and I enjoyed helping Antonio herd the cattle up onto one of the high pastures, stopping to check that the water holes were clear and the fencing tight. Sometimes I would be assistant mechanic, passing wrenches or pumping brakes while Robin fixed engines, brakes, or clutch pads to the accompaniment of country music on the car's tape recorder. Once in a while we'd be asked to take a sick child to the hospital, or to help a young couple move house. In exchange for these favors someone would make sure our horses were properly shod, or bring us a bag of peanuts or a leg of pork.

Once a week we made the long trip to Muriaé to pick up supplies and make our phone calls. We tried to do it on a Tuesday, which meant that Monday was devoted to writing the weekly Iracambi bulletin to be mailed to our families. In the early evenings we would rendezvous in the dairy, where the staff collected their milk and everyone exchanged news. Robin would scan the milk records, I would check the medicine cabinet, Antonio would sit on a low stool doing the milking, and Fia would bottle-feed the calves. Occasionally one of our neighbors would trot up on his horse and engage Robin in one of those lengthy rural conversations that never seemed to go anywhere. When we made it home with a two-liter bottle of fresh milk, it was time to light the woodstove and put the supper on to cook, as the light faded and the frogs started their evening chorus.

Sometimes I would take Consolo out in the evening and ride up the Graminha valley through the forest and over the stream, returning by starlight under the canopy of the Milky Way with the Southern Cross beckoning me home. However dark it was, Consolo would never stumble, and Fia solemnly assured me that horses could see through their hooves.

It was a gentle rural rhythm, and things took time. Food was cooked from scratch, and no one had phones, so if you wanted to find someone you had to get on a horse or into the car and go look for them, and when you got there they might be out.

I hadn't any idea how we were going to find any stonemasons for the Iracambi Building Project, but Albertinho had been asking around and had located Dona Ana's family in one of the nearby villages. They were available immediately, and would live with us while they worked.

"Best if you go over to collect them," Robin told me. "I'm going to be tied up with John the Baptist. We're making plans for the new dairy. He says he can be getting on with it when he's done the foundations for the house. And he told me we need to get the stonemasons here as soon as possible because they're incredibly slow. So if you wouldn't mind running over there?"

"No problem." I nodded. "Over where, exactly?"

"São Domingos. Edmar's place, next to the prefect's farm. You'll need to make two trips because there are nine of them altogether."

"Nine of them? Where are you going to put them all?"

"In Antonio's granary."

"Isn't it a bit small for nine people?"

"They'll find it a lot better than some places they've lived," said Robin. "At least it's got electric light."

I set off next morning for the tiny village of São Domingos. I'd been there before on a sand-buying expedition. To get there you went out of the *fazenda* gate, up the steep hill to São Pedro, past the house of João Red Face and on until you got to the Limeira turning. Instead of going right you headed left toward Belisário, and after a couple of miles you turned off on a road that was so narrow that it didn't look like a road at all.

São Domingos consisted of a couple of cobbled streets with a chapel, a public telephone, a bar with a pool table, and a little store that sold sugar, oil, soap, and a few cans of tomato paste. When I'd gone there to buy sand I hadn't been able to see anywhere that sold building supplies, and I thought that Robin must have gotten it wrong. After driving up and down a couple of times I stopped outside the bar just as a very old man came lurching out, smelling strongly of liquor.

"Excuse me," I began, but he paid no attention, staggered toward his horse, and stood there swaying and muttering to himself.

"It's no good trying to get any sense out of him," came a voice from inside the bar. "He can't hear a word you're saying. Deaf as a post, he is."

I looked inside and saw a young woman in a shiny pink top standing behind the counter. "Thanks!" I laughed. "Maybe you can help me. I'm trying to buy some sand for building."

"Sand, eh?" She swabbed the top of the counter with a cloth. "Well, you could try Zé Antonio. Last house on the right. Next to the chapel."

I walked down the road to the neat little house next to the chapel. There was no sign of life and no doorbell, either. So I clapped my hands, according to local custom, and shouted, *"O de casa!* Hey there! Anyone home?" Nobody appeared, so I ventured around the back. A sweet-faced woman was energetically slapping her washing in a concrete sink.

"Are you looking for Zé Antonio?" she asked, wiping her hands on her apron. "You'll find him down by the river. Just this side of the bridge."

It was only when I found him digging in the riverbed that I realized where the sand came from.

But sand wasn't the errand of the day this time, and, following

Robin's instructions, I drove over the bridge, along a rutted road, through an avenue of eucalyptus trees, and into Edmar's farmyard. A small boy directed me to a dilapidated wooden shack in the middle of a cornfield where Dona Ana's family were having their lunch.

Once I had driven into the field, I climbed out of the car and walked toward the house, clapping my hands to signal my arrival. A black face appeared at the window and invited me in. I pushed open the wooden door and found the whole family assembled. A short, stout woman in a blue head scarf was sitting on a three-legged stool peeling an orange. An old man, perched on a sack of rice in one corner, was sharing his food with two small children. A teenage boy in a faded blue shirt was leaning against the window, and four little girls with cornrow braids were seated on a bench swinging their legs. There was a pot of fresh coffee on the wood-stove, and everyone had a tin plate piled with rice and beans.

"Dona Bianca?" The woman looked up at me. "I'm Ana, and this is my husband, João. We'll just finish our lunch and then we'll get our things together. Can we offer you a *cafezinho*?" One of the little girls came shyly toward me with a glass of dark, sweet coffee, and after much whispering and shushing room was made for me on the bench. Everybody fell silent and concentrated on finishing their food.

At a signal from Dona Ana the children jumped up and bustled about collecting the plates and glasses and pulling down the few items of clothing that were hanging from a string stretched across a corner of the room. The eldest boy, who told me his name was João Pedro, supervised the packing and loading. One of the girls snatched up the three-legged stool, two others carried the bench outside, and a fourth came running up with a large tin washbasin on her head. Old João hobbled over with two straw mattresses, and soon the car was packed high with sticks of furniture; sacks of rice, beans, and cornmeal; bundles of clothes and bedding; a box of kitchen utensils; and a pink plastic chamber pot. The little girls climbed into the cab beside me and João Pedro vaulted into the back as Dona Ana came puffing up with a squirming sack. "That damned pig," she explained breathlessly, thrusting it into the arms of João Pedro. "The *filha da puta* wouldn't let me catch her."

D ona Ana and her family settled into Antonio's granary with the ease of long practice, and it soon became apparent that she was the brains behind the business. One of her most delicate tasks was organizing the illegal purchase of explosives. This involved regular trips to a quarry on the outskirts of Muriaé where she had an arrangement with one of the guards on the gate. She would ask to be dropped off on the main road and always waited until we'd driven away before going off on her errand. On our return journey we'd find her seated under a tree, the picture of innocence, next to a basket covered with a spotless white cloth.

Every morning she marched her family out the door at seven o'clock sharp. Three of the bigger girls set off on the long walk to school in São Pedro, while the other children spent the day sitting in the shade of a tarpaulin, patiently chipping rocks into gravel to be mixed into the cement. Old João spent many hours at the forge, sharpening his tools, and young João helped his mother lay the dynamite. They were supposed to warn us before they did the blasting, but they usually forgot, and the peace of the day was regularly disturbed by the sound of an explosion.

R obin had been concerned that he wouldn't get any consulting jobs because it was so hard for potential employers to contact him. But the problem was miraculously solved when the Muriaé post office acquired the first fax machine in the area, bringing us suddenly in touch with the big world. All letters, packages, or faxes were delivered in a sealed mailbag to the Limeira bus—an ancient vehicle brightly painted in red, blue, and yellow with her name picked out in black: OUR LADY OF PERPETUAL SUCCOR, commonly shortened to Our Lady's bus. The mailbag would be off-loaded at the Limeira post office, and anything urgent would be sent along care of the next passing horseman.

Our first fax was delivered by Jair, who made sure to hang around long enough to discover whether there was any exciting news such as a death in the family. He didn't bother to conceal his disappointment when he heard it was the offer of a trip to Mexico. For all he knew, Mexico was somewhere beyond São Paulo.

Robin and I sat down together and went over everything in detail: bills, vaccinations, milk records, fertilizer, cow food, and building supplies for the new dairy.

I was a little apprehensive before he left, but once he was gone I found it easier to manage things than I had feared. Albertinho took upon himself the role of foreman, and started dropping around of an evening for a chat. João kept himself to himself and gave no trouble, while Antonio was as good tempered as ever. But even his patience was sorely tried by Dona Ana. "That woman is a damned nuisance," he complained. "Always after me to run errands for her when I'm dropping off the milk in Limeira. One of the kids comes running up, 'Uncle, could you buy us a needle? We've broken ours. Please, uncle, one of my sisters has a fever and we need some aspirin from the *farmácia*. We're out of cooking oil. Could you bring us some? Thank you so much and God bless you.' She knows I can't refuse the children."

"Such a kind man, Antonio," Dona Ana remarked to us later. "I made him some of my corn cake last week as a little thank-you for everything he does for us."

* * *

I was modestly pleased with progress on the farm by the time Robin returned from Mexico, full of plans for the house. Albertinho and João started digging and hauling the earth for the walls. John the Baptist built the concrete columns for the corners, and, under Robin's direction, a wooden frame for the arch. It was the first arch ever seen in the neighborhood and, viewed from the valley, the combination of arch and columns gave the building site a pleasing resemblance to the Manhattan skyline.

Every building project has its challenges, and building in mud has more than most. One of them is the question of installing water pipes and wiring for the power sockets. Since you can't bang holes in mud walls without damaging them, you have to locate all the wiring and plumbing inside the walls during construction—which leaves plenty of room for error. If you don't use good-quality piping you'll end up with leaks inside the walls, and if you miscalculate over the wiring you'll find yourself with wall sockets that can't be connected up, or no place for telephone wires.

We hired some extra hands to start on the building and as the walls started to rise—four meters high and fifty centimeters thick—the house site became something of a tourist attraction. One of our most regular visitors was Jair. As the source of all local gossip he could always find an excuse to drop by and check on progress. He appeared one hot afternoon on his mule. "Wanted to come and see these earth walls," he explained, dismounting and hitching the reins over the pommel of his saddle. "How do you make sure they are straight?"

"With a plumb line," said Robin. "Just like any other wall."

Jair wandered around poking the walls with his whip. "Hmm," he said, "what happens when it rains?"

"What do you mean?"

"Mud walls like these, what's to stop them falling down?" Jair grinned. "Remember I told you the garage roof was going to fall down at the blue house?"

"Yes, I remember," said Robin. "And you were right, it did. In fact, it fell down on top of the Toyota. But that was because the roof joists were rotten—eaten by termites. Termites don't eat mud walls."

"Termites will eat anything," said Jair flatly. "But tell me something. Why don't you build a proper house out of brick?"

"Several reasons," said Robin patiently. "First, because it's cheaper to build with earth. Earth doesn't cost anything."

Jair raised a bushy eyebrow.

"Second, because it's an excellent building material," Robin continued. "Earth houses keep cool in summer and warm in winter. And third, because I've always wanted to build a house out of earth."

Jair was not convinced. "It's a very large house for two people, isn't it?" he asked. "A big house like that, it's going to cost you a lot."

Robin winked at me.

"Wood beams." Jair was counting on his fingers. "Windows— glass windows, so I hear. Roofing tiles. Cement. That's a terrible price these days."

"It is," agreed Robin.

"But it'll be a fine house," said Albertinho, leaning on his shovel.

Jair sniffed. "That's as may be," he said gloomily. "If it ever gets finished."

CHAPTER EIGHT

A Christmas Christening

Maria's youngest baby needed a godmother, and I was drafted into the job without being consulted. "You don't suppose they'll be expecting me to pay for her schooling or anything?" I said to Robin anxiously.

"Goodness, no," he told me. "They've only asked you so you'll take her to Ervália to get her christened. They have group christenings on Saturday mornings."

"Why don't they christen her in Limeira?"

"Because the padre in Limeira won't baptize children without preparation, and neither Maria nor Albertinho ever go to church."

"If they don't go to church, why bother to christen the baby?"

"*Tradição*," explained Robin. "It isn't a proper baby until it's been christened. I told them we'd go next Saturday because I want to go there anyway and buy a chaff cutter. They're cheaper in Ervália."

Ervália was a small, undistinguished town twenty miles away across the mountains. The quickest way to get there was by taking the horse trail over Graminha, but it was too narrow for the Toyota so we had to make the detour through Limeira and follow the spine-jarring road that led, eventually, to the state capital, Belo Horizonte. For years there'd been talk of paving the whole section of road from Muriaé to Ervália; earnest speeches were made in the state legislative assembly about the importance of tying our region to the capital, and pilot projects were set up to study the question. After ferocious bidding, a contractor would arrive, set up camp, start to realign the road, and send in some heavy machinery to scrape off the top layer of hard-packed dirt. This usually coincided with the beginning of the rains in October, rendering the road impassable for weeks on end, and in due course funds would run out, the contractor would depart, and the road would revert to its normal wretched state.

We were discussing the Ervália trip over breakfast when our daughter, Juliet, emerged from her room, yawning. She'd been studying in London and could hardly wait to get back to Brazil for some sunshine. Her brother was off with his classmates to a ski slope in France, but she was determined to help us celebrate our first Iracambi Christmas. "It's not like I'm that great a skier," she told us. "And anyway, Gus didn't invite me."

She was delighted with the progress we had made. "This is pretty cool," she said. "A lot different from Washington, but it's coming on nicely."

She firmly declined the offer to accompany us to Ervália. "Why on earth would I want to sit for hours in a car with a yelling baby?" she demanded. "It's not as if I like babies. If they're not throwing up at one end they're peeing at the other. Or worse. You go off and enjoy yourselves and I'll take one of the horses out for a gallop."

I was wishing I could join her when one of Maria's children showed up with a message. Did I, she wanted to know, have a christening dress for the child? I did not. Tell her to use the dress she used on the last child, I said. I wondered in a brief moment of panic if I had let myself in for some lifelong role that I was unwilling to assume. Juliet, who was studying human sciences, was no help. "Kinship ties," she said darkly, "can be complicated."

I was not in the best of tempers when the expedition set off—Maria and the baby in front, Albertinho and the other three children in the back, together with grandfather Olavo and the child's godfather.

"I'll leave you to do the honors," said Robin when we arrived at the church. "I'm off to collect the chaff cutter. See you later." He drove off before I had time to protest.

I looked around at the hopeful little family and endeavored to put myself in a more charitable frame of mind. "All right, Maria," I sighed, "let's go see what's happening."

There was nothing happening. The church was empty. I turned to Maria. "What time did you say the service was?"

"I don't know," muttered Maria.

I looked around the church. It was full of tacky plastic images and fairy lights, and I could make no connection between the surroundings and the fact that we were there to dedicate a new life to the Creator of the Universe.

I glanced over at Albertinho. He was leaning against the church door. What was going through his mind? Or Maria's? Why did a baby have to be christened in order to become a proper baby? What was Maria thinking as she sat there with her four children? I looked at my godchild. Despite Juliet's warnings, she had slept peacefully all the way. What will become of you, Viviane? I thought. What will your life be like? Will you go to school, and if you do, what will you learn? Or will your mother keep you home to help with the other little ones?

My thoughts were interrupted by a tap on the shoulder. It was the godfather, Ailton, one of Adão's sons from next door who had occasionally helped out on the *fazenda* when we needed an extra pair of hands. He was dressed in an immaculate white shirt and jeans and a smart pair of suede ankle boots, and was painfully shy. He covered this by speaking exceptionally fast, and I caught only about half of what he was saying. He indicated that it was time to register the child, so I followed him out of the church and up the steps to the parish office. The padre didn't look up as we went in.

"What is the name of this child?" he inquired.

"Viviane Fátima do Carmo Rodrigues," said Ailton.

"Very well," said the padre. "Now I would like the godparents to sign here. First the godfather."

The godfather picked up the pen and signed his name, slowly and laboriously.

"Now the godmother," said the padre. "Can she sign her name?"

"Yes, she can," I said crisply.

The padre looked up in surprise. He adjusted his glasses. "That," he said, "will be twenty-nine thousand. Plus a thousand for the notary. Thirty thousand, in all."

Viviane Fátima do Carmo Rodrigues, I thought. For $1.50 we are buying your ticket to heaven.

We returned to find that the church had filled up and there was a long line of mothers and babies ready for baptism. The padre swept in, looked at his watch, made a perfunctory sign of the cross, and started off at high speed. Twelve sets of parents and godparents mumbled the responses, swearing solemnly to reject the Devil and all his works.

"Right," said the padre, "all the children to the font, please." Maria thrust Viviane into my arms. Viviane took one look at me and started bawling. I rocked her and she yelled louder. It started a chain reaction among the babies, and the other godmothers looked at me in contempt.

"I baptize you . . ." the padre raised his voice above the bawling of the babies, looking to the godparents.

"José Maria," muttered the first.

"Edmar dos Santos."

"Maria Aparecida."

"Maria das Graças."

"Ana Maria."

"Antonio José."

"Rosângela."

I listened to the litany of names, concentrating on getting Viviane to keep the volume down. Maria was darting me anguished looks, and the next-door godmother was digging me in the ribs. I rocked the child more vigorously. My neighbor was hissing something at me, but it was drowned by Viviane's renewed wailing. I caught the padre's eye. He was glaring at me.

"What do you name this child?"

"Viviane Fátima do Carmo," I blurted out.

The padre focused his attention on the next baby. By now all the babies were crying in chorus.

"I baptize you," bellowed the padre, "In the name of the Father and of the Son and of the Holy Spirit, *amen!*"

We drove home through torrential rain, the car making slow progress through the thick mud. The *fazenda* was in darkness—something must have gone wrong with the generator. Albertinho shepherded his family into the house and reappeared almost immediately. He had changed back into his rusty brown jacket and had a flashlight in one hand and a wrench in the other.

"I'll just see what's happened with the lights," he said, and went off whistling into the darkness.

We found Juliet cuddled up on the sofa next to Splittie, listening to the BBC World Service through a hissing of static. The room was lit by two stubs of candle and the glow from the wood burner. "Hi there," she greeted us. "We've just had the mother of all storms, the roof has been leaking like a sieve, and now all the lights have gone out. Welcome home."

"I think," I said, shaking the water out of my hair, "we all deserve a drink."

"Good idea," said Juliet. "After all, tomorrow *is* Christmas Eve."

Next morning we were woken at first light by Antonio. "I can't find the goat," he reported.

"Do you mean Mrs. Thatcher?" asked Robin.

"Oh, no." Antonio grinned. "Not her. I've just chased her out of your vegetable patch. No, I mean the brown billy goat."

There was a rocky outcrop behind the generator house where Antonio had built up a colony of native goats. Mrs. Thatcher, who was a pedigree Toggenburg, refused to mix with the native goats and lived an independent life—although, despite repeated assurances from Zé Viricius, she never displayed the slightest dislike of water. Zé Araujo from behind the hill had acquired a handsome male of the same breed, and we dreamed of raising a flock and maybe making goat's cheese. The billy had twice been to visit, chauffeur driven in a bright green VW Beetle and spending several days with Mrs. Thatcher. But although she had become positively skittish in his presence, nothing had ever come of it, and Robin decreed that if she didn't produce kids she would have to go. "This is a farm," he said. "Not a holiday camp."

"Last time I saw the brown goat was yesterday morning," Antonio told us. "But there's no sign of him today. Then I said to myself, 'I wouldn't be surprised if somebody wasn't after a nice goat to put in the pot, seeing as it's Christmas.' So I'm off to Graminha to make a few investigations. I'm not naming names, but there's some people around here who'll stoop to anything."

"Talking of Christmas, Antonio," I said, "could you ask Fia to catch us a guinea hen for dinner?"

Fia had been raising a flock of guinea hens at Robin's request. He wanted them to control the ticks in the pasture, and told me they bred like rabbits. "Our place in Kenya was overrun with guineas," he told me. "Those things are practically indestructible." But for some reason Brazilian guinea hens proved to be as delicate as Victorian ladies. The hens refused to sit on their eggs, which had to be snatched away from the nest and put under a broody chicken. Once hatched, the chicks would follow their adoptive mother everywhere like little spotted feather balls, but they couldn't stand to get wet, and if they did, they died. If they managed to make it to adulthood, they were likely to be eaten by something—bush dogs, wild cats, even ocelots. But Fia had persevered and succeeded in raising a flock of twenty-seven, and Robin was determined to have one for Christmas dinner.

Later that evening one of Antonio's children delivered a small parcel wrapped in newspaper. It turned out to be the mangled corpse of a spotted bird.

"It's all bloody," exclaimed Juliet in disgust. "You're going to have to cook it, Daddy. We vegetarians are having stuffed eggplant. By the way, Mummy, where did you put them?"

"Put what?"

"The eggplants, silly."

"I was wondering that myself," I said distractedly. "You don't suppose I forgot to buy them?"

"Anything is possible," said Robin, studying the slaughtered bird. "I've figured out what the problem is here. Antonio has blasted it with his muzzle loader."

Y es, you did," reported Juliet later.
   "Did what?"
"Forget to buy the eggplant."
My face fell.
"Never mind, Mummy. Who says you need them anyway?"
"Well, the Christmas pudding looks great."
"It does," said my husband loyally. "And it will be even better when I've made the brandy butter."

C hristmas Day dawned fine and windy, and I found a Christmas stocking on the end of my bed. There was a tap on the door and Juliet peered in. "Happy Christmas, Mummy," she said. "Let's open our stockings."

Robin came in carrying a tray with three mugs of fragrant coffee and three gold-wrapped chocolates. "Happy Christmas, everyone," he announced.

We all climbed into bed and sat up, balancing our coffee mugs and opening our presents. Splittie hurtled through the door and made a flying leap for the bed, scattering wrapping paper in all directions. My stocking was full of all sorts of small luxuries, not easily obtainable. It was beginning to feel like Christmas.

"So what's the plan?" asked Robin, biting into his chocolate with immense enjoyment.

"Let's do the present run first," suggested Juliet. "Then, when that's over, we can sit in the sun with a glass of champagne."

"I vote we go for a swim this afternoon," I put in.

"Best do that early," advised Robin. "There's rain about."

"Not on Christmas Day," said Juliet firmly, looking out at the cloudless sky.

"We'll do presents and carols this evening. Is that okay with everyone?" I asked.

"Sounds good to me," said Robin.

We ate our breakfast in the sunshine, and then sat down to wrap the presents for the farm children. Robin volunteered to blow up the balloons, I had another surreptitious look for the eggplants, and Juliet sorted through the presents: dolls for the girls, toy cars for the boys, and T-shirts for everyone. "Let me check them one more time," she said. "Albertinho: three girls and a boy; Antonio: two girls and a boy; João: two girls and a boy."

"That's right," said Robin, blowing up the last balloon. "I hope we've got enough. There are bound to be some extra children hanging around."

"Did you remember old Olavo?" I asked him.

"Couldn't possibly forget him." Robin smiled. "He's building up quite a collection of balloons. Hangs them all in his kitchen."

"Surely they'll pop in the heat?" said Juliet.

"Oh, no," laughed Robin. "He lets all the air out."

A ntonio swears that cow is going to calve today," said Robin as we headed off to deliver the presents. He pointed to a small Brown Swiss grazing peacefully in the pasture. "I told him he's wrong. Her udder's almost empty. She'll be some time yet."

"Is that the one you call Edelweiss?" asked Juliet.

"No, it's Edelbraun," said Robin. "The staff call her Morena. She looks like her sister but she's much darker."

"Well, I hope she doesn't calve during Christmas dinner," I said. "We don't want to have to go down to the corral on Christmas night."

"Oh, I don't know," said Robin. "Seems to me that Christmas is just the time for being in the stable with sleepy cows and asses. But in any case she's not calving today. I'm certain of that."

The first house we visited was Albertinho's. The house was bursting with friends and relations, including lots of small children. We didn't have presents for everyone, but fortunately the candy bag was large enough to go around, and Sandra took charge of the balloons like an old hand.

The next house was Antonio's, and his small kitchen was crammed with people, including all of João's family. They were in the middle of lunch, and the only concession to Christmas was the fact that they'd been to Mass the night before. Although there was a large plastic Santa Claus in the main square of Muriaé, it was to be several years before Western-style Christmas arrived in our part of the mountains. Presents were restricted to weddings and sometimes birthdays, and those who could manage it bought new clothes for Easter. But the truth was there was little money to spare and many children still went barefoot.

Handing out presents was a wonderful way to spend Christmas morning, and I was in high spirits when I stopped off at the dairy to collect some milk. Antonio moved his milking stool away from a large black-and-white cow, and gave me a broad smile.

"Everything okay around here?" I smiled back. "And what's the news on the goat?"

"Well," said Antonio, running his hands through his hair. "The damnedest thing. Remember I told you some people will stoop to anything? I was thinking of that fellow Cesar. Lives up the mountain beyond Fia's parents. A bad lot if ever there was one. He'd steal anything he can lay hands on. Well, I rode up to his place and his wife asked me in for coffee. There was a big pot bubbling on the stove and I said to her, 'Dona Joana, that smells wonderful.' And she told me she'd always been fond of a nice bit of wild pig, and offered me a taste then and there."

"What did it taste of?"

"It tasted of pig."

"And where do you suppose he got it from?"

"From our forest, I wouldn't be surprised."

"Well, at least it wasn't our goat."

"No, it wasn't. And the funny thing was that when I went to check on the goats after I got back, there was the brown billy together with all the others. Must have been there all the time. But I'm damned if I saw it yesterday."

"Well, that's good news," I said.

Antonio grinned. "And that's not all. You can tell the boss he was wrong about Morena."

"She's calved?"

"That's right." Antonio nodded. "A Christmas calf."

I don't believe it," said Robin when he heard the news. "Let's go see."

"She's not one of those cows that goes after you, is she?" asked Juliet.

"You never want to get too close to a new mother," Robin told her. "But this one's a placid soul. She won't give any trouble."

Edelbraun was standing in the pasture cleaning her calf. As we watched, it staggered to its feet and nuzzled around looking for a teat.

"We'll let it suckle," said Robin, "and then we'll take it up to the calf pen."

We waited till the calf had drunk its fill and settled down in the grass. "Right," Robin instructed us. "Here's what we'll do. You open the gate to the corral, Jules, and I'll drive Edelbraun in."

"She won't leave her calf, surely?" queried Juliet.

"No way," said Robin. "We'll have to kidnap it."

Juliet opened the gate and, to everyone's surprise, Edelbraun walked straight in and made for the feed trough. Her calf staggered along behind her, and then collapsed onto the grass.

"Okay," whispered Robin, "I'll grab the calf, and you guys be sure to slam the gate behind me. Don't open it before I get to the road, okay?"

"Okay."

No sooner had Robin snatched the calf than Edelbraun set up a heartbreaking bellowing and tried to break out of the corral. Robin had made it to the road and was walking up the hill to the dairy when Edelbraun burst out of the open gate and thundered across the pasture after him. Robin quickened his pace, but the calf was awkward to carry and heavy, and Edelbraun was closing fast.

All three of them disappeared over the brow of the hill, and Juliet and I set off as quickly as we could, our hearts in our mouths. We arrived panting hard, but all was well: Edelbraun was licking her calf, Antonio was hosing down the yard, and Robin was leaning over the rail, breathing heavily. "Well, Antonio," he said, "you were right and I was wrong."

Antonio hid a smile and turned away.

Robin may have been wrong about the calf, but he was right about the weather. As we walked down from the dairy I noticed thick clouds coming in fast. There were storms about.

B ut it was cozy and Christmassy in the kitchen that evening as we added the finishing touches to our dinner. The tree was in one corner, surrounded by the presents. The smell of roasting guinea hen mingled sweetly with the rich aroma of Christmas pudding overlaid with a heady suggestion of brandy butter, against a background of woodsmoke. There was a bottle of champagne cooling under the running tap, and Juliet had made a creamy brown chocolate soufflé. It was hard to believe we were in the Brazilian rainforest.

It seemed a million miles away from the European Christmases of my childhood. I remembered myself, as a small child, holding tightly to the hand of a very old man and carrying a lighted candle down the long dark aisle of a Gothic cathedral in England. In the sharp cold I could see my breath coming in clouds, and somewhere in the darkness a voice was singing, very softly, about a silent night. We walked through row after row of people, all standing quietly, until we came to an immensely tall tree that smelled of pine needles and winter. The voice ended its song and for a minute there was nothing in the whole world except the two of us standing in the candlelight. The old man whispered something in my ear and together we touched the flame to a candle on the tree. Suddenly, miraculously, the tree was lit by a thousand points of light, and the choir burst into the most glorious music I had ever heard. The cathedral was full of people, smiling and wondering, and at the end of the music the old man turned to face them, and declaimed in a loud voice, "The people that walked in darkness have seen a great light; they that dwell in the land of the shadow of death, upon them hath the light shined."

I felt again the glory of that moment, and gave thanks to be in a warm kitchen with Robin and Juliet. Robin retrieved the bottle of champagne from the veranda, eased the cork out, and very carefully filled three glasses. "This is remarkably civilized, wouldn't you say?" He toasted us both and the three of us raised our glasses.

"To Gus on his ski slope," said Juliet. "And may he make it through without breaking anything."

Robin and I caught one another's eyes. "Amen," we said simultaneously.

There was a distant rumble of thunder.

"How about we have our presents next?" Robin suggested.

"How about we eat first, Daddy?" countered Juliet. "I'm starving."

"Right," said Robin. "Let the banquet commence."

"I'll light the candles," I offered.

"I'll turn on the music," said Juliet. "And after dinner we'll sing carols round the piano like we always do. It's a pity we haven't got Gus here. You'll just have to sing his part, Mummy. Unless we can persuade Dad to stand in."

Robin raised an eyebrow. "When have you ever heard me singing, Jules?" he remarked.

Juliet grinned. "Well, Dad," she said. "What with your new life and all. Maybe you've finally found your voice."

"No chance," said Robin. "But I will say grace."

We closed our eyes while he prayed for families everywhere, and those without families, while a pure voice floated through the speakers bringing us the story of Royal David's City. For a moment we were part of the millions of believers across the globe and throughout the centuries celebrating the time when the light came into the world. We smiled at one another, Robin carved the guinea hen, and Juliet carved the eggplant stuffing. Our Christmas celebration was finally beginning.

I had just taken the first forkful when there was a loud clap of thunder, a rattle of rain on the roof, and the lights went out.

There was a moment's silence and then we all started laughing.

"Happy Christmas, everybody," said Juliet. "Here's to life in the land of milk and honey."

CHAPTER NINE

The Barefoot Vets

I hear you're looking for another dairy hand." Old Sebastião from across the valley reined in his horse and leaned down to shake our hands. "I'll send my boy Valdeci over to see you. He's a good boy. Reliable. Worked with cattle all his life. And there won't be a problem about housing because he's got a house of his own."

"Thanks, Sebastião," said Robin. "Please ask him to come and talk to me."

Sebastião nodded and trotted off.

The next morning Valdeci came around to see us. He was very young and very shy but we immediately liked the look of him, and after some discussion agreed to take him on a month's trial.

Fia, as usual, had all the gossip.

"Valdeci used to be a wild one," she told me as she helped me thin the lettuces in our vegetable patch. "But then he fell in love with Marinha, and she's from a family of Believers, so Valdeci converted. They go to that little church on the road to Belisário, and they have to show up every Sunday without fail, otherwise they get into terrible trouble."

"Is that the church where the women wear veils over their heads?" I asked her.

"That's right." She nodded. "And long sleeves, and skirts below the knee. They're not allowed to cut their hair and they can't wear makeup or jewelry, and they say," she leaned forward confidentially, "they make love with their clothes on."

We caught one anothers' eye, and burst out laughing.

Antonio and Valdeci had known each other since they were children, and it wasn't long before the dairy settled into a comfortable routine. Antonio knew exactly when each cow had come into season, when she had been bred, and how much milk she gave. But he had a hard time keeping records because he couldn't write very well. His 5s looked like Ss, his 8s didn't join up properly, and his 3s lay down on their backs with their legs in the air, so we had to pretend we'd left our glasses behind and ask him to decipher them. But Valdeci was a good reader, so Robin was spared the chore of having to keep the milk records and decipher the medicine labels, and was able to turn his mind to more important issues like improving the herd.

The quickest way to do this would be by moving over to artificial insemination. Although widely adopted in the south of the country, it was a technique that was virtually unknown in the region. The local colonels thought it was sissy, and preferred to have bulls, while the small farmers resisted modern technology and insisted on doing as their fathers and grandfathers had done before them. One point that provoked scorn among our neighbors was our practice of separating newborn calves from their mothers. Jair was quick to point out that we were giving ourselves twice the work—milking the cow, filling the bottles, and bottle-feeding the calves. Robin explained that it was a way of checking milk production as well as ensuring that the calves got the right quantity to drink, but Jair remained unconvinced. Even Antonio and Valdeci were doubtful, but when Robin insisted they nodded politely, and did what they were told.

Insemination was another matter altogether. First of all, it was a complex process that required a trained technician. Second, you had to pay for the semen instead of getting it free from the bull. Third, it wasn't guaranteed. They couldn't see the point of it.

But it was the quickest and most effective way of improving the herd, and Robin was not to be deflected. After considerable effort, he managed to track down a salesman who could supply us with a nitrogen tank and semen. The purchase price included a free training course in Rio, and this proved to be the first sticking point. Neither Antonio nor Valdeci had ever been to Rio and neither wanted to go. Valdeci pointed out that he couldn't leave his young wife and Antonio pointed out that he couldn't read.

After some discussion we managed to convince Valdeci, who allowed himself to be enrolled for the training course a month ahead. But Robin wasn't happy at the prospect of leaving the entire insemination program in the hands of one person. "What happens if a cow comes on heat and it's Valdeci's day off?" he said. "I'll talk to the extension people and see if they can get us a training course."

"If they do will you attend it?" I teased, knowing that Robin was uncharacteristically squeamish when it came to things like that.

"No, I won't, but you could," he retorted.

I tell you what," said Antonio as we were discussing it one afternoon over the milking. "About this business of insemination. How about we ask Rosana to come up and give us a demonstration? Then we can see how it's done right here in our own dairy."

"Good idea," said Robin. "Let me know next time you have a cow on heat."

Rosana was a niece of Lenin's whom we had met a few months earlier. We had instantly struck up a friendship. She had studied animal husbandry at the local agricultural university, and her passion in life was cattle: cattle breeding, calf rearing, animal health, pasture rotation, dairy management—anything and everything to do with cows. "There's nothing so rewarding as a cow," she would say with eyes shining. "You feed her well and keep her in health, and she'll give you milk and calves and meat and dung. You'll never go hungry if you keep a cow."

Rosana lived with her mother about an hour's drive down the mountain from Iracambi. After graduation she had looked for a job in the neighborhood. But girls from her background weren't expected to take paid jobs, and Rosana ended up working on the family farms in exchange for handouts. One of her uncles bought her a Volkswagen Beetle and gave her carte blanche to use his account at the local gas station. Her mother allotted her a percentage of the new calves born on the *fazenda* and gave her a small allowance. But Rosana had set her sights higher than that, and dreamed secretly of going to the States.

One sparkling morning I set off down the mountain to Fazenda Copacabana where Rosana lived with her mother, Teresinha. The rain had washed the sky clean and new, and the air was so clear that everything was in extrasharp focus. The road was muddy but manageable. From the top of the pass near Belisário the blue mountains stretched as far as the eye could see, and the road wound down in a series of crazy bends to the highway. I drove through the village of Itamuri, and instead of taking the paved road toward Muriaé, I took the dirt road north to Rosana's house.

As I drove up, the dogs rushed out to greet me, followed by

Rosana, elegantly clad in the briefest of shorts. "Hi there, Bianca," she said warmly. "How lovely to see you! What's new?"

"I've come to kidnap you." I gave her a hug. "We're moving over to insemination but we're not set up for it yet, and one of our best cows has just come into season. Would you be able to come up and give us a demonstration?"

"Sure I'll come," she said. "It's a great day for a visit. Is it a Holstein? I've got some extraspecial semen here. Imported from Canada."

Rosana's garden was brilliant with color. "That's because my mother is nuts about flowers," Rosana confided. "She gets the farmhands to do the gardening. I can't tell you how many times I've fought with her about it! We've only got three men here, and two of them are in the dairy. The third guy should be in the fields, but every time I turn my back she's after him to do something in the garden. It looks wonderful, doesn't it? Just don't look too closely at the pastures."

I followed her onto the back veranda. A well-fed black woman in a long white apron was standing by the wood burner, stirring a pot of something that smelled delicious. She turned and held out her arms. "So you're Bianca," she said. "I'm Maria José. Delighted to meet you. Rosana's told me a lot about you."

I gave her a hug, breathing in the fragrance of wood smoke and molasses.

"One of these days," she continued, "I'm going to come up to your place for a visit. I've always liked the climate up there in the mountains. It's nice and cool."

"Please do come," I said. "Get Rosana to bring you."

"Want to try some of the house special?" offered Rosana, pointing to the contents of the pot.

"I certainly do," I said. "It smells wonderful."

"It's a local dish," Maria José told me. "Made of grated sweet corn and peanuts."

"Say no more," I said happily. "Two of my favorite things."

B ack at the *fazenda* Valdeci had hosed down the dairy and tied a pretty little black-and-white cow to the railings. Antonio was chopping cane, Fia was scrubbing the milk churns, and Robin was poring over the milk records.

"Looks like you guys are really well organized." Rosana smiled. "Now, when you're all ready I'll show you how to inseminate. There's no mystery about it—just one or two little tricks, and you'll pick those up with practice. The crucial thing is good hygiene. Everything must be clean as a whistle. Who is going to be my helper?"

"I am," offered Antonio.

"Okay," said Rosana. "First thing is to tie her tail out of the way. Otherwise she'll try to flick it and you could easily drop the syringe. And remember the most important thing is hygiene—everything must be sterile."

We crowded around while she demonstrated her equipment. "This is the nitrogen tank where the semen is stored," she began. "The temperature inside is so low that when you take the lid off, it looks like it's smoking. Who wants to open it? Okay, Valdeci, unscrew the lid carefully and let the steam out. Can you see those little baskets? They're for storing the individual doses of semen. Each one is labeled because you'll be keeping different semen for different cows. Pull up the basket and take out the vial, like this. Then you load it into the syringe, okay?"

All attention was focused on the syringe as Rosana carefully loaded it. She looked around and smiled. "Okay, that's the first step. Now what we're going to do is to see where to deliver the semen. Hold the syringe between your teeth and pull the plastic glove up your left arm. You'll be going up her intestine."

That doesn't sound very attractive, I thought to myself. But at least cow shit smells a lot better than the human variety.

"You need to clean her off, just like wiping a baby's bottom." Rosana caught my eye and grinned. I could swear she was reading my thoughts. "Once the passage is clear you can very gently move your hand around inside the intestine until you feel the mouth of the uterus right next to it. It'll feel like a rubbery ring. Take your time, there's no hurry."

I closed my eyes and tried to imagine going up to my armpit inside a cow's intestine. Surely she wouldn't like it? Wouldn't she do everything to push my arm out? And how on earth could I aim straight if I couldn't see what I was doing?

"Once you've located the cervix you'll insert the syringe with your right arm, and guide it into place with your left." Rosana answered my unspoken questions. "Sounds difficult, but it's simple when you get the trick. For some reason I find it's easier when I have my eyes shut. Okay, here goes."

I closed my eyes and tried to visualize the diagram of the female reproductive system that I had studied in high school biology class, attempting to superimpose upon it the digestive system with its yards of intestines neatly coiled in the abdomen. I peered through my lashes and found myself back in the cemented yard, the cow standing quietly and the small group hushed as Rosana picked up the syringe. I noticed that Robin was standing off to one side, averting his eyes. He'd been staunch enough when his children were born, but he never enjoyed any kind of medical procedure. I suddenly felt a surge of competence. I could do this, even if he couldn't.

Rosana's movements were gentle and practiced, and the cow stood calmly while she was working. "When I've finished I like to give her a good massage to relax her," she told us, "and leave her for a bit to settle down."

Two weeks later Valdeci went off to Rio for the first time in his life, and despite his qualms, thoroughly enjoyed himself. "It's very simple," he told us on his return, as he wielded the insemination equipment with impressive speed and skill. "My professor told me I was one of the best in class." He took to starting his sentences with "When I was at the university," or "At my university we do it this way," and his shyness vanished, never to reappear.

But he wouldn't let anyone else do anything beyond tying the cow's tail. "You can't just let *anyone* inseminate," he told us. "It has to be a skilled technician. When you've done your course I'll be able to help you improve, but in the meantime you just need to watch carefully."

Robin kept checking with the extension agency about the promised course, but there was never any word. Until the day we had a visit from Edson. A vet by training, Edson came from a farming family, and was one of the few in his department who preferred being in the field to sitting in their hot little office in Muriaé. Edson always wore a blue check shirt, neatly pressed jeans, and cowboy boots; had the whitest, most even teeth; and smelled of aftershave. He had the happy knack of turning up when you needed him and had helped us out on several occasions when we had a sick calf or needed advice on animal nutrition.

He arrived in a small white car, just as we were taking an afternoon coffee break. "Well, hello," said Robin. "How nice to see you!"

"Hello there," said Edson, extending his hand. "I've come about the insemination course."

"That's wonderful," said Robin. "We've been waiting to hear about that. What's the news?"

"We're all set." Edson accepted a slice of my no-fail chocolate cake and a mug of coffee. "Took a little time to get the funding, but it's all okay and we're starting on Tuesday."

"Okay," said Robin. "We've got three candidates. There's Antonio the cowman, Fia his wife, and there's Bianca—if you have room in the course."

"We certainly do," said Edson. "I'll reserve three places for you. Now let me tell you how it works. It's a four-part course. We start on Tuesday with an evening meeting in the school to explain what it's all about. People have lots of funny ideas, so we let them ask as many questions as possible, and we answer them as best we can. The next session is a practical one, learning how to handle the equipment and using organs we get from the slaughterhouse. Then we have two practice sessions, and by that time you should have gotten the hang of it. You'll have to bring your own cow—the ideal is two cows per inseminator. You won't want to bring your good cows, so you'd better use some of the ones you were planning to cull. And you can't touch any cow that's in calf."

"I can't possibly find six cull cows," said Robin. "I sold off a bunch last week. But I'll do what I can."

"Fine." Edson smiled. "See you Tuesday evening at seven. If there's any change I'll leave a message at Murilo's bar."

T he insemination course started with a bang. Fourteen men and two women turned up in the Limeira school, and crammed themselves into one of the classrooms to hear Edson explaining about genetic improvement of the stock.

One old man in faded jeans and battered felt hat raised his hand. "I've heard," he said, exhaling a cloud of smoke, "that a cow can only calve three times with insemination."

"I've heard there's cows that don't take," said another.

"It's expensive, right?" asked a young boy.

"You say it's cheaper than keeping a bull." A wizened little man looked at Edson accusingly. "Tell me one thing. If I sell my bull, how do I know when the cow is in season?"

"All right, all right," laughed Edson. "Let's take your points one at a time."

Lesson Two took place on one of the local farms. A large table was piled high with slippery internal organs donated by the slaughterhouse, and we were each handed a syringe and shown how to insert it through the neck of the womb into the vagina. It was a hot afternoon, flies were buzzing around, and vultures were circling in the sky. I pictured myself in scrubs and a surgical mask, under the harsh lights of the operating room. All attention was focused on the patient on the operating table, whose life depended on the skill of the operating team. I rolled up my sleeve, drew on the long plastic glove, and fired up my syringe.

The next stage in our training required practicing on a real cow, and this was where we ran into difficulties. Despite our entreaties, Valdeci wouldn't let us near any of the cows except one—a sassy little heifer who obstinately refused to come into calf. "You can take Virginia," he told us. "She's the only dry cow we have." The final lessons of the course were to be held on a farm about five miles away, and since cows don't like to be driven without a companion he agreed, reluctantly, to let us take Emilia. "She's two months in calf," he said. "So she's not to be touched."

It was a glorious sunny morning when Antonio and Fia set off on horseback driving the two cows. "We start at ten, so don't be late," shouted Fia.

"Don't worry," I shouted as I headed for home. But of course I was. As usual everyone wanted something. Albertinho flagged me down to complain that Mrs. Thatcher had trampled on his tomatoes, Valdeci asked me to pick up some horseshoes, and Dona Ana wanted me to buy her a bag of sugar. By the time I managed to get away I barely had time to make it to class.

I shot through Limeira at high speed and took the muddy road toward the farm where the course was being held. The trainee inseminators were milling around inspecting one another's cows, sipping little cups of coffee, pulling on their plastic gloves, and loading up their syringes. Edson and a helper were strolling up and down offering advice and encouragement. Faced with the reality of a restlessly stamping cow who was depositing liberal amounts of dung over my feet, I motioned to Antonio to hold the tail and gingerly approached my task. I thrust my arm up her intestine and felt a strong contraction as she tried to expel it, and then tentatively searched for the mouth of the uterus. To my relief I could feel it through the wall of the intestine—a series of rubbery rings. I guided the syringe toward the spot, took a deep breath, and released the semen. Feeling thoroughly pleased with myself, I withdrew the syringe, then massaged the cow's backside and handed the equipment to Antonio with a big grin on my face.

During our coffee break, Fia told me all about their adventures driving the cows to class. They'd gotten as far as Limeira without incident and Fia had run into the bar for a couple of cheese pasties while Antonio drove the cows through the square. Up until then Virginia had been a model of good behavior, but suddenly, with no warning, she galloped off through an open gate, sending a small child screaming into its mother's arms. "Trampled Dona Alice's vegetable garden," Fia told me with a big grin. "She'd only just planted it, and of course she was mad as a hornet. I had to promise her a nice fresh cheese to make up for the damage."

The next day was our final class and we were all issued a certificate. Written in beautiful cursive, it attested to the fact that we had completed the course, but made no mention of our level of competence. I drove home in high spirits, leaving Antonio and Fia to follow with the cows. They had decided to go through Limeira so that they could deliver the cheese, and promised to make sure that no damage was done.

It wasn't until next morning that I heard about the return trip. Fia told me about it, laughing uproariously as she clamped the teat of a bottle into the mouth of a newborn calf. "We were determined to keep the cows out of trouble," she said, "and we did. They walked past Dona Alice's garden as good as gold. But you won't believe what happened then."

"We were just going by João Bosco's," put in Antonio, "when we saw Dona Alice sitting by the road with a sack of rice spread out to dry in the sun. I trotted ahead and gave her the cheese. Said I was sorry about the damage to her garden, and she said it was no problem, it could happen to anybody."

"And then I came up with the cows," said Fia, laughing helplessly.

"And damn me if they didn't walk right over her rice," said Antonio.

"And sprayed it with dung from one end to the other," completed Fia.

CHAPTER TEN

Cremating the Cow

For months there'd been talk about rural electrification. Robin hadn't been in favor of it, pointing out that there were plenty of waterfalls in our area and that we could get all our power for free by putting in small generators. He said it would cost the state hundreds of dollars per family to connect up the remote farms where people couldn't afford to do more than have a single lightbulb, and that the money would be far better spent on the roads.

I disagreed. Our little generator did a valiant job of lighting the houses, but the voltage fluctuated as the water levels rose and fell. It barely generated enough power to run the blender, and when I switched on the electric shower all the lights went out. I complained to Robin and he told me he'd find a *jeito,* and so he had. One of the local builders installed an ingenious system of iron pipes inside the wood burner, known as a *serpentina*. Most houses kept the fire going all day and had plenty of hot water, but we only cooked in the evening and could never heat more than a few gallons. If you could face having a shower at night—keeping a watchful eye open for hairy spiders or worse—you could run the scalding hot water off into a bucket and mix it with cold, but it wasn't very satisfactory, and although Robin talked brightly of solar heating and tried several experiments with coiled black hoses on the roof, they never quite worked. I dreamed of hot showers, and prayed for the day when we'd be connected to the county power supply, but I didn't provoke Robin by talking about it.

And then the miracle took place—we returned to Iracambi after a short break in Rio to discover that the power lines had reached the farm gate. The next steps were to register with the electricity company office in Muriaé, and figure out how to pay their large bill—something in the region of three thousand dollars for the posts, the wiring, the transformer, and the installation. A few months later the power company changed the rules and offered to buy back the transformer in six annual installments at the original price. Inflation was running at several thousand percent per annum at the time, and the first year's payment to us was the equivalent of one hundred dollars. The second year's payment was three cents—but we never got it.

The power supply turned out to be fairly reliable, but sometimes there were lightning strikes and the power went out with no warning. We had our hydropowered generator, so we were in good shape, but most of our neighbors went straight from kerosene lanterns to the county power supply. Since they didn't understand it very well they were inclined to poke the wires with bamboo poles, and one of Jair's nephews electrocuted himself.

Albertinho was considerably more careful. He had already wired up the dairy, and was in the process of running a line down to our house. A new era was dawning, and I was overjoyed. We'd be able to use the blender without dimming the lights, I could finally have a hot shower, we could install a refrigerator, and, best of all, we could buy a washing machine. Gone forever the days of scrubbing muddy jeans in a sink of cold water and praying that the voltage stabilizer would protect the computer when there was a power surge. Robin forgot his reservations and started scheming with Albertinho to trade the diesel engine that powered the chaff cutter for an electric motor, and I even caught him studying a brochure for milking machines. Valdeci and Antonio lobbied for a milk cooler and I unearthed the electric frying pan that we had kept since our student days. Things were shaping up.

On the staff front, however, there was some turbulence in the air.

"There's something funny going on with Albertinho," Robin told me. "He's asked for a few days off to go and visit some relatives in Ervália."

"What's funny about that?" I asked. "He's entitled to take some days off just like everyone else."

"Here's what's funny about it," said Robin. "First of all, Albertinho never sets foot off the *fazenda* if he can help it. He goes up to visit his father every second Sunday and very occasionally he goes to Limeira, but this is the first time there's been any mention of relatives in Ervália. Why does he want to go and see them all of a sudden? There's more to this than meets the eye."

"Maybe he's planning to move to the city," I laughed.

As it turned out, Albertinho never left the farm. The next thing we heard, he was confined to bed with an acute bellyache.

"That's odd," I remarked. "Not at all like Albertinho. I hope he hasn't got appendicitis."

The patient certainly wasn't looking too ill when I went over to see him, my barefoot doctor's manual under my arm. "Now then, Albertinho," I began. "There are a couple of things I'd like to check. Just lie back and let me feel your stomach."

Albertinho paled.

"This won't hurt," I told him. "I'm just going to apply a little pressure here above the groin." Albertinho braced himself while I prodded experimentally but he didn't feel the sudden sharp pain I was looking for, and there was no sign of fever or vomiting. "Stay quiet for the rest of the day," I said, "and I'll drop by in the evening to see how you are."

"I'll be fine," said Albertinho decisively.

And he was.

W ell, what do you suppose that was all about?" I remarked to Robin several days later. Albertinho had returned to work the day after my sickbed visit, and there had been no further mention of the Ervália trip.

"I think I've got it figured out," he told me. "You know he's a bit of a loner? Seems there was a disagreement among the work crew when they were carrying fencing stakes up the hill. It's a heavy job, and they'd tried to borrow Jair's oxen, but they weren't available. Albertinho turned up late, which is unusual for him, and when someone teased him about lying in bed he said he wasn't going up there because he had a hole in his boot and he might step on a snake. Particularly since he'd had some milk for breakfast and that always attracts snakes. He was grumbling about this and that, and then the others started laughing at him and saying he was just a weak woman and finally he stormed off in a rage. After *that* he couldn't quite see how to get back without losing face, so first of all he invented the fictitious relative in Ervália and then he invented the bellyache."

"Well, I fixed that one for him," I laughed.

"Let's hope it's the last we hear of it," said Robin.

S enhor Robin!" came the voice outside the window.

"In the dairy," I said automatically.

"I've just come from there," said the voice.

"Try the barn then," I suggested, sticking my head out to see who it could be at this early hour. It was Neri, Jair's son, a young man I couldn't bring myself to like. He'd done several small jobs for us, and while his work was good his charges were exorbitant, and we'd agreed not to hire him again.

I went out to fill the kettle for coffee, only to discover that the tap had run dry. Our water came from a spring in the forest via a system of bamboo pipes and channels connecting to the hose that delivered water into the concrete sink on the back veranda. The water pressure was so strong that we had to leave the tap running, otherwise it would blow the connectors apart, and the system worked well except for the rare occasions when a horse stepped on the pipe or it was blocked by leaves.

I pulled on my boots, took a shovel, and set off to investigate, following the pipe as far as I could. I couldn't find any leak—there must be a washaway farther up the channel. It was dark and cool as I entered the forest, there was a piercingly sweet smell from a flowering tree overhead, and specks of dust were dancing in the slanting shafts of sunlight. Splittie was chasing mottled gray lizards on the path, and a yellow butterfly flitted through the trees ahead. I splashed along the channel until I found the weak spot where the water was leaking through the channel wall into the river below, patched it up as best I could, and resolved to ask Albertinho to fix it later.

On the way back I met Robin. "Did Neri find you?" I asked.

"Yep," said Robin.

"And?"

"Made an outrageous bid for the fencing contract. I told him to forget it."

Back at the house the water was running once again. "Where's the coffee?" Robin shook the empty thermos flask.

"Haven't made it yet. There wasn't any water but I fixed it. The coffee won't take a minute." I lit the flame on the gas ring. It sputtered and died. "Robin," I said sweetly. "Do you mind changing the gas cylinder for me?"

Robin changed it cheerfully enough. He would do anything for a cup of coffee.

We took our breakfast into the front room to catch the morning sunshine. Two minutes later Antonio appeared. He was looking distinctly flustered.

"Is Neri around?" he asked.

"He left about ten minutes ago," said Robin.

"Filho da puta!" exclaimed Antonio. "One of the goats is missing and I'll swear it's that damned dog of his."

"Not again?" I said.

"That dog is a bloody nuisance," muttered Antonio furiously. "It ought to be shot."

"All right, Antonio," said Robin. "I'll have a word with him about it."

"You can tell him from me," said Antonio, "that if the bugger comes anywhere near my goats again, I'll blast its head off."

I was balancing two full coffee mugs when I heard a cough outside the door. It was Valdeci.

"Hello, Valdeci," I said. "What can I do for you?"

Valdeci blushed. "I wanted a word with you."

"What's the problem?" Robin breezed in from the kitchen.

"I'm going to have to hand in my notice," said Valdeci quickly, looking fixedly at his feet.

"Come and sit down, Valdeci," I said, "and tell us all about it."

Valdeci removed his boots and I noticed, for the first time, that they were lined with straw, and made a mental note to find him a pair of socks. He perched himself on the sofa and took a deep breath. "It's because of the long hours," he told us. "And my house being so far away. I leave home when it's dark and I don't get back till late, and my wife doesn't like being alone all day. I think I'll have to look for another job."

"Valdeci," said Robin gently. "Do you like working here with us?"

Valdeci brightened. "Yes, I do."

"You're doing a good job," Robin told him. "So if we can sort out another house for you, do you reckon you'll be okay?"

Valdeci nodded.

"Leave it to me," said Robin. "I'll think of something and we'll talk about it tomorrow."

I'll have a chat with old Sebastião," Robin told me later. "He's got a couple of empty houses on his place. Maybe he'll rent us one. Of course, I don't know whether Marinha gets along with her mother-in-law."

"That reminds me," I put in, "I finally got the story straight."

"What story?"

"About the family feud, silly. Between Jair's family and Sebastião's. You know, not speaking for years? Well, Fia told me. Do you remember there used to be a school next to Sebastião's house? Sebastião's wife wanted to do the school lunches—that way she'd get a job for life. And a pension. But Jair's wife got there first. There

was a violent quarrel about it, everyone took sides, and it turned
into a blood row. Sebastião's wife swore if she couldn't have the job
nobody would, and next thing someone started playing pranks on
the teachers. They were only young girls, had never been away
from home before, and they used to sleep in a little room at the
back of the school. All of a sudden there was a banging on the windows at night and lights going on and off, and they got so scared
they refused to stay there. Fia swears it was Sebastião's wife, and
she swears it was Jair's wife, but nothing was ever proved. People
started saying it was the evil eye, the kids were afraid to go to
school, and in the end they closed it down."

"What a sad story," said Robin, laughing.

Since I had taken one of the horses out for a gallop, I missed
the next installment of the day's news. Robin told me about it
when I came back.

"This business of the evil eye," he told me. "Maybe there's something in it after all."

"What's up now?"

"It's João. Told me he was leaving. I was just getting ready to go
and talk to Sebastião when João showed up. I took one look at him
and I knew something was wrong. Well you know how difficult it
is to get a straight sentence out of him, so I was quite taken aback
when he told me his cousin wanted to take a job in São Paulo cutting cane and had asked him to go along, too. I asked him if he
really wanted to go all the way to São Paulo and he said no, he
didn't. And he didn't want to cut cane all day, either. And then it
turned out the real problem was that he needed a bit of land to
plant up, and he didn't feel right if he didn't have his little patch of
maize and beans.

"I said we could arrange that, and while we were at it, how was

he getting on over the hot lunches? He said it was fine in Albertinho's granary but he'd really like his own house and was there a
chance that he'd be getting one soon? And I said, of course, his
house was the next on the list. In fact, his house would be ready
long before mine. So one way and another he seems to have talked
himself out of handing in his notice, and just as well, because he's
a good man and an excellent worker. And after that, I just hope
that Albertinho doesn't get it into his head to walk out."

I was sitting in the sunshine digesting all this information when
a small boy arrived, panting, to deliver a message. I didn't recognize him and he didn't stay long enough to introduce himself.

"My mother says that Valdeci says that João Bosco says . . . ,"
he gabbled.

"Yes?" I inquired.

"That João Bosco says please to call the man."

Which man? I wondered as he bolted down the path.

There was only one way to find out. I got into the car and went
in search of João Bosco. With considerable difficulty and at unrea-
sonable expense we had managed to obtain a Limeira telephone,
which we kept in João Bosco's shop. There was no question of
running a line five miles out to the *fazenda,* so although it wasn't
very convenient, it was the best location we could manage for now.
It was easier for us to make our calls from there rather than from
Murilo's bar, where everyone could hear the conversation, and once
in a while someone would call in and leave a message.

João Bosco had been trained as a veterinary technician, and
was always willing to lend a hand with a difficult calving or to give
advice on how to treat a sickly cow. He had trouble with his eyes,
and was saving up for an operation in the state capital, but he could
never raise quite enough money. When he ran his motorbike into

the ditch, gossip had it that it wasn't solely due to poor eyesight: People said he had a problem with the local moonshine, and years later when his pretty wife ran away she said he'd been impossible to live with.

His store was in the main square near the house of Armir Toko, the Coffee Baron, and he had recently bought a television that was his pride and joy. An avid fan of environmental programs, particularly anything connected with Africa, João Bosco loved to collect interesting facts: Elephants in Western Kenya ate salt in caves; there was a giant turtle in the Mombasa zoo that had adopted a miniature hippo; did we know that wolves ate rats?

I found him sitting in front of a large pile of invoices with a calculator in one hand and a glass of coffee in the other. "*Olá*, Bianca," he greeted me. "I'm glad you got the message. The man said it was important."

"Which man?" I asked.

"The man from the bank. I've got his number here somewhere—just a minute, I'll see if I can find it." He opened a drawer that was overflowing with untidy scraps of paper and started rummaging around.

I took a deep breath and inhaled the friendly smell of molasses and cattle feed. Things were piled up higgledy-piggledy all over the place, but João Bosco could put his hand on anything important in a second. Scraps of paper were something else entirely. Coils of rope, sacks of grass seed, and rolls of wire lay on the floor. There was a large pile of horseshoes in one corner. Brightly colored woven string girths hung next to braided reins, quilted saddle blankets, plastic fuel cans, and lengths of chain. The shelves were stacked with little bottles of medicine and vaccines, sprays, dips, and wormers.

"Here we are!" he said triumphantly, producing a piece of paper. "Looks like it's a number in Brasília. The code is 061."

Relief washed over me. Far from being a mistake with our current account, it was confirmation of the consulting job Robin had been waiting to hear about. He'd already been several times to Mozambique and Mexico, and now he had set his heart on visiting an irrigation project in the south of Brazil. It was an interesting assignment and we needed the money. Besides, I was getting more confident about managing the farm.

I t was a particularly busy time of year, but I had discovered that I didn't really need to supervise; I just had to be around in case of trouble. I was, however, doubtful about one of the temporary hands, a taciturn fellow named Walther. He was a great grumbler, and although I could find no fault with his work, I felt instinctively that he was a troublemaker.

My first run-in with Walther took place on the day of the anthrax scare. Robin was fifteen hundred miles away on the borders of Paraguay, and things on the *fazenda* were going remarkably smoothly. The building project was making steady progress, and John the Baptist was working on the internal walls. Following Valdeci's advice I had bought a couple of loads of sugarcane for supplementary feed for the cattle, and, best of all, I had discovered that Albertinho had a natural aptitude for driving the truck. And then one of the heifers died. One day she was perfectly all right, and the next day she was lying on her back with her feet in the air and blood coming out of her orifices.

"What on earth did she die of?" I asked Valdeci anxiously. "When did you last see her?"

"I had her in the corral on Monday for spraying. She was fine then."

"It wasn't a snakebite, was it?"

"Couldn't see any sign of it."

"Perhaps she ate a poisonous plant," suggested Antonio. "It does happen sometimes."

"I doubt it," said Valdeci. "That pasture's been recently cleaned out. I had a look around last week before I let the cows in."

"It couldn't be anthrax, could it, Valdeci?" I asked. "She's been vaccinated against that, hasn't she?"

"I'll check in the book," said Valdeci. "But I think she was done a few months back. I wish you'd go and take a look at her, Dona Bianca. We'll have to get her buried this morning."

I stumped gloomily back to the house to get my veterinary book, wishing for the hundredth time that someone would write a book for barefoot vets. (They did later, but by that time I'd learned the basics by trial and error—mostly error.) I poured myself a coffee and sat down on the sofa to study causes of sudden death.

ANAPLASMOSIS AND PIRAPLASMOSIS: Tick-borne diseases. They didn't apply in our region.

FOOT AND MOUTH: We lived in the endemic area, but we vaccinated twice a year.

RABIES: The thought of rabid cows rampaging through the *fazenda* was scary, but I thought it unlikely. (Later we were to gain experience in bovine rabies, and discover that cows didn't develop furious rabies like dogs. But I didn't know that at the time.)

TUBERCULOSIS, TETANUS: Not applicable.

MINERAL DEFICIENCIES AND NUTRITIONAL PERTURBATIONS: Mineral deficiencies don't kill cows overnight, I said to myself. But a nutritional perturbation

could, I suppose. If she'd accidentally eaten some poisonous plant. Still, Valdeci had ruled that out.

ANTHRAX: Acute form: no symptoms. The animal is
found dead with blood issuing from the orifices.

Blood issuing from the orifices? I read on. "The corpse is swollen with blood running from the nose and anus. The carcass must
be burned, together with any material contaminated with blood or
feces. Take extreme care in handling, since the disease is transmis-
sible to humans."

Shit! Now what? The corpse lay at the top of the steep hill above
the generator house. It was all cleared pasture, and there was no
firewood within easy reach. The vultures were circling in the sky.
I made my way up the hill puffing hard, my thoughts whirling.

I looked at the swollen body, at the blood trickling from the
nose and hindquarters. I wish, I wish there was a vet nearby, I
thought. I wish I had a phone. I wish I knew what to do.

I ran down to the house and consulted my medical manual.
"Malignant pustules," I read, "Edema, fever, hemorrhage." Dear God!
I pounded up to the dairy in search of Valdeci. "You've got to burn
that corpse, Valdeci," I shouted. "Right now!"

Valdeci's eyebrows shot up expressively. "I was going to bury
her, Dona Bianca," he said.

"No, Valdeci," I insisted. "You've got to burn the body. And
you mustn't touch the carcass, because you might catch anthrax
and it'll make you very ill. It could even kill you."

Valdeci nodded. "We'll need another pair of hands. Can you
ask Albertinho to help us?"

"All right," I muttered.

Later that afternoon I looked out and saw a pall of smoke on
the top of the hill.

"Did you manage that okay?" I asked Valdeci that evening.

"It's very difficult to burn a cow," he said reproachfully. "We had to dig a pit and drag a lot of wood up there, and Albertinho had to get some gasoline to start the fire."

"Well done, Valdeci. Thank you."

"Walther has been grumbling all afternoon that we were having a barbecue up there," said Antonio, laughing.

"I hope you told him that anyone who eats the meat of that cow could die of a very nasty disease?"

"I told him, all right," said Antonio. "But he said it was nonsense and he could have told us that she had died of poisoning. Any fool could have seen that, that's what he said."

"What do you think, Antonio?" I asked.

"To tell you the truth, Dona Bianca, I don't know. Better safe than sorry, that's what I say."

In the morning Valdeci reported that the corpse had still not been completely cremated. I had a sudden flashback to my Scottish great uncle, veteran of the Indian Army. He had decreed in his will that his body should be disposed of on a funeral pyre by the banks of the river in his garden. But the local health authorities would permit no such thing. I could see why. To dispose of a body takes a long time and a hot fire.

As I left the dairy I ran into Walther, plodding stolidly up the hill with his hoe over his shoulder.

"Walther!" I called out. "I'd like you to give Albertinho a hand today. You'll need to take a few more loads of wood up there to finish burning the cow." Walther looked at me sourly and I heard the ghost of a laugh from Antonio.

I turned back and saw Antonio gesturing at me. "*Psst!*" he said. "Look at this." He was carrying a small innocent-looking plant.

"What is it?" I whispered.

"Ratsbane. If a cow eats this she's dead in five minutes."

"Where did you find it?" I demanded.

"Up in that pasture," he said. "But I don't think we'll tell Walther."

"No, Antonio," I replied. "I don't think we will."

CHAPTER ELEVEN

The Brazilian Blues

We'd been at Iracambi for just over a year and I was suffering from a monstrous case of the blues. Try as I might, I didn't seem to be able to shift it. Sometimes I found life at Iracambi wrenchingly difficult. I missed giving concerts, I missed my friends, I was lonely and frustrated, and I felt that life was passing me by. And, although I knew we could use the money, I couldn't help being resentful that Robin was the one who got to go to exciting places and I was the one who stayed back to mind the store.

It wasn't that I minded roughing it—although neither of us ever expected to stay so long in the blue house. Had we known that we'd live there for several years, we might have done a bit more in the way of home improvements. The house was too small and too dark, and when it rained hard the roof developed serious leaks. The woodstove was unpredictable: Sometimes it was friendly and cooperative, other times moody and downright difficult. And despite Albertinho's work on the road there were still days when the car would get bogged down to the axles and it took all hands to dig it out.

The blue house wasn't much of a house, but I can bear most things as long as I'm warm. It wasn't the simple lifestyle that was the problem. It was the culture shock. We had thrust ourselves into a completely different society where people were reserved and suspicious, women were repressed, and men were macho in the extreme. Robin used to laugh when Valdir the cattle dealer came to the house, never addressed a word to me, took his coffee without so much as a thank-you, and then gave me his empty glass. But I didn't find it very funny.

We had few friends, we were living miles from nowhere, and our methods of communication with the outside world were highly precarious. It was hard to get anywhere because the roads were so bad. It was hard to get in touch with anyone and virtually impossible for anyone to get in touch with us. With no form of communication, things took twice as long to happen. If a cow was sick, we couldn't call the vet for advice. We couldn't check if the feed had arrived at the feed store. If we wanted to contact someone, we had to get in the car and look for him, and if we needed to make a telephone call, we had to go to João Bosco's shop and wait patiently for the operator to answer. More often than not the line was engaged, and if we did get through, it often cut out midconversation. If the Limeira telephone was out of order we could try Belisário, but the line there wasn't much better. In the end it was more effective to wait for our weekly shopping trip to Muriaé, and make all our calls in one go.

We were trying to lead a twentieth-century life in a nineteenth-century environment, and while Robin was accustomed to the leaden pace of the developing world, I found it hard to adapt to. I was used to being in a situation where if you worked hard you could change things. Here we worked hard and things didn't change. I kept asking myself if we were having fun yet.

Robin bore my discontent manfully, but sometimes even he had his down days. Days when nothing went right. When the cows got sick and we couldn't figure out what to do, when the staff got irritable and wouldn't say why, when it rained from dawn to dusk, and when people asked for favors that Robin was too nice to refuse.

"Just say no," I urged him when old Olavo dropped by one morning to ask if we could help him move a load of maize.

"No problem," said Robin. "It won't take me long." But it did. The maize was in the field and had to be collected, weighed, and put into sacks. It took most of the day, and then Robin got the car stuck in the usual muddy place by the river and had to walk home.

Valdeci's brother's wife announced that she was going to have a baby and would we please take her into Muriaé. "That's something that won't wait for our next trip to town," Robin told me. "Not from the look of her."

"But she's had nine months to get ready," I pointed out. "She could have taken herself into Limeira a little ahead of time."

"You're a hard woman," said Robin to me, smiling.

"We've got to define our boundaries," I muttered. "After all, if we weren't around they'd have to think of something else. And life's difficult enough as it is."

The truth was, I was finding it tough to handle so many unknowns. High inflation meant that we never knew what our money was worth or what price we would get for our milk. It was hard to get the things we needed for the *fazenda,* and often the quality was terrible. We supplemented the cattle feed with bone meal and discovered it was adulterated. The grass seed didn't germinate, we couldn't get spare parts for the chaff cutter, and there was an outbreak of calf pneumonia that killed three of our best calves. As if that wasn't enough, I got covered with minute tick bites that itched so badly I couldn't sleep, and one night when I got up for a drink of water I stepped on a gigantic cockroach.

Robin took me in his arms and brushed the hair out of my eyes. "I hear what you say," he told me. "And I know it's tough. But life *is* tough and unpredictable out here in the real world."

"Just a minute!" I snapped. "We chose to come and live here, remember? To do what? To run some little one-horse outfit in the back of nowhere surrounded by a bunch of predatory peasants?"

Robin knew better than to open his mouth.

"It's a lot of hard work and we don't seem to be getting anywhere," I finished.

"This sort of thing takes time," Robin told me. "But things *are* coming together. Remember how it was when we arrived? There was nothing here. Albertinho was living in a tumbledown mud hut looking after a handful of cows. And now look at us. Our staff are living in decent houses with electric light and running water. We're providing employment and producing something that people need. Don't tell me that's not more constructive than sitting in an office and pushing papers around."

T hat's all very well," I took up the conversation at supper that evening, "but if you want to know what I need, it's a friend." The fact was, I was just plain lonely. Later I learned that lots of people in situations like ours suffer from loneliness; if I'd known that before, I might not have felt so bad.

Robin tried to encourage me to talk to the local women. Get out more, he told me; they all love to talk to you. But, God help me, they weren't the kind of friends I needed. I needed someone who understood where I was coming from and how I felt, someone to help me process the culture shock of living in the backwoods with backwoods people. I wasn't going to find such a person living in my mountains, and I couldn't imagine there would be anybody like that in Muriaé. But I was wrong. My friend had been living there all along. And one day I found her.

It happened one sleepy Sunday afternoon. Robin was going off to Mexico on a job and I had just dropped him off at the bus station in Muriaé. The road up the mountain was in particularly bad shape, and I was in no hurry to tackle it again. I drove around the cobbled streets in search of a treat—mangoes, avocados, ice cream, chocolate. Nothing. The stores were tightly shuttered; there was nobody in the streets. It was as dead as a Sunday in Scotland.

And then I had an inspiration: I'd look up the Peace Corps volunteer people kept telling me about. Maybe she'd like to come up and spend a few days on the *fazenda*? I'd been meaning to find her, but somehow there'd never been enough time. Whenever we came to town there were a million things to do: send off the mail; make our phone calls; go to the supermarket; buy cattle feed, veterinary medicines, and building supplies; fill up the car—a constant battle against the clock that left me exhausted and irritable. But today I had time to spare. Checking my notebook, I found her address in a small apartment building in a quiet leafy street behind the bank. I parked under a tree, walked up the stairs, and rang the doorbell.

There was a long silence.

I leaned on the bell. Nothing. I knocked on the door. No reply. Stupid of me to imagine she'd be at home on a Sunday afternoon.

I was just turning to leave when the door was opened by a stately white-haired woman in an ankle-length red robe.

"Good afternoon," I said, momentarily startled. "I'm so sorry, I think I've got the wrong house. I was looking for the Peace Corps volunteer."

"Honey," she said, in a rich Southern accent, "you have found her. Come on in."

Trying to hide my surprise, I went in. The apartment was clean and airy, with bamboo furniture and potted plants everywhere.

"Let me introduce myself." She smiled. "Louise Gardner. Known as Luiza."

"I'm Binka," I said, taking her hand. "Known as Bianca."

Luiza offered me a chair, poured tall glasses of lemonade, and lit a cigarette. "I know exactly who you are," she told me. "Everyone knows about the *ingleses* who live in the mountains near Limeira. But let me tell you a little bit about myself."

She had joined the Peace Corps in the 1970s when they started taking older volunteers. She'd just come out of a difficult marriage, had no kids and no commitments, and needed a change of scene. They promised to send her to Mexico but somehow she ended up in Brazil and went to work in Sete Lagoas, north of Belo Horizonte. She was helping out in a rural cooperative, and one of her colleagues was Julia Monteiro, who was a rural extension agent.

"I expect you know her; she works up in Limeira." Luiza smiled. "Ever since she told me about you I've wanted to get up there and meet you, but my car's getting old. Like me. We're neither of us very good on mountain roads."

After finishing the Peace Corps she went back to the States, she told me. But somehow she just couldn't settle back in. Everything was too predictable, and she found she was missing Brazil. So she decided to come back. As it turned out, Julia had married and moved down to Muriaé. She suggested that Luiza might like to come live with her family, but that wasn't Luiza's style at all; she was far too independent. So she bought an apartment in the same building and it worked out just fine. She kept busy by creating finely detailed paintings of birds and flowers and giving English lessons—resulting in a small but significant group of young Brazilians in town who spoke with the courtly tones of the Deep South.

"This is great," I told her. "You can't believe how good it is to find an English speaker in this neck of the woods."

When Robin returned I told him about Luiza. "Sounds like the answer to prayer," he said. "What was she doing in the Peace Corps?"

"Home economics or something, I think."

"Perhaps she can teach you to sew." Robin grinned at me.

"Don't be an idiot," I told him crisply. "But she might be a whizz at baking brownies."

"Now you're talking. I could do with a bit of spoiling."

"Me, too," I agreed.

Two weeks later Robin was summoned to Mozambique to look at the government's new agricultural plan, leaving me once again in charge of the *fazenda*. Luiza promised to come up and spend a few days, and my spirits were much higher as Robin and I went over the list of jobs to be done. It was the beginning of the rains and everything had to be planted at once: tree seedlings, sugarcane, corn, beans, and improved pasture grass. The new batch of calves had to be vaccinated and wormed. Work on our house had stopped because of the rains, and John the Baptist was planning to get on with the promised house for João, which meant I would need to make sure the building supplies were on hand since he only remembered to ask for things after he'd already run out.

Robin and I took a couple of horses out for a ride up to the high pasture, returning just as the light was starting to fade. Fia met us with news of a new calf, and we walked down to the pasture together to inspect it. The calf was lying in the long grass with its mother standing by protectively.

"Let's see if we can get them up to the dairy," whispered Robin. "It's almost dark and I'd like to have them safely tucked in for the night. Fia can give us a hand. You two take care of the cow and I'll grab the calf." But the cow refused to cooperate. She was a big crossbred Gir and she wouldn't budge.

"She's not going anywhere," I told Robin. "Better send for Antonio."

Fia loped off to the dairy, and I backed away from the cow and squatted down in the grass. The setting sun was lighting the topmost peaks and the sky was aflame with color. "Just look at that sunset," I said to Robin, and as he turned the cow charged and knocked him flat.

I shouted at her, and she stood her ground. Robin didn't stir, but he wouldn't with an angry cow standing over him. I yelled again and she moved back to her calf. I sprinted over to Robin and found he was out cold.

"Robin!" I shouted, and I saw his eyelids flutter. He couldn't have hurt himself falling in this long grass, could he? As I bent over him he opened his eyes and struggled to sit up. "Must have tripped over something," he mumbled. "The weirdest thing."

Antonio and Fia came running up and together we helped Robin to his feet. He stood there swaying. "Feeling a bit dizzy." He shook his head.

"Let's take him to Albertinho's house," I urged. We helped him across the pasture and up the steps. Maria swept the children off the sofa and found a pillow, and Robin lay back and closed his eyes. Albertinho's gray horse was tethered outside, and I jumped onto its back and galloped home to find the little bottle of arnica tincture that I used for shock. With shaking hands I seized my barefoot doctor's manual, leafed through it until I came to the section on concussion, studied it carefully, grabbed a flashlight, and galloped back.

Maria and the children were clustered anxiously around Robin. His face was drained of color and his eyes were closed. "Robin!" I shouted. "Are you okay?"

Robin opened his eyes and looked at me. "Of course I'm okay," he said. "Shall we go home?"

"Just let me check something," I told him, shining the flashlight into his eyes. One pupil contracted, the other remained dilated. I checked again. No change.

I drew Albertinho to one side. "We need to take him to hospital right now. Can you come with me?"

"*Ah eh.*" Albertinho nodded.

"I'll run back and collect the car. Lend me a blanket, Maria, and some pillows." I shot back home, snatched my wallet and the car keys, shut up the house, and gunned the Toyota as fast as I dared. Albertinho helped Robin onto the front seat and surrounded him with pillows, and I concentrated on avoiding the worst of the potholes as the road stretched endlessly into the darkness.

At the hospital they x-rayed Robin's head to check for fractures and suggested he spend the night there. "Probably just a simple concussion," they said. "But we'll keep him under observation. Just to be on the safe side." I sat with Robin until he fell asleep and then took Albertinho off to Luiza's apartment for some mothering.

I was back at the hospital at first light to find Robin sitting up in bed looking very cheerful. "Stupidest damn thing," he told me. "I'm absolutely fine. Except I can't see straight."

The door opened and in swept the neurologist on his Friday morning rounds. He took one look at Robin and had visions of foreign money.

"This little problem with double vision," he said smoothly, "I'll order a CAT scan to check for any swelling or bleeding in the brain so that we can rule out surgery. Back in a few minutes."

Surgery? In Muriaé! My heart was racing. When we'd first arrived in Brazil a few years earlier, the then president-elect had died a long, slow death because of hospital infection and medical incompetence. Robin and I had sworn to avoid Brazilian hospitals at all costs, and here was the neurologist talking about brain surgery. Robin caught the look on my face. "Ridiculous nonsense!" he told me firmly. "I'm just fine."

Five minutes later the neurologist was back, smiling benignly. "I've got you an appointment," he told us. "Said it was urgent, so we got you in for Wednesday at nine. In the Itaperuna hospital, sixty kilometers from here. I'll let you go home today, but if there's any change you must get in touch immediately. And the charge for the CAT scan will be five hundred dollars."

"What a load of crap," said Robin to his retreating back. "I haven't got five hundred dollars. And anyway, if I close one eye I can see perfectly fine."

"Let me run over to Luiza's and collect Albertinho," I told Robin. "And then we'll go home."

D on't you fret, honeychild," said Luiza when I told her the neurologist's diagnosis. "We'll put Julia onto the case."

Julia was indignant when she heard the story. "Five hundred *dollars?*" she snorted. "*Filho da puta!* That's outrageous! Now let me think. Okay, here's what we'll do. First we'll call Itaperuna and find out what they charge for a CAT scan. I reckon we can bill it to the health service, all it takes is a *jeito.*"

Back at the hospital Robin was dressed and ready to leave. "Just after you left I had a visit from one of the Sisters of Charity," he told me. "She asked me if I wanted confession, and I thanked her very much and told her I wasn't a Catholic. She looked at me as though I had horns and a tail and bolted out of the room."

I laughed. "Did the neurologist come back?"

"You bet he did. Dreaming of his fat fee. Told me to stay quiet and come see him after the CAT scan."

"I think we've got some news on that front," I told him. "Julia's working on it, and she reckons it won't cost even half what he quoted. We may be able to get it for free."

B ack at Luiza's Julia was on the phone, speaking very fast and gesturing. She gave Robin a thumbs-up as Luiza settled him on the sofa with a plate of chocolate chip cookies. He grinned at her and ate three in swift succession.

"Thank you, Luiza. I'm okay now. No need for the CAT scan."

"Don't be an idiot," said Luiza firmly. "Of course you need a CAT scan. It's all arranged."

"That's right," Julia cut in. "Now here's the deal. My hairdresser's sister has a cousin by marriage who works in the Itaperuna hospital, and she's just checked out the price. Exactly half what the neurologist quoted. But that's not all. She's rescheduled your appointment and figured out a way to bill it to the rural health fund. That way you'll get it for free. Problem solved."

F rom that point on everything ran smoothly. Robin discovered he could see fine if he wore a patch over one eye. His spirits rose by the hour and I even caught him admiring himself in the mirror. A couple of days later we drove to the Itaperuna hospital and were greeted by the cousin of Julia's hairdresser's sister who was on the lookout for us.

"The neurologist was spitting mad when he heard you'd canceled your appointment," she laughed. "But I've got a friend in town who can read the X-ray for you and let you know if there's anything to worry about. He'll look at it this afternoon and I'll figure out a way to get his report back to Julia. No call for you to drive all the way back here."

Two days later Jair delivered a brown envelope marked URGENT.

I tore open the envelope and pulled out the X-ray and the scrawled note, which read, "No sign of any trouble. Suggest you check with the ophthalmologist. Could be you've bruised the ophthalmic nerve."

"All well then?" Jair asked solicitously. "I heard that Robin was sick," he tapped his forehead, "and they'd sent him down to that place in Itaperuna."

What place in Itaperuna, I wondered.

"You know, the place for people when they have—er—*problems,*" he added.

I stared at him for a moment and then burst out laughing. Itaperuna was the site of the regional psychiatric hospital. "It's nothing like *that,*" I told him. "He had a concussion and went for an X-ray. He's fine, just fine."

Jair stood his ground. "I heard he was wearing an eye patch," he told me.

"That's right. But his head's working okay. He just can't see straight." Jair raised a bushy eyebrow and grinned.

Later that evening Valdeci came over somewhat diffidently to invite us to a service held by the Believers. "It's tomorrow," he told us, "at the house of Jerson and Maria, up in Graminha. I hope you can come."

"Of course we'll come," said Robin. "Thank you."

Fia was around early next morning to borrow a cup of sugar. "Did you hear about the Believers service?" she inquired.

"I certainly did," I replied. "And we're planning to go. But tell me something. I thought your parents are Catholics?"

"So they are," said Fia. "But they didn't want to offend the Believers so they agreed to have the service there. After all, it's the same God, isn't it?"

"Of course it is," I told her. "Oh, and one more thing . . ."

"Yes?" said Fia, her eyes sparkling.

"You don't suppose we have to wear veils?"

"No, we don't," she laughed. "I asked Valdeci about that. First thing I thought of."

"What time is the service?"

"Eight o'clock. We Catholics are holding a meeting of our own beforehand."

"That must be to ward off foreign gods," remarked Robin later.

B etter dress decent," Robin advised me that evening.

"Better dress warm," I told him. "Fia says they're expecting so many people that Jerson has run an extension light out into the yard. What time do you think we should leave?"

"Eight thirty will be plenty of time. These things always run late. And we'll have supper first. You never know, it'll probably go on for hours."

The car was fully loaded with Antonio's family and all the Valdecis as we set off up the mountain by the light of a perfect moon. It was clean and cold and I was glad to have my jacket and scarf. Jerson's house was right under the peak, and the rock face gleamed pale against the black sky. We could hear the sound of singing from far down the valley.

A line of horses stood by the fence, and seventy or eighty people were clustered under the lightbulb in the yard. Men stood on one side, women and children on the other, invited guests mingling with the Believers except for a few young men hunkered down apart, chatting and smoking. The master of ceremonies was a little old man dressed in a threadbare blue suit, holding a Bible and leading the prayers. The Believer ladies huddled together, draped in white veils and shouting "Amen!"

There was something deeply touching about that earnest little band assembled in the chilly moonlight, and I suddenly knew without a doubt that God would hear their prayers.

"The Lord is my fort where I can enter and be safe," intoned the leader. "No one can follow me and slay me. He is a rugged mountain where I hide. He is my Savior, a rock where no one can reach me, and a tower of safety."

The choir struck up, somewhat raggedly: " 'You are my hiding place. You always fill my heart / with songs of deliverance. Whenever I am afraid / I will trust in You.' "

I glanced over at Robin, rakish in his eye patch. I looked up at the mountains and the old words came back to me with a new intensity:

I will lift up mine eyes unto the hills,
from whence cometh my help.
My help cometh from the Lord, which made heaven and earth.
He will not suffer thy foot to be moved:
he that keepeth thee will not slumber.
Behold, he that keepeth Israel
shall neither slumber nor sleep.

CHAPTER TWELVE

Policemen and *Pistoleiros*

A nother year had passed, we were coming up on our third
Christmas, and Limeira was in a ferment of excitement. For
years people had dreamed of turning the district into an independent county with its own funding, instead of being forever dependent on Muriaé. The moving force behind this was the Toko
clan, headed by Coffee Baron Armir, who saw it as a way to consolidate his power—although it didn't turn out that way.

But before this dream could be translated into reality, several
concrete steps needed to be taken. First was to hold a referendum
to see whether there were enough voters in favor. Since this would
require a minimum of two thousand voters, and since the entire
population of the district was barely four thousand, it was important that every adult sign up. The next step was to organize a petition and send it to the state governor in the distant city of Belo
Horizonte. If this petition was successful, the people of Limeira
would have to wait for the next election year and then select a prefect and nine town councilors.

There were several good reasons for pursuing independence.

Politics in Muriaé had long been controlled by two rival families of colonels, the Carvalhos and the Canedos. Both families concentrated their efforts on the urban areas, where they drew the majority of their support. The Carvalhos dreamed of setting up an industrial area and bulldozed a large tract of land on the edge of town. They plowed roads, installed electricity, and erected large signs on which their names figured prominently. But nobody wanted to move there—it was too far out of town, and the townspeople preferred to conduct their business where they had always done so: in their backyards. The Canedos installed an elaborate one-way traffic system that meant that everyone wasted a lot of time getting from one part of town to another, and followed it up by putting traffic lights in the main square, which served only to slow the flow of traffic still further. They caused a minor stir by demolishing several illegal shacks that had been built on the airstrip, and when the padre started his Sunday homily by vehemently denouncing injustice they called up the bishop and had him transferred to another state. The airstrip was fenced and paved and there was talk of setting up a local air service, but nothing came of it, and it became the de facto private landing ground for the state congressman. Meanwhile, the rural roads were frequently impassable, the town had no proper drainage system, the river was a floating cesspool, there was no fire brigade, and the animals in the town zoo were half starved.

The county representative for the district of Limeira was Bertoni, the coffee farmer who lived in the house with the white satin sofas. Like his fellow councilors he gave extravagant parties and plentiful handouts at election time. For the balance of his term he was long on talk and short on delivery. His constituents grumbled but they didn't know how to change things; the teachers' salaries were always in arrears, there was no medicine in the clinic, and the roads were in such poor shape that the isolated farms were completely cut off during the rains.

An isolated rural district with few voters and a small tax base, Limeira was at the bottom of the list of priorities for the prefect of Muriaé. If, however, it could become an independent county, it would qualify for the federal funding to which every county was entitled—to provide schools, a proper health service, and improved roads and communications. Such funding would be administered by the prefect and councilors, and it was vital that Limeirans elect a candidate of integrity who would hold the interests of the county above those of his family. It was an important moment, and the most exciting thing that had happened in the area for a long time.

W e discussed it in the dairy one evening. Antonio and Valdeci were seated on low stools milking into metal buckets, while Fia was bottle-feeding the calves.

"What do you think about Limeira becoming independent?" I asked as I scanned the milk records attached to the clipboard.

"I think it's worth a try," said Antonio slowly, straightening up from his milking stool.

"It depends on who's elected prefect," said Robin, who was checking the medicine cabinet.

"Whoever it is, he couldn't be worse than the one we've got now," Fia pointed out. "The only time he shows his face around here is the week before the election."

"What's the deal about Limeira joining up with Belisário?" I asked. "Sounds like it would make sense."

"It'll never happen," said Antonio decisively. "Belisário doesn't like Limeira and never has. They want to set up a county of their own but they haven't got a chance. Not enough voters."

There was a moment's silence while Antonio finished the milking and Valdeci let the cows out into the yard.

"Speaking of chances," Antonio said casually, "I hear that Fazenda Graminha is for sale."

Stretching from our western boundary to Graminha peak, Fazenda Graminha was a wild, forested piece of land with a river running through it and a nice old house under the hill. Robin and I had talked several times of buying it if the opportunity arose. We needed an area to plant trees, and we were getting short of pasture.

"Are you sure, Antonio?" Robin demanded.

"Quite sure." Antonio nodded. "Silvério's got money problems."

"Not just money problems," added Fia. "They say his wife threw him out of the house. On account of his new girlfriend. Young enough to be his daughter, so I hear. Of course, everyone knows what she did to his last woman."

"What?" I exclaimed.

"Had her rubbed out," said Fia.

"No kidding!"

"It's God's truth," Antonio assured me. "You don't go fooling with Silverio's wife."

"I see," I said, breathing deeply.

T he next morning we had a visit from Silvério himself. Dressed in leather chaps and a felt sombrero, he had jet black hair and cut a fine figure as he cantered up on a glossy black stallion.

"You probably know why I'm here." He leaned down and shook Robin's hand. "It's about Fazenda Graminha. I'm putting it on the market and I wanted to give you first refusal, seeing that we're neighbors. It's a beautiful piece of land, and I wouldn't dream of parting with it if things were otherwise."

Robin and I avoided each other's eyes.

"At my time of life a man has to put his house in order," Silvério continued. "Never know what tomorrow will bring, isn't that the truth? I'm seventy years old last birthday, but you wouldn't know it to look at me."

"Not a white hair on your head," said Robin admiringly. He himself had kept a fine head of hair but was graying at the temples.

"It's my Indian blood," Silvério told him. "Indians don't go gray. May I invite you to ride up with me to Fazenda Graminha?"

"I'll come with you," I offered. "It's such a beautiful day, I was planning to take my horse out anyway."

Robin preferred cars to horses. "Good idea," he told me. "Go get your horse and Silvério and I will take a look at the map. I'd like to see where the boundaries go."

Silvério and I trotted our horses up the road toward the jagged peak of Graminha. A steep cut took us twice across the river and then along the shoulder of a hill with a view clear down the valley to Iracambi. We were up in the high country, it was cool and clear, and the peaks were very close. As we turned our horses onto the rough track that led up the side of the mountain we could see the Fazenda Graminha farmhouse nestled down in the valley beneath us. The horses were breathing heavily as we reined them in and looked out across the blue mountains. Below us stretched a mosaic of dark green coffee fields, patches of forest with purple and yellow flowering trees, neat little farmhouses, and steep green pastures dotted with miniature cows. We tethered the horses in the shade and walked along an overgrown path into the dense forest, then crossed the river and came out onto a natural grassland with a long view down the valley.

"When I was a kid there used to be a settlement up here," Silvério told me. "Funny, really, the whole place gone back to forest like this."

"Woodcutters?" I asked.

"Yes, exactly. And occasionally a truck would make it in to take out the timber. There was one family that kept a couple of cows and they used to make the most delicious cheese."

I looked around at the forest and tried to imagine people living up here. Instead of houses all I could see were trees; instead of the voices of children all I could hear were the calls of the birds. Parrots chattered overhead, somewhere in the distance a bellbird tolled. A little wind blew up from the valley and felt cool on my face, and I took a long pull from my water bottle.

"I love this place," said Silvério simply. "I feel more alive up here. Breaks my heart to let it go. But I'll feel better if I know it's gone to you and Robin. And it'll make an excellent addition to your farm—in fact, you'll be just about the biggest landowners around here. Robin could run for prefect of Limeira."

"I don't think he's interested in that," I told him.

"Don't you be too sure," said Silvério. "The nice thing about being prefect is that you can vote yourself a good fat salary."

T he news was around the valley before we had even signed the contract, and several of our neighbors came over to offer us their services in clearing pastures and fixing fences. There was a lot of discussion in the dairy about what should be done with the land and who would go up and live there. "Hold on!" laughed Robin when the subject came up again. "We haven't got the title deeds yet."

And there we ran into a hitch. It was all to do with being foreigners, and wanting to enlarge our landholding. We would have to get authorization from the Institute of Land Reform—an archaic and largely bankrupt agency, heavily burdened with bureaucratic rules and regulations, that was in charge of all land deals. In order for the sale to proceed we would have to get fifteen different documents, one of which had to come from the Brazilian Institute of Statistics in Rio de Janeiro.

It was the job of the Institute of Statistics to say whether the land in question was where the Institute of Land Reform said it was. This was a difficult calculation, since most of the land had never been properly titled, and title deeds were written much as they had been in colonial days, e.g., "The boundary runs along the crest of the ridge for three leagues, turns north to the marker stone by the rocks, and follows the river down." To add to the confusion, the area hadn't actually been surveyed and the only maps were hand-drawn.

As a result, the process took a very long time and many visits to the local notary public—an old man who sat a high desk in a dusty office full of yellowing papers. He would adjust his glasses on his nose, send the boy to collect our file, study it with painful slowness, and tell us to go to the bank. We would spend an hour or two standing in line to pay a small sum of money, then go off in search of a working copy machine, make six copies of the receipt, have them authenticated by the notary, and finally deliver them to Land Reform—if the office was open. Located in a hot little cubbyhole above the bus station, Land Reform had a crumpled piece of paper permanently stuck to the door promising it would open in twenty minutes. Even if someone was there, nothing could be done without referring to some mysterious and undefined higher authority, who couldn't be contacted because there was no phone. It was like playing chess with an invisible opponent. But persistence paid off and eventually they grew tired of seeing us and issued the document.

Robin took all this in his stride, but it did spur him to apply for his naturalization papers. "If we want to buy more land, one of us will need Brazilian citizenship," he told me. "And it's better if I do it. Next time we go to Rio I'll check with the federal police. It can't be as complicated as getting permanent residence."

We'd started the process of converting from diplomatic visas to permanent residency (the Brazilian version of the U.S. green card) while we were living in Recife, where Robin had access to fix-it men who did the paperwork. For some reason we had been invited for an interview by the Captain of the Port. He had received us with the utmost courtesy; had shown us a picture of himself taken many years earlier, standing beside the queen of England on the royal yacht; and had delicately intimated that there were one or two formalities to be observed before he could send our files to Brasília. He then handed us a sealed envelope. When we opened it later we discovered it was a request for a medical exam. In order to be considered for permanent residency we would need to be tested for two things: syphilis and schizophrenia.

B ack on the farm, João put in a bid to move to Fazenda Graminha. "Someone needs to be living up there," he told us. "On account of that fellow Duca next door. Not that it's my business, but you need to watch him. And those two boys of his. Won't do an honest day's work, any of them, but come the full moon they'll be out there hunting in the forest. And stealing anything they can lay their hands on."

This alarming description turned out to be all too accurate, and over the following years our new neighbor was to set fire to our forest, steal fish from our ponds, and make several unsuccessful attempts to rustle our cattle. Happily for us, his health was severely affected by his taste for the local moonshine, which kept him out of action for days on end and finally killed him.

Officially known as *cachaça*, and colloquially referred to as *pinga* (which translates as "a wee drop"), moonshine was freely available in every bus station and bar, where a shot was sold for a few cents. Men would gather in the roadside bars for a drop of *pinga* and a game of pool, but most women didn't touch it, except for the medicinal kind that was mixed with all sorts of bitter herbs and tasted terrible. I once mistakenly helped myself to a glass, under the impression that it was water, and nearly fell over on the spot.

I t was Robin who brought the next item of news to the *fazenda*. He'd been to Limeira to collect some bags of cement, and though on his way home he passed Jair whipping his pony cart into a gallop to get there first with the news, the pony cart was no match for the Toyota, and Robin arrived before him.

"Hey there," I said as he drove in, "what's new?"

"What's new? Murder and mayhem, that's what. One of our new neighbors, too."

"Tell me quick," I demanded.

"Hold on! Let me put the car away and get some coffee and I'll tell you."

"Well?" I waited impatiently for him to get himself organized. "Tell!"

"You know Zezinho Rosa, up on the southern boundary of Graminha?"

"The one with the big old Toyota? Met him at the feed store once—I thought he lived in Muriaé?"

"So he does. But he owns a little farm on our boundary, and the place next to his belongs to Joaquim Gomes, father of the man who drives the milk truck. So it's Tuesday evening and João Bosco is in his store when Zezinho drops by to pick up a sack of grass seed. He's loading it into his truck, and João Bosco is just writing up the bill, when all of a sudden Joaquim Gomes comes screeching up on his motorbike and takes a potshot at Zezinho. Hits him in the leg. So Zezinho yelps like a stuck pig, reaches inside the glove box, pulls out his revolver, and fires right back. Next thing they're both shooting at one another, and João Bosco is flat on his stomach behind the counter. 'Thank God I was at the back of the store,' he told me. 'Otherwise I'd have caught a bullet myself. There I was in the middle of a shootout and what the hell was I supposed to do?'"

Well, João stays quiet until things settle down, and next time he looks out there's Joaquim Gomes lying on the floor with his eyes shut, bleeding like a pig, and Zezinho Rosa propped up on a sack of grass seed not looking too good, either. João helps him into his truck and drives him over to Murilo's bar. Tells them he's taking Zezinho down to the hospital and they'd better find the policeman and get him to do something about Joaquim Gomes because he's in pretty bad shape.

Robin poured himself some more coffee, taking his time.

"This is like the movies," I exclaimed. "Go *on*."

"Wait a second, it gets better. Next thing is, they end up in hospital, right next to each other in intensive care. Luckily the nurses have the sense to remove their guns."

"And what's the story?"

"Apparently they'd been enemies for years. Something to do with water rights. So the doctors keep them in Muriaé for a couple of days, and then transfer Zezinho Rosa to Juiz de Fora to remove the bullet from his chest. It's right next to his heart, and it's touch and go whether he'll make it."

"What about Joaquim Gomes?"

"They reckon he's a goner," said Robin. "So they left him where he was."

All this was a far cry from Washington, D.C., that was for sure. Or at any rate from the part of town that we had lived in. There was, I reflected, something both exciting and scary about living on the frontier amid a culture of guns, where everyone knew the local hit men, and people talked routinely about vendettas and crimes of passion. It added an edge to life, so long as it didn't come too close to home.

And then, a few months later, it did. Luckily for me I was away when it happened.

Robin had been in Mozambique and returned a few days earlier than expected to find that someone had broken into our house and made off with a few bits of equipment that were important to us but of little use to anyone else—a laptop, a camera, and a chain saw. He reported the theft to Limeira's fat policeman and suggested he might care to check for fingerprints or other traces. The policeman told him that he was very busy and in any case had no forensic equipment of any kind. He recommended that Robin install a padlock on the front door.

Splittie had been staying with a friend in Muriaé and Robin hadn't had a chance to collect him. So he was alone in the house on the night the robbers came back. He was sleeping soundly when there was a loud crash and the wooden shutter burst open. Half awake, he fumbled for the light and went to the window when all of a sudden something struck him a glancing blow and knocked him to his knees. It took him a couple of seconds to realize what was happening—someone had fired a shot at him, which had ricocheted off the side of the wooden window frame and grazed the side of his head.

I was hundreds of miles away in the Amazon, with Juliet who had recently graduated. We'd been doing some research for a book I was planning, and had stopped off in Brasília after a three-day bus journey from the far western state of Acre. After cleaning up we'd gone to a cocktail party at the UN office, where Juliet had talked her way into a job at the upcoming Earth Summit. We were writing up our research notes when Robin called, offering to meet us in Belo Horizonte and save us another eight hours journey.

Two days later he was there at the bus station, all smiles, and when I inquired about the scar on the side of his head he laughed and said it was just a scratch and didn't we need some breakfast after that long bus trip? It wasn't until we'd tucked into a large plate of scrambled eggs with ham and cheese that he told us the story.

"My first reaction was blind rage," he said. "If I'd had a gun I'd have shot right back. But I didn't. I lay on the floor for a second wondering if someone was going to come after me, but nothing happened. I finally had the sense to turn off the light, and after a while I looked out, but I couldn't see anyone. Eventually I crept out the back, got into the car, and drove to Limeira to tell the policeman. He was no damn help. Asked me what I expected him to do at three o'clock in the morning. Told me I didn't look too good and maybe I should take myself down to hospital."

Juliet and I stared at each other in horror. "Just a minute." I turned to Robin. "Someone *shot* you? Were they trying to kill you?"

"I think it was a mistake," Robin told me.

"Don't be an idiot. You don't shoot people by mistake."

"I've had plenty of time to think about it," he said. "And here's what I think happened. Word must have got out that there was nobody in the house, so one of the local baddies thought he'd break in. He couldn't find anything interesting apart from the chain saw, so he took the computer case, which just happened to have my camera in it also."

"The laptop should be easy to trace," Juliet pointed out. "It's probably the only laptop for miles."

"My hunch is they wouldn't know what it was," Robin told her. "Probably dumped it somewhere in the woods. And I'm pretty sure they were coming back for the desktop, thinking it was a TV. They could sell that."

"Someone shot you, the laptop's gone, and what the fuck are we going to do now?" I stared at my plate, my appetite gone.

"First of all, we're going to order another pot of coffee," said Robin, "and then we're going to have a council of war."

We argued back and forth, drank far too much coffee, and finally came to an agreement. We would buy a revolver and learn how to use it. It was either that or live in fear. Juliet was remarkably calm about the whole thing. "Like Dad says, it was probably some small-time thief," she told me, "and we're not going to let that sort of thing drive us out. So I'm with Dad. If people know we've got a gun they won't bother us again."

Neither Juliet nor I had ever handled a gun, whereas Robin had been raised with a rifle and had been the star of his college shooting team. But after that discussion we went out and bought a .38, and Robin taught us how to fire it. We both turned out to be fair shots, and Juliet was in high spirits as she set off to start work for the Earth Summit. "I'm well equipped for the job." She grinned. "I can speak Portuguese, I can fire a gun, and it won't take me long to earn the money for a new laptop."

But it wasn't something I could easily put out of my mind. There we were in the back of nowhere trying to build something from nothing. Some small-town criminal had all but murdered my husband, and the police had done nothing. *Nothing.* I announced to Robin that I was going to tackle the police chief in Muriaé. "Go ahead, if it makes you feel better," he told me. "It won't do any good."

"We're talking attempted murder," I said hotly. "You can't just sit back and do nothing."

I stormed into the Muriaé police station and told the police chief my story. "It's a case of attempted murder, and nothing has been done in the way of an investigation," I raged. "So what are you going to do about it?"

The police chief wasn't planning to do anything. "I understand your problem, *senhora*," he told me. "But unfortunately I am not in a position to help you at present. Due to budget constraints I have only one working vehicle in the county. I regret deeply."

"I'm fully aware of your difficulties," I said, gritting my teeth and lying freely. "And I want you to know that I hold the Brazilian police force in the greatest admiration. May I make a suggestion?"

He looked at me warily.

"I suggest," I said, pressing my advantage, "that the *senhor* sends a couple of detectives with me. I will provide them with a car and fuel, and I will give them accommodation."

It was past the hour for the police chief to have his lunch. He was hungry and irritable, and I was standing over him in a way that made him feel uncomfortable.

"Very well," he said reluctantly. "I will send them next week."

R obin had left for Mozambique, and Luiza invited herself up for a few days. A great fan of murder mysteries, she was delighted to hear about the visit of the detectives, and insisted on coming with me to collect them off the bus. They were a good-looking pair in their smartly pressed uniforms, and their arrival in Limeira did not pass unnoticed: Jair was standing outside the bar when they got off the bus and climbed into the Toyota, and the tale was around the village in a matter of minutes.

The two policemen, Sidney and Vanderlei, were all set to make the most of their unexpected break from routine. They visited every house in a radius of eight miles, waded across the flooded river to talk to João at Graminha, seized an unlicensed hunting rifle from our neighbor Duca, and questioned him closely about the activities of other illegal hunters. In the evenings we played bilingual Risk and traded tips on security, and on their last afternoon Luiza told them she'd been on her college rifle team and gave us a demonstration to prove it.

"Good shot!" exclaimed Sidney, hiding his surprise. "How about you, Bianca? Can you handle a gun?"

"Watch me," I told him, firing a couple of rounds at the target and hitting it squarely in the middle both times.

Sidney smiled.

"Any ideas as to who took a potshot at Robin?" I asked him.

The two detectives looked at one another. "We checked out the known troublemakers and didn't come up with anything conclusive," said Sidney. "The thing is, it could have been any one of a number of people. What's important is to avoid further trouble. You'll need to be on your guard. Keep your eyes open for gypsies. And hunters, of course. And don't forget the *pistoleiros.*"

I realized, with a start, that I no longer found anything unusual at the mention of *pistoleiros*—which showed how well I must be acclimatizing. Our part of Minas was known for *pistolagem* and *coronelismo,* guns and colonels. Both professions ran in families and both commanded a certain respect in the community. Not that the better sort of *pistoleiro* was available for hire by just anybody—he would be associated with a certain family of colonels and would do what was necessary to protect the honor for the family, in return for which he would be shielded from any unpleasant consequences. Second-class *pistoleiros,* on the other hand, would hire themselves out to whomever would pay.

"Which *pistoleiros* did you have in mind?" I asked.

"The taxi driver, for one."

Old Antonio? From time to time I had taken a ride in his battered white Beetle, and he'd reminisced about his days in the security business. "My eyes went, and I had to retire," he told me once as he peered shortsightedly over the steering wheel. After that trip

I began to worry about his driving skills but I never stopped to think about his former profession.

Vanderlei nodded. "Now, Dona Bianca," he said. "There's just one thing. If you have any problems here, shoot first and talk afterward. If you're unlucky enough to shoot someone in the back, which as you know is illegal, turn them over and shoot them in the chest."

"And don't bother to tell us," added Sidney. "Just throw the body into the river."

I looked at him suspiciously. Was he pulling my leg? No, perhaps not. "Let me get this straight," I said cautiously. "It's perfectly okay to shoot someone from the front, is that right?"

"Perfectly okay," he assured me. "In self-defense."

"Of course, it's better if you don't kill them," said Vanderlei. "But aim for the body anyway. You wouldn't want to miss."

"Oh, no," I said. "I wouldn't want to miss."

CHAPTER THIRTEEN

The Rain It Raineth Every Day

It was February and the rains were supposed to be trailing off, but they weren't. It had been raining nonstop for three weeks, and according to local lore it was all the fault of Saint Peter—although I never succeeded in finding out why.

"You might ask him to lay off," I said to Antonio as we waded through a puddle so deep that the water spilled over into my boots.

Antonio smiled. "We need the rain, Dona Bianca," he said as he squelched away, holding his shoes aloft.

Antonio was right, but nevertheless, Saint Peter was overdoing it. Each storm found new holes in the roof, and when we weren't putting buckets under the leaks we were covering the furniture with tarpaulins. Weeds grew up overnight and mold sprouted in every corner. Green mildew grew on the bathroom walls, the cement floor in the kitchen sweated, the house was full of muddy footprints, we couldn't dry the clothes, and everything smelled of damp. The salt grinder corroded, the wood burner smoked sullenly and gave out no heat, and if I left food out of the refrigerator overnight it developed the most alarming colored fungus.

The road was such a quagmire that the horse could barely make it through the mud to deliver the milk, and we couldn't get the cement up to Fazenda Graminha to fix João's house. Work on our own house had stopped. We couldn't get the fertilizer into the fields or the tree stumps out of them; the ox got foot rot, and the staff fell sick one after another. The Limeira bus couldn't make it up the mountain, the mail service was disrupted, and the phone went out. I decided that life in the rainforest was overrated.

"We ought to be doing something with all this water," I grumbled to Robin over coffee one dank and dripping day.

"What did you have in mind?" said Robin, adjusting one of the leaking tiles with a broom handle.

"I don't know," I snapped. "What do *you* suggest?"

"How about fish? We could put a couple of ponds in the swamp."

"Go on."

"One or two people in the area are raising ornamental fish," he continued. "But I'm more interested in carp. Or maybe catfish. I've heard there's a place on the road to Rio where they sell fingerlings, and I'm thinking of going over there sometime to see what they have."

No sooner had the idea of fish raising been suggested than suddenly everyone was talking about it. "You don't have to invest everything in cows," said the people from the extension agency. "Fish give you a far better return per hectare. And they mix well with cows. You can locate the fishponds next to the dairy to take advantage of all that good manure that's going to waste."

"Fish don't eat manure, do they?" I asked.

"No, they don't," they said. "But the manure feeds the plankton and the plankton feed the fish. And if you're going into fish raising seriously, you need to stock several different varieties; some that live on the bottom, some that live in the middle levels, and some that browse on the grass."

"I never heard of fish browsing on the grass," I said to Robin.

"Don't you remember the carp in Indonesia?" he asked. "They were grass carp."

I did recall admiring the neat little fishponds in Java, and the processions of ducks walking in single file along the bunds. "I thought they were oversize goldfish," I told him.

"Goldfish *are* carp," said Robin patiently.

Just below the blue house there was a swamp where our neighbor Adão had several times asked to plant rice. Robin had always refused. "I like the birds," he said. "Particularly the rails and spinetails. I don't want anyone messing about with the swamp—might frighten the birds off."

Across the road from the swamp there was another large boggy field. "If we flooded that bit," said Robin, "and if we flooded the bit in front of the house—and I'm not saying we will—that'd give us five acres of ponds. They should hold about six thousand fish to start with, and we can put in more as the weed on the bottom rots down. That's what I read."

"How long do the fish take to grow?"

"Depends on the variety. Carp mature quickly; catfish take a little longer. But the yields are good. Half a ton per acre the first year, double that the second year, and up to two and a half tons per acre thereafter. We'll be coining money."

We'd need a tractor to build up the road between the two ponds, and a technician to put in the sluices to control the water flow, otherwise all the fish would be swept away next time the river flooded. The tractor driver who had worked with us before had moved away, but Jair told us there was another one working over near Belisário. He wasn't easy to find, since he moved around from one job to the next, only visited his family between jobs, and had no phone. But Valdeci sent a message to his cousin's brother in Belisário, and eventually contact was established and the tractor arrived. Unfortunately, so did the rain.

The tractor driver was a nice man and so was his assistant, but they spent a lot of time getting bogged down and having to make repairs to the tractor, and they had to be billeted with Albertinho and fed by Maria. They also had to be collected off the midday bus on Monday and delivered back on Friday, and I sometimes wondered if they were worth the trouble.

But the ponds gradually took shape. Albertinho spent an afternoon experimenting with the water levels, after which Robin took some water samples and sent them to Muriaé for testing, and then declared that we were ready for the first delivery of fingerlings.

The fingerlings arrived in oversize plastic bags that had to be immersed in the fishponds for an hour or so until the water inside the bags reached the same temperature as the water outside. Robin had a thermometer, but Albertinho could tell by feel, and it was Albertinho who solemnly untied the string and released the first batch into the water, Albertinho who elected to manage the project. Every evening he would wheel a barrow of maize meal across the dam and stand there admiring the ponds and smoking a corn-leaf cigarette.

Robin needn't have worried about losing his birds. The rails and spinetails stayed around, and they were joined by other water birds: three varieties of kingfisher, two kinds of purple moorhen, several pairs of elegant chocolate and lemon web-toed lily-trotters, six pairs of ducks, and a solitary long-necked lesser grebe. A large crested heron took to fishing in the lower pond, and once, when I was sitting by the swimming hole, an otter streaked out of the clump of giant bamboo across the water and poured himself into the river like molten bronze.

T he youngest field hand, Ailton, volunteered to deliver the manure to the fishponds. The eldest son of Adão next door, he had been my fellow godparent at Viviane's christening. He was a good-looking young man with a ready smile, but he'd recently fallen in love and found it difficult to focus on the job. Antonio caught him one day driving the manure cart right into the fishponds and reported back to Robin. "Damn nearly drowned the oxen, stupid boy," he spluttered. "Gave him a piece of my mind, I can tell you."

"He's young," said Robin. "He'll learn."

Antonio sniffed.

The next day Ailton turned up while we were having our coffee break. "I wanted to ask you something, *senhor*," he said politely.

"Yes, Ailton?" said Robin.

"You see, I'm getting married."

"Well *that's* good news." Robin smiled.

There was a pause.

"Yes," said Ailton, "and I was wondering if you could build me a house?"

"I can't do that right now," Robin told him. "But I'm sure I can find you one. I'll ask around."

W here are we going to find a house for Ailton?" I asked Robin later.

"Sebastião's got an empty house on his place," he told me. "The one where Valdeci used to live. I'll go over there this evening."

But Sebastião would have none of it. He told Robin a long story about one of his sons who'd gone to São Paulo, broken his leg falling off a motorbike, and might need to come live in the house. "First I've heard of a son in São Paulo," I remarked. "What do you suppose all that was about? You don't think it's something to do with the murder, do you?"

"Which murder?"

"Just think a minute. Sebastião's sister-in-law's uncle murdered Ailtons's grandfather, right?"

"Oh, *that* murder. Ridiculous, really, since Sebastião and Jair aren't even speaking. But they do say that blood is thicker than water."

We looked around and found the perfect place to rent on the next-door property. It was a pretty little house by the river, set in the valley leading up to Graminha, ideal for honeymooners. We sent a builder up there to make a bathroom, and the day he finished Ailton turned up with a long face and said his fiancée didn't like the house.

"Well, that's too bad," Robin told him. "You're welcome to find another. But you'll have to pay your own rent on it."

I n the meantime, Robin's naturalization process was winding its way slowly forward. Part of the trouble was that nobody was quite sure of the correct procedure, and although the president had passed a law that said you didn't need a tax clearance certificate every time you applied for a document from the government, the federal police appeared not to have noticed. Robin, who held a law degree from Oxford, had combed the law books, found the relevant decree, and brought it to the attention of the police, who thanked him very politely and forwarded his file to Brasília. But the people in Brasília didn't know about the law, either, and nine months later they sent him a fat envelope covered with impressive-looking stamps inside which was a request for a tax clearance certificate.

Undaunted, Robin pressed on with his quest. The next document required was a declaration from the police that he had no criminal record. This had to come from the federal police in Recife and involved a thirty-six-hour bus ride each way. He returned from that trip elated to learn that his age and his status as foreigner precluded him from compulsory military service and that his dossier was now complete. But he was still required to provide a certificate of exemption. The officer in charge would call military headquarters and the matter would be speedily resolved.

A few weeks later Robin was off again on a job, heading for sunny Mexico. Down on the ranch it was raining harder than ever. The fishponds were full to overflowing, and every evening Albertinho patrolled the dam, wielding an ancient black umbrella. The road turned into a morass, and we restricted travel to the bare minimum. If I needed to go somewhere in the Toyota I took Albertinho with me. I felt more secure when he was around.

The day of Ailton's wedding set in grim and gray, with rain clouds hanging heavily on the hills. The entire farm staff was bidden up to Adão's house for lunch, and somehow we all managed to squeeze into the Toyota. As we headed up the hill the rain set in, but a stout tarpaulin had been erected over the trestle tables in the yard, and spirits were high, since rain at a wedding was traditionally considered to be a good omen.

Men were standing around in small groups, chatting and smoking; children were running everywhere laughing and chasing one another; and young mothers were cradling their babies and taking shelter inside the house. The bridegroom's mother, Orisa, was in the kitchen, adding the finishing touches to the feast, and I arrived just in time to help carry out the steaming pans full of chicken stew, rice, and polenta, with black bean paste, roasted manioc flour—a local delicacy that tasted like a mixture of gravel and sawdust—and shredded greens on the side. Ailton's smallest brother, frowning in concentration, was handing around glasses of Coca-Cola, and Adão was dispensing home-brewed *cachaça*. He insisted I take a sip. It tasted raw and fiery, and I declined a refill. There was a concerted move toward the food, and as soon as a plate was emptied it was snatched up, rinsed under the tap, and given to the next person.

After lunch the guests disappeared one by one into the house and emerged in their wedding finery: stiffly ironed denims and straw hats for the men, knee-length bermuda shorts and brightly colored tops for the women. Most of them weren't planning to attend the wedding ceremony but were heading directly for the reception at the bride's house. Women and children were bundled into pony traps, horses and mules were saddled up, and those who had no transport set off on foot, chatting animatedly.

"Where is the bride's house?" I asked Adão.

"Over there." He gestured toward the misty mountains.

For a minute I wished I could go there with everyone else, but for me there would be no free lunch—my job was to ferry the wedding party to the church in Limeira. I trudged down to the truck and backed up as close to the house as I could. Four or five adults and a great many small children settled themselves in the back, looking anxiously up at the lowering skies.

"What delicious food," I said to Orisa as I fished in my pocket for the car key. "Won't you be coming with us?"

"Oh dear, no." She shook her head distractedly. "I have to do the dishes."

* * *

W e bumped over the corrugated road to Limeira, unloaded our passengers in the square, and toiled up the sixty-six steps to the church. The interior was dominated by a statue of the Virgin, crowned with a halo of lightbulbs, some of which had burned out. There was a small vase of flowers near the altar, but no special wedding preparations appeared to have been made, and there was nobody inside. Half a dozen young men were leaning against the outside wall, passing a cigarette from hand to hand. From the church door I looked down at the square where a cowboy was driving a bunch of steers over the cobblestones. Our Lady's bus drew up with a flourish and its occupants headed for the bar. An old man on a black mule trotted up and parked his mount outside the church door. Finally Antonio's taxi appeared, bearing the bride and her mother.

I slipped in through the side door of the church and looked around for a familiar face. Fia beckoned me to her side, just as the bride began to make her way up the aisle. She was dressed in close-fitting lace and looked very pretty and very young. "Doesn't she look nice?" I whispered.

"That dress is too tight," sniffed Fia. "Not surprising, really, in her condition." Coming from Fia, who had brought an illegitimate child to her marriage with Antonio, the remark was less than charitable.

After the service I joined the line to congratulate the young couple, and by the time I had walked down through the rain the Toyota was crammed full of people, most of whom I had never seen before.

"Okay, guys," I said. "How many of you live along my road? I can take fifteen at the most."

Nobody said anything.

I made a quick head count: nineteen adults, four small children, and two babies.

"Fifteen is all I'm taking," I told them firmly. "And I'm heading for home."

"No, no!" said one small boy, smiling up at me. "We're going to the bride's house for the party."

"Not me," I told him.

One or two people started climbing out, and I was fumbling in my pockets for the key when I felt a hand on my shoulder. I turned around and saw Adáo. "Dona Bianca," he said, "we're counting on you to come to the party."

"I wasn't planning to go," I told him. "But I'll drop you off there, okay?"

That couldn't take long.

We set off into the gathering gloom, along a steep road that led into the backlands behind Fazenda Graminha. Halfway up the first hill there was a sudden wind and the rain began to fall in fat drops. The mud was slick as ice, and every time I hauled the Toyota around a corner I expected to land in the ditch. My passengers didn't share my concern; although liberally spattered with mud they were in a party mood, passing a bottle of *cachaça* from hand to hand, singing and laughing.

Adáo had climbed in the front and was peering though the muddy windshield. "Are we nearly there?" I asked him several times.

"Nearly there," he echoed. But we both knew we weren't.

Forty minutes into the journey we came to a patch of deep mud. Engaging low gear, I cautiously made my way through and rounded a sharp corner, almost piling into the Volkswagen taxi that had stopped in the middle of the road and was showing no lights. I stuck my head out of the window to see what the problem was, and Antonio, the gunman turned taxi driver, emerged from the driver's seat, looking glum.

"There's a landslide up ahead," he reported. "Damn great tree across the road. There's no way through."

"I'm carrying lots of strong men who want to go to the wedding," I told him. "Maybe they can move it."

He brightened. "In that case you can take my passengers. It's their wedding."

Ailton pushed the seat forward, climbed gingerly out into the mud, and headed in my direction. "Lucinha!" he shouted to his bride. "Come over here!"

"Ailton!" I remonstrated. "Whatever are you thinking of? She'll ruin her dress. Go back and carry her."

Ailton hoisted Lucinha as if she were a sack of maize and deposited her on the front seat next to Adão. She smiled shyly, and told me her father's house was very close.

I drove cautiously on through the mud and slid to a halt in front of the landslide. Just as Antonio had said, there was a large tree blocking the road. But my passengers were determined to get through, and it didn't take them long to haul the tree clear of the road. Twenty minutes later, as the clouds lifted, we came to the bride's house, with its triumphal arch of banana leaves and long line of parked pony traps. A salvo of fireworks heralded our arrival, and half my passengers jumped off before we got to the front door. Ailton helped Lucinha out and escorted her inside, holding her hand tightly.

The house was freshly whitewashed and brightly lit, with picture-book red roses growing up the front walls. A hundred or more people were jammed into the front yard, and celebrations were in full swing. Somebody produced a box camera, and the bridal party lined up for ceremonial pictures. After a long interval, the bride and groom disappeared into one of the bedrooms and flung open the wooden shutter. Inside, on the bed, was the largest cake I had ever seen, measuring three feet by four. There was a spontaneous round of applause, somebody produced a knife, and Lucinha cut the first slice. Served on tiny paper napkins, the cake was very pink and very sweet and was accompanied by glasses of sugary lemonade. Everyone tucked in with great gusto, scattering cake crumbs and paper napkins on the ground, where they were trodden into the thick layer of mud. Jair picked his way through the crowd to stand beside me. "Well, Dona Bianca," he remarked, "I never expected to see *you* here. You'll have a job getting home tonight. The road is in a dreadful state."

"I'll be fine," I said, more confidently than I felt.

Cassilda pushed her way to my side. "How do you like that dress?" She gestured toward Lucinha, who was standing in the window, smiling up at Ailton.

"I think she looks lovely," I told her.

Cassilda sniffed. "Hired it in Muriaé, can you believe it? Couldn't find anything in Limeira good enough for her."

"It's awfully pretty," came a voice from beside me. I turned to see Maria, and remembered how she had eloped with Albertinho. No pretty wedding dress for her.

Orisa edged her way around to where I was standing. She was dabbing her eyes with a scrap of handkerchief. "Well, Dona Bianca," she sighed, "wasn't that a lovely wedding?" I looked at the crowd of shining faces, the young couple laughing together, the children stuffing themselves with cake.

"Yes," I said, "it was, wasn't it?"

CHAPTER FOURTEEN

The Tale of the Telephone

We had been trying for more than two years to get a telephone installed on the *fazenda,* and the whole business was enough to try the patience of a saint. Had we lived in town it wouldn't have been such a nightmare—in fact, it would have been relatively simple. We could have either registered with the government-owned telephone company and waited months to be allotted a line, or bought one on the black market at great expense. Brazilian telephones weren't very good—the joke ran that it was easier to call New York than to call next door—but they were the best available.

If you lived in the countryside, though, things were considerably more complicated. After a lot of hassle we'd managed to buy a Limeira telephone line from the fat policeman and had installed it in João Bosco's shop. He got more use out of it than we did, but it was a step in the right direction. There was only one line in the whole village, and naturally everyone listened in. Very few of the outlying *fazendas* possessed a telephone—which didn't bother their owners, who mostly lived in town. Lenin had an ancient hand-cranked machine with a separate mouthpiece and earpieces, but it was hard to get through and next to impossible to hold a coherent conversation. One or two farms nearer to Muriaé had a radio call up service—like something out of the Australian outback. But the system worked only during office hours, and we were beyond its range. There was only one other option, a microwave radio connection, but it was difficult to find, difficult to install, very expensive, and not very reliable.

Robin refused to be defeated. "We need a phone on the *fazenda,* and we are going to get one," he said firmly. "There are one or two hurdles to overcome, but nothing is impossible. Let me show you the plan of action." He produced a large sheet of paper that read:

Iracambi Telephone Project

Please note that this process is liable to be lengthy and frustrating. It is important to maintain a sense of humor throughout.

1.1.   Obtain a radio frequency from the Ministry of Communications in Brasília.
Note: This could take many months, and may finally prove impossible since we are foreigners and Brazilians are concerned about national security issues.

1.2.   Submit a written project (almost certainly in multiple copies) to, successively (a) the state telephone company, (b) the national telephone company, and (c) the Ministry of Communications.
Note: These submissions cannot be simultaneous since approval from (b) and (c) depends on approval from (a) and (b) respectively.)

2.1. Source equipment (radio transmitter and receiver, antennae, and tower).

Note: The equipment is expensive and poor quality. Unfortunately it is illegal to use imported equipment, which is greatly superior and significantly cheaper. Even if we were tempted to break the law we could never get a radio frequency for imported equipment.

2.2. Locate competent technicians for installation of equipment.

3.1. Obtain permission from the state telephone company to install the transmitter in their facility.

Note: While there is nothing in their operating procedures to say that this cannot be done, there is nothing to say that it can. Since ours would be the only private transmitter in the area, they are liable to be unwilling to do so, and will certainly not provide technical assistance if and when the equipment breaks down.

3.2. Obtain a line with a working number from the state telephone company.

Note: There are a limited number of lines and it can take up to three years for a line to be allotted. The normal procedure is to buy one from (a) the black market, or (b) a customer who is deceased, and whose line has been inherited by numerous heirs.

3.3. Install the receiver at a high elevation on the farm that is within line of sight of the transmitter and also within reach of the house. The receiver will be housed in a small cabin located next to the telephone tower where the antennae are mounted.

Note: Both radio cabin and antenna tower must be fenced to keep the cows from causing accidental damage. It is also important to install ample protection from lightning since the system can easily get fried.

3.4.   Connect the radio to the house by an underground electric cable and an overhead telephone wire.

Note: The underground cable should be encased in plastic piping to keep the water out. It must also be buried sufficiently deep that it can't be damaged if a cow steps on it. There is little we can do to stop it being chewed by rodents, which is why we shall install circuit boxes so that we can identify which section of cable is damaged.

Expected Project Duration until Installation: Minimum of one year and possibly longer.

Estimated Cost: Astronomic.

"Looks like a complete nightmare," I commented.
"Well, yes."

The telephone office in Muriaé didn't install microwave radios. Not for private citizens. No, they didn't say it couldn't be done—they just said they couldn't do it. Robin was not discouraged. He asked around and finally came up with the name of a man in the distant city of Belo Horizonte who professed to be able to handle it. The people in Muriaé were not very hopeful that it would work, but Robin was determined to give it a try.

Six weeks later we had a visit from a telephone engineer called Enoque. He came all the way from Belo Horizonte and brought a couple of technicians with him. They climbed the steep hill behind the house, did some tests, and produced a lengthy contract for us to sign. "We'll have you on the air within three months," they promised, departing with a hefty deposit.

Weeks passed with no sign of the phone, despite regular promises that everything was on track. Robin called every week, and every week he was assured that Enoque would be back as soon as he had all the requisite permissions from the authorities. Five months and two days after his first visit, Enoque reappeared with the radio receiver—a miniature Eiffel tower that he erected at the top of the hill—and six coils of wire that he stacked neatly in the barn. "I'm off to Muriaé to check out the transmitter," he announced. "Back in the morning."

Next evening he returned, with the transmitter packed in a Styrofoam box. "I need to take it back to my office for a few adjustments," he told us. "I'll be back within a week." With that he collected another installment of his money and drove off. And that was the last we saw of him.

The telephone company in Muriaé was only mildly sympathetic. "A bunch of cowboys," they sniffed.

"But there's no one else," said Robin, who still nursed the hope that somehow things would come out all right. He paid a visit to Belo Horizonte to talk to Enoque, but the truth was that the radios were duds, and Enoque's company was on the verge of bankruptcy. Robin contacted the small claims court, but the lawyer there wasn't too hopeful. "I'll look into it for you," he said kindly. "But the contract is a bit woolly. It talks about supplying telephonic equipment, but it doesn't say anything about getting the telephone to work."

"Well, there you are," said the people from Muriaé. "We told you so."

Eighteen months later Robin received a letter from another company in Belo Horizonte. He showed it to the people at the telephone company in Muriaé. "José Pedrosa," they said. "Now there's someone who knows what he's doing. This time you could be lucky."

Robin called Zé Pedrosa and he promised to send his engineers down to run some tests. We would have to cut our losses and start over.

Time wound on and nothing happened, and we told ourselves there was no point in worrying about things we couldn't change. From time to time we called the lawyer to see if there was anything to be gotten out of Enoque, and each time he told us to call back in a month.

So we had almost forgotten about the whole business when a small, heavily laden truck appeared on the *fazenda,* and out jumped a couple of Zé Pedrosa's engineers. They came into the house all smiles and told us they were going up the hill to see if they could communicate with the transmitter. It might take a little time because they'd have to get the angle of the antenna just right, but they were confident they could do it.

It was a long day, and neither Robin nor I could settle to anything. We kept assuring each other that there was no point in running up to see how they were getting on, but finally Robin could bear it no longer and strode up the hill just as they were coming down. "Good news," they told him. "We finally got a signal through to the transmitting station, and tomorrow we'll go over there and run some tests. We're just heading off to Muriaé and we'll be back in the morning, okay?"

The next day they were back by early afternoon to tell us that everything was in order at the other end and now it was just a question of synchronizing the two radios. Robin drove them up the steep track and twenty minutes later he reappeared, beaming. "Eureka!" he shouted. "We're on the air! This is the first time in history that a telephone call has been made from Iracambi Heights."

"I can't believe it!" I jumped up and gave him a bear hug. "Who did you call?"

"Luiza."

"What did she say?"

"Nothing," reported Robin. "She was out. I spoke to the maid. But then, history is full of such anticlimaxes."

Two hours later the engineers came back and assured us that everything was fine. They just needed to run back to Muriaé and collect the other radio, and then they'd take both radios to their workshop in Belo Horizonte and synchronize the frequency. If all went well we'd be on the air within a matter of weeks.

"If I were you I'd put the whole thing to the back of your mind," Robin advised me. "It's going to take a long time and cost a fortune. Just as well I've got that job in Mexico coming up."

Two weeks later he was off. "Good-bye," he said, as he loaded his suitcase into Antonio's taxi. "Look after yourself, and keep praying for rain. We could use a good long rainy spell. Shan't see any where I'm going."

It was true we did need the rain, and sure enough it started that very night; once again I thought Saint Peter was overdoing it. It rained for twenty-three days without stopping, and then, unexpectedly, the clouds lifted, the sun came out, and everything started to steam. Luiza sent a message offering to come over and keep me company. I mopped the mud off the floors, hung out the bedding in the sunshine, and set out to collect her off Our Lady's bus.

The next afternoon was so sparkling and clear that Luiza and I unanimously elected to take ourselves down to the waterfall. I was gathering up my things when I heard the melodious whistling that signaled Albertinho's presence. "Bother!" I said to myself uncharitably. "I hope it's nothing important."

Albertinho swung into sight, smiling radiantly.

"Hello, Albertinho," I said, regretting my meanness of spirit.

"We've got a stuck truck on our hands," he informed me.

"Well, that's too bad," I countered swiftly. "I'm going for a swim."

Albertinho cleared his throat and spat into the long grass. "I think," he said, looking at me sideways, "it might be the telephone."

There was a minute of total silence.

"*What?*" I shouted. "Albertinho! Why didn't you say so before?"

"I guess that puts paid to our afternoon's swim," said Luiza tranquilly, picking up her book. "You two go see what's going on and I'll mind the store."

I was galvanized into action. "Where are they stuck, Albertinho?" I demanded. "The usual place?"

Albertinho nodded.

"We're going to need a chain."

"*Ah eh.*"

"Shovels," I continued, "the Hi-Lift jack, mud tracks, planks . . ."

"Leave it to me," said Albertinho masterfully. I crammed my feet into boots and my hair into a cap, and set off to inspect the situation.

The ancient and heavily laden Dodge truck sported a large sticker on the windshield that read JESUS LOVES YOU. Securely lashed to the truck bed was a tower that was twice the size of the existing one, together with ten bags of cement and a couple thousand feet of heavy-duty wire. Two engineers were standing on the bank, while the driver revved his engine, burying the wheels ever deeper and liberally splashing everyone with mud. Several of our neighbors, dressed in their Sunday best, were lined up in their pony traps waiting to get past. One of the passers-by began to dismantle the fence so that he could drive his horse through the field.

Albertinho wandered around scratching his head and muttering to himself, and everyone was giving contradictory advice. I glanced down the road and saw Jair trotting up on his mule. "This *is* a fine mess," he said happily. "That truck isn't going to get out of there in a hurry."

Albertinho ignored him and started to excavate a channel in front of the wheels, dispatching all available hands to cut green branches and round up logs to lay across the road and provide traction. "We'll get you out with the Hi-Lift jack," he told the driver. "And put some rocks in front of your wheels. In the meantime, you'd better start unloading."

"What you need," said Jair unexpectedly, "is a stout plank."

"There's one in the dairy," I remembered.

Two of the bystanders trotted off to get it, and Albertinho squatted down in the mud and dug a hole under the axle, covering himself from head to foot in thick red mud. He had just extricated himself and lit a corn-leaf cigarette when the plank arrived on the shoulders of two teenage boys. "Next thing I need is some rocks," he told them. "You'll find them in the river by the Casa Sozinha." The two boys trotted off obediently and Albertinho took a deep drag on his cigarette.

Twenty minutes later all was ready. Albertinho disappeared under the truck and guided the end of the plank into position. At first the combined weight of four men on the other end appeared to have little effect. The plank buckled slightly, but the truck remained firmly stuck. And then, almost imperceptibly, the axle began to emerge from the thick mud. "Steady there, boys." Albertinho grinned. "Hand me down those rocks and I'll pack them in underneath."

At a signal from Albertinho I climbed into the Toyota, checked the tow chain, engaged the lowest gear, revved the engine, and slowly let in the clutch. For a heart-stopping moment nothing happened. Then the truck popped out of the mud like an emerging dinosaur, slithered a few yards, and promptly buried itself in another hole.

Everybody groaned. "No problem," said Albertinho. "This one isn't nearly so deep." He hoisted his shovel onto his shoulder and marched off toward the truck. I took a long breath and looked out through the muddy windshield. The mountains were misty and veiled in rain clouds, and a rainbow stretched clear across the valley.

It was getting dark as we finally eased the truck onto terra firma and parked it outside Albertinho's house. Maria came out with a flask of coffee, and the helpers went in relays to the tap on the back veranda to wash off the mud.

The two engineers were sitting by the woodstove eating slices of corn cake. "Where are you staying tonight?" I asked one of them.

"Belisário," he replied.

"In that case you'd better take the Toyota," I said, handing him the keys. "See you in the morning."

"Thanks." He smiled. "We'll be here by nine."

"Albertinho," I said, as the engineers drove off, "how in the world are we going to get that telephone tower up the hill?"

There was no way the truck could make it up the steep mountainside, and I didn't trust the Toyota to get there, either. Robin had told me I could drive it up the side of a house if I engaged low, low gear, but its brakes were unreliable, it had recently developed the habit of popping out of gear, and I wasn't about to risk my neck even for the sake of the telephone.

"We'll have to do a *jeito*," said Albertinho grinning. "Borrow some oxen and donkeys. Call in a few favors."

According to the code of the countryside one good turn deserved another, and it was finally payback time.

T he next morning at first light I looked out the kitchen window and saw a line of oxen and donkeys toiling their way up the steep hillside. Albertinho had dismantled the tower and the antennae, and Antonio was supervising the loading onto the oxcarts. Donkeys and mules were harnessed with panniers to carry bags of cement, barrels of water, and loads of sand and gravel. John the Baptist was marking the line for the underground cable linking the house with the telephone cabin, and João was cutting poles to string the telephone line. By the time the engineers showed up, work was well under way, and children were scrambling up and down the hill with lunch pails and water. Luiza sat under the gourd tree with a pair of binoculars, monitoring progress. "Do you know what this reminds me of, honeychild?" She smiled. "Building the pyramid of Cheops."

Work continued for several days; the engineers erected the tower and the antennae and buried a large number of copper rods for lightning arresters. João strung the telephone line, Albertinho dug the trench for the cable, and John the Baptist built four cement junction boxes at hundred-meter intervals so that we could test for potential problems in the underground cable. Meanwhile, Saint Peter was good to us, and the days were dry—although there were several thunderstorms in the evenings.

But there was never enough sun to dry out the road, and Luiza advised me to get hold of the road crew. "The engineers are working like crazy," she told me, "but I bet they can't wait to get home. And we're going to need help getting them out of here. We could really do with a Caterpillar tractor."

"Tell you what I'll do," I told her. "I'll go to Muriaé and have a word with the prefect."

"If he gets that truck out of here," remarked Luiza, "it'll be the first constructive thing he's done since he was elected."

The next morning I picked my way through the mud to the spot where the engineers had parked the Toyota, and drove down the mountain to Muriaé. It wasn't until I got there that I realized I had forgotten to take any other footwear, so I arrived in the prefect's office in my rubber boots. A neatly painted sign welcomed me to the county building, where a long line of petitioners was waiting to be attended to. I ignored them and walked on in.

The prefect was seated in an ornately carved wooden chair, underneath a large and highly flattering portrait of himself. Surrounded by his staff, he was simultaneously signing papers, talking on the phone, drinking coffee, and issuing instructions. I approached his desk and cleared my throat. The prefect looked up and frowned.

"Bom dia." I flashed him a dazzling smile. "I trust the *senhor* is in good health?"

The prefect nodded impatiently.

"I am here at the suggestion of the state governor," I lied fluently.

"Yes?" I had gotten his attention.

"One of the state vehicles is stuck on the road near Rosário da Limeira," I told him. "The road is impassable and the vehicle needs to return to Belo Horizonte as soon as possible. So if the *senhor* could arrange for the road crew?"

"Very well," said the prefect, signaling to one of his staff. "See to it."

L uiza and I were drinking our coffee the next morning when an aged man tottered up the path. He was pushing a muddy bike and carrying a hoe. *"Bom dia,"* he wheezed. "We've come to fix the road."

I tried not to laugh. He looked as though he was ready to lie down for the rest of the day. "How many men do you have?" I asked him.

"Ten," said the old man.

So much for our Caterpillar tractor.

"We'll have our lunch first," he quavered. "And then we'll get started. Oh, and we'll need Albertinho to shift a load of earth for us."

After breakfast the clouds came down and a fine drenching rain settled in. Albertinho came to report on progress. "The engineers reckon they'll be finished by the weekend, if they work straight through."

"This calls for a celebration," said Luiza when I told her the news. "I'm going to make a chocolate cake."

T wo days later the weather cleared, the sun shone brightly, and the driver managed to ease his truck along the newly repaired road. The tower stood proudly against the skyline, and the engineers called their families and told them they were coming home. Everyone voted Luiza's chocolate cake the best ever.

"Good work, honeychild!" she said as we waved them goodbye. "Let's try the phone."

Five minutes later I was talking to Robin in Mexico. I could hear him as clearly as if he were sitting in the same room. "Doing well here," I told him casually. "Good rains. Four new calves. Albertinho has fixed the brakes on the Toyota, the road has been repaired, and . . ."

"And?"

"We've got the *phone*!"

"*What?*"

"We've got the phone!"

I could hear Robin draw a deep breath, just as the line crackled and went dead.

CHAPTER FIFTEEN

Where Farm and Forest Meet

Rumors were flying thick and fast around the area.

"It's the government, they're going to take away our land."

"All the land above one thousand meters."

"Set up some kind of park."

"Fine us for cutting trees."

"Stop us planting maize."

"What are we going to do?"

"I'm not leaving my land."

"Me, neither."

"They'll have to carry me out feet first."

"What's it all about?" I asked Fia when I arrived one afternoon to find the dairy staff anxiously discussing the latest rumors.

"Nobody knows, that's the truth of it," she told me. "The forestry people have been nosing around here, but everyone avoids *them* because they mean trouble."

"They're passing a new law." Antonio straightened up from his milking. "About cutting trees."

That was always a sensitive issue. The forest laws were so strict that you couldn't even cut a dead tree without getting a license. And what were you supposed to do when you needed some wood for building? Or making a new corral? The law said you were supposed to keep one-fifth of your property under forest, and yet you couldn't use the wood. Of course the law was ignored.

Old Olavo used to smile blandly and swear he never cut a stick of wood, yet every year his coffee field expanded a little farther into the forest. Fia's father, Jerson, would cut anything that grew and would do so quite openly, and there were plenty more who made charcoal out of the native forest. Most of our neighbors paid lip service to looking after their trees, at any rate in our presence. But when the forest police appeared unexpectedly and fined several of the charcoal makers, people said it was our fault—and so were the new laws, like as not. We didn't approve of cutting trees, they complained, or hunting, or fishing, or even capturing songbirds. We were making a forest reserve, we were allowing the forest to grow back, and instead of planting food crops we were planting trees. As if trees were more important than people.

Worse still, there'd been sightings of a jaguar. Adão saw it in his coffee field one night—it frightened him out of his wits. People were blaming it for everything that went wrong. Zé Viricius's goat went missing, just when he was planning to sell it to us. Jerson's dog mysteriously disappeared, and Sebastião lost a newborn calf, right out of the pasture. And where had it come from, all of a sudden? It had been a good ten years since there'd been any sign of a jaguar in these parts. Could it be something to do with Iracambi?

"Hey, what do you reckon's going on?" I remarked to Robin one evening after Fia had run in breathlessly to report seeing a strange animal drinking in the river. "Could it really be a jaguar?"

"More likely an ocelot," said Robin. "A jaguar has an immensely large range and it wouldn't stick around here for several days."

"Unless it's acquired a taste for goats," I pointed out. "Or dogs, or calves. Of course, it *could* happen. Remember when the leopard took the farm manager's dog in Kenya?"

"That was Kenya," said Robin firmly. "But this talk of new laws—I've discovered what it's all about. They're planning to set up a conservation area, but they didn't go about it very well. Someone drew a line on the map—all the land above one thousand meters. Something like thirty-five thousand hectares. Problem was, when they looked closer they discovered there were a couple thousand families living there, so they had to halve the area. But even so, it's a good chunk of land, and if they're serious about saving what's left of the Atlantic Forest it's not a moment too soon."

Most people had never heard of the Atlantic Forest, and that included the people who lived in it. When the Portuguese arrived in 1500, the Atlantic Forest extended for more than six hundred thousand square miles, from Rio Grande do Norte up near the Amazon, clear down to Rio Grande do Sul on the borders of Argentina. It was a treasure trove of hardwoods, fibers, fruits, and medicine, including the highly prized Brazilwood tree that yielded a red dye and gave the country its name. After cutting these trees almost to extinction, the Portuguese set about clearing the remaining trees to plant sugar, raise cattle, and found settlements. The forest was so large that it seemed it would never end, and when forest clearings lost their fertility they were abandoned and new land was conquered, with no need to care for the land that was already cleared.

Five hundred years later, the forest had been reduced to 7 percent of its original extent, and if the last remnants were to be saved there was no time to be lost.

R obin went off to Muriaé to talk to the State Forestry Institute and returned smiling broadly. "Looks like it's true," he announced.

"What?"

"They're really going to set up the state park. Looks like it'll be about fifteen thousand hectares, but there'll be a buffer zone all round it that will include Iracambi."

"Will it be part of the Atlantic Forest Project?" I asked.

"Yes, it will. They've been talking about it for years, but they never could find the money."

"They're not going to throw us off the land or anything?"

"Oh dear me, no. They've finally realized you can't get away with that sort of behavior any longer. In fact, it's a good thing to have people living in the buffer zone to help protect it."

"So what does it mean for us, exactly?"

"Well, we'll be in the buffer zone and that should give us some level of protection. Government backing for what we're trying to do already—figuring out how farming and forests can work together."

"Farming the forest?"

"Well, yes, in the sense of managing it. And, of course, foresting the farm."

"Farming the forest and foresting the farm. I like it."

One of the problems with conservation was that most Brazilians just didn't see the need for it. For a start, the majority of them lived in the towns and considered the countryside fit only for peasants. Or Indians. In their haste to become a serious country, successive governments had focused on cutting the forests, mining the soils, and harnessing the rivers for hydroelectric power. Lured by the dreams of city life, thousands of small farmers abandoned the land to try their luck in the cities, where, lacking the necessary survival skills, they usually ended up in the *favelas*.

But things were starting to change. The Earth Summit was the beginning of a new age for Brazilian conservation, and our family, represented by Juliet, was involved in the discussions. In the air-conditioned convention center, government delegates hunched over their computers and hammered out Agenda 21, a bright new road map for sustainability. Meanwhile, half a million environmentalists from across the globe came together in Flamengo Park in Rio to figure out ways to make change happen.

Slowly but surely that change was beginning to trickle down into the interior of the country. The city of Muriaé set up an environmental council and invited Robin to join. They even talked of providing environmental education in the schools. Cynics pointed out that this sudden interest in conservation was likely connected to new "green" tax bonuses; when one of the councilors asked the prefect about the objectives of the environmental council, he was told to mind his own business.

But nothing could diminish Robin's enthusiasm, and when the first meeting of the environmental council took place on a brilliantly sunny afternoon, he set off all smiles, determined to do his bit to save the rainforest. "I've got lots of ideas," he told me happily. "I'm going to put in a plug for conserving the Itajuru forest—they're talking about making it into a municipal park. Probably because of the tax benefits, but the outcome will be the same. See you later. Bye."

By nine thirty that evening there was still no sign of him. It was a beautiful night and I was sitting on the front steps listening to the chorus of frogs and trying to recognize the pattern of stars in the night sky. I knew better than to worry about Robin; he was sometimes delayed coming home but he always made it sooner or later. I checked my watch. Maybe there was a problem with the car?

I was on the point of calling Luiza when I heard the distant sound of a car engine. But it wasn't the Toyota—it sounded like a Volkswagen Beetle. Perhaps he had taken a ride in Antonio's taxi. I peered through the banana trees as the sound drew closer, and saw a car crossing the causeway between the fishponds.

The moon came out from behind a cloud just as an unfamiliar

dusty Volkswagen drew up outside the house. Robin uncurled himself from the driver's seat and yawned. "Sorry to be late," he called. "Ran into a spot of trouble."

He settled himself in the rocking chair and accepted a plate of food.

"So what happened to the Toyota? And whose car is that?"

"Belongs to the notary public," he told me between mouthfuls. "The Toyota's in the garage. The sodding axle broke."

"What?"

"Like I said. I was on my way home and just driving round that sharp corner by the Pirapanema cemetery when all of a sudden the sodding axle broke. Luckily there was no one on the road. So I walked up to old man Baess's farm to get someone to keep an eye on the car—couldn't just leave it there, otherwise it would be stripped. He gave me a warm welcome and offered me some of his homemade *cachaça* and when I told him my problem he produced a wild-looking fellow who he said was a famous *pistoleiro* and just the man for the job. Nobody would fool with him and the car would be in good hands, that's what he said."

"No relation to Antonio the taxi driver, I don't suppose?" I asked.

"Could be." Robin poured hot sauce onto his beans. "Problem was, when he saw where the car was, he flatly refused to stay there. Not unless I gave him my gun. What gun? I said. I don't carry a gun. That's all very well for *you*, he said, but wild horses won't persuade me to stay outside the cemetery at night without a gun. Because of the ghosts.

"So he went off and got the most terrifying-looking blunderbuss, and settled down quite happily in the driver's seat. I walked back to the telephone to call the garage, and they said they'd come up straightaway. I was just trying to figure out how I was going to get home when the notary came along on his evening walk. I told him my story and he offered to lend me his car—said he never used it anyway. Of course there wasn't a drop of fuel in it, but I managed to find some and here I am."

"What an adventure!" I exclaimed. "Now tell me about the meeting."

"It was surprisingly good. They've got one or two people who are really interested. A self-taught biologist, a friend of Rosana's called Gabetto—interesting guy. Mad about trees and has a little forest nursery with all sorts of species. Then there's a vet called Aline, and a couple of others whose names I never caught. Mind you, we didn't get onto the really substantive issues. In fact, we spent most of the time talking about garbage recycling. That and planting more trees in the main square. But it was a good start, and we plan to meet once a month."

T he following Saturday dawned dry and sunny—a perfect day for an adventure. "Let's go up into the forest," I suggested to Robin.

"Okay," he said. "How about we climb Itajuru?"

"How far can we take the car?"

"Depends on the road; we'll just have to see."

We drove up the steep hill beside the fishponds, stopping to peer up into the tall tree where Albertinho had reported seeing a sloth. We craned our necks and squinted up, training our binoculars on several dense clumps of foliage that might possibly conceal a sloth, but we could make no positive identification. "You'd have to watch it for hours to see if anything moved," Robin told me.

"They come down once a week," I said helpfully.

"Could have been yesterday." He let in the clutch and drove on.

The rough track took us across the river, past the little house where Ailton and his bride were living, then up through the next valley past the school, the chapel, and Aparecida's old house to the farm belonging to Fia's parents, Jerson and Maria. I jumped out to open the gate while Robin negotiated his way through a family of squealing piglets, then jumped back in before we pulled steeply up a winding track that led onto an even narrower and more rutted trail across the mountains.

Heavy wooden gates barred the way, fastened to their posts by strips of leather or wooden hinges, and to our left rose the shoulder of Graminha peak. We dipped down over a rickety bridge past a pink-washed mud house where a widow lived all by herself. She'd had no children, and when her husband died she refused to move, even though several people had offered her a home; she told everyone she'd been in that house for fifty years and couldn't see any reason to leave it. A tiny old woman, brown as a walnut, she was sitting on the front steps sorting beans, and waved cheerfully as we passed. Through a ramshackle gate the track emerged onto a broad pasture, and far beneath we could see the road twisting up the valley. Stopping under a tree laden with smooth-skinned oranges that tasted wonderful, we looked across to the sheer rock face of Itajuru with its slopes clothed in dense forest. The track deteriorated steadily, steep and gullied, running through dense scrub on land that had once been cleared and was reverting to forest. On our right a simple wooden cross marked the grave of a wild boy who had run away from home and hidden out in the forest. They say he used to come down at night and milk the cows or steal eggs from the chickens, but nobody knew who he was, and one day he was found lying dead under a tree.

Shortly after the wild boy's grave we reached the top of the pass. On one side of the track a large rock had been used as a shelter from the rain, with a makeshift fireplace made of sooty stones at its base. On our left stretched the forest; on our right a large area had been recently devastated by a wildfire and was now covered with a thick growth of vines and brush creeping up the granite flanks of Itajuru, the Place of Sorrows. The main track led on through the forest to a small settlement on the other side of the mountain, but our way took us along an overgrown path, scarcely wide enough for a horse to pass. Hiding the car in thick bush, we took to our feet.

To our left the dense forest of the Serra do Brigadeiro stretched away across the mountain tops. The path was fringed with flowering fuchsias, orange watsonia, and palest pink begonias. Suddenly the silence was shattered by the barking of howler monkeys, starting low and progressing up the scale in a cacophony of whoops. We stood quietly, scanning the canopy, but could see nothing, and minutes later the sound came again, this time from another group on the next mountain.

Robin passed me a handful of scarlet berries that tasted like the European wild strawberries I used to collect when I was a child. I motioned him to keep still as the howlers started up again, farther away this time. I stooped to fasten my bootlaces and saw a procession of leaf-cutting ants marching across the path, looking like miniature windsurfers.

We squelched along the boggy trail, bright with wildly patterned leaves. On our right the splashing of water beckoned us to a hidden rock pool, perfect for cooling thirsty throats and washing sweaty feet and faces. Our way headed downhill with a sudden view over range upon range of hazy mountains. On one side, dense forest; on the other, an exuberant growth of vines clothing charred tree trunks, site of an old forest fire. In their profusion they seemed to mimic the impenetrable forests of Africa, uncertain refuge of the last mountain gorillas. A flash of white in one of the dead trees was followed by the musical call of a bellbird. The rock face loomed above us, veiled in mist, and suddenly, illogically, the track plunged sharply down toward the sound of rushing water. Slipping and sliding downhill, we came to a mountain stream whose water tasted strongly of peat and smelled of woody vegetation.

Across the rocks the trail beckoned us into the forest, its shade pierced by an unexpected flash of purple flowers glowing in the slanting rays of the sun. Scrambling up the rock face, I tipped a bromeliad to drink its stored water, then hauled myself up by clutching at grassy tussocks and wedging the toes of my boots in clefts in the rock. Robin had disappeared into the forest above me and I was on my own. A coral snake slipped across the path—or was it a false coral? Deadly venomous, or completely harmless? Better not to know, since there's no effective serum for its bite. Breathing heavily, I trudged upward through the misty forest. Slender vines caught at my ankles and tiny thorns stung my hand as I grabbed a tree trunk to steady myself. Moss hung from the trees, the ground was spongy, and black water seeped through my boots. The air felt hot and heavy, and my every sense was on full alert for thorns and spines, hairy caterpillars or worse.

Suddenly I was clear of the forest and out on the heathery grassland above the tree line, the air pure and cool. Robin was sitting on a rock, admiring the view. On every side the mountains stretched to the horizon; below us were the dark forest and the brilliant green of the pastures, above us the scudding clouds, where a pair of vultures soared high and wild on the wind.

Later, as we picked our way back carefully down the slippery path, I became aware of a whole new set of muscles, and later still flopped gratefully into the sandy rock pool, feeling the water seep into my every pore. On the homeward trail we passed the house of old Olavo and were invited in for glasses of thick sweet coffee. He introduced us to his wife, Dona Maria, a sweet-faced old lady who darted about stoking the fire and plying us with corn cake while Olavo and Robin talked about the plants of the forest and I sat comfortably by the woodstove, battling to keep my eyes open as sleepiness stole over me.

Our trip to Itajuru sharpened our resolve to do something to protect the wonderful forests around us, and Robin had much to discuss when he set off to meet the newly appointed Municipal Secretary of the Environment. The secretary had recently transferred from the National Department of Roads and was determined to make his mark by setting up the first conservation area in the county.

"The preliminary studies are complete," he assured Robin. "Itajuru Park has been a pet project of the prefect for some time and now he's got the council to vote a budget."

"That's great," said Robin. "Have you completed the management plan?"

"Management plan?"

"Maybe I could help you with that," said Robin, remembering the sad state of the animals in the town zoo.

The secretary brightened. "I've got the architect's drawings for the park facilities." He rummaged in his filing cabinet. "Here they are."

Robin cast a quick eye over the drawings. They showed an impressive building with classrooms, library, and computer room. There was also a parking lot, although there was no road access. "What's the budget?" he inquired.

"276,000 cruzados."

Robin pulled out his pocket calculator. Around three thousand U.S. dollars. "Per month?"

The secretary shook his head. "Per annum," he said. "I'm trying to get it increased, but you know how it is."

Robin nodded. "How do you plan to finance the construction?"

"That's the problem. At the current level the first two years' budget will go on the architect's drawings."

There was a silence. "But I do have the biological inventory," the secretary continued. "I'll make you a copy if you like."

Robin smiled. "Thanks very much. I'd like that a lot."

T hat night Robin showed me the inventory. It was illustrated with blurred black-and-white photographs, had been produced on a typewriter, and was signed by a Professor João Francisco.

"Who is this guy?" I asked. "Is he from the University of Viçosa?"

"I don't think so." Robin shook his head. "It's not very professionally produced and it doesn't mention anything about the university. I expect he's from one of the local high schools – the teachers always refer to themselves as professors."

I studied the inventory. It listed an impressive array of species—160 of them, including birds, mammals, and reptiles. Some of them were extremely rare, including the cock of the rock, the collared sloth, and the giant armadillo. "Wow, look at these." I showed the list to Robin.

He looked at it closely, shook his head, and laughed. "This is complete fiction! I doubt this professor actually went into the field at all. First of all, the cock of the rock. It's extremely rare and only exists in the Amazon. That particular sloth, *Bradypus torquatus,* is from southern Bahia, and the giant armadillo lives in the savanna. Makes me wonder what else he's got wrong."

"He claims to have spent ten months on the survey," I remarked.

"That's as may be. But people round here will tell you exactly what you want to hear. All it takes is for someone to show up with a photograph and ask them if they've ever seen that particular animal and of course they'll say yes. First of all, they're not used to recognizing things in photographs, they're used to seeing the real thing. And second, they've got work to do and can't waste their time answering stupid questions."

Several years later, when the Serra do Brigadeiro Park became a reality, a proper survey was commissioned. It noted the existence of a previously unknown group of highly endangered woolly spider monkeys, as well as several undescribed species of bromeliad and amphibia. But there was no sign of the cock of the rock, nor the collared sloth, and the nearest confirmed sighting of the giant armadillo was more than three hundred miles away.

CHAPTER SIXTEEN

A Woman's Place

W e might have laughed at the idea of a schoolteacher claiming that giant armadillos were roaming in our forests, but all the talk of forests and conservation provided just the stimulus we needed to get on with the next phase of the Iracambi development plan. Robin had discovered that we could put some of the best old-growth forest on Fazenda Graminha under permanent federal protection as a private forest reserve. This would require a lot of paperwork, and someone from the Ministry of the Environment would have to come down and inspect it, but the government was keen to encourage landowners to set up reserves, and ours would be the first in the region.

We also planned to plant trees on the steep slopes, but hadn't been able to decide which varieties would be most suitable. Robin's first choice had been the araucaria pines that had once grown so abundantly in the southern reaches of the Atlantic Forest, providing hardwood as well as pine nuts that tasted like a poor man's version of *marron glacé*. But although we lived in the southeastern region of Brazil, we were too far into the tropical zone, and the professors at the Forestry School at the University of Viçosa reckoned that araucaria wasn't suitable for our conditions. They recommended different varieties of pine, but they didn't flourish, either, and Robin finally came to the conclusion that our best option was eucalyptus.

"We'll be planting native hardwoods, too, of course," he told me. "But even in this climate they take thirty years to grow and we need to be able to eat in the meantime. Eucalyptus takes seven years to mature and you can coppice it for another two cycles."

"Coppice it?"

"Cut it about fifty centimeters from the ground and leave it to grow back. We can get seedlings from the forestry institute in Muriaé, but they only carry *Eucalyptus grandis* and I'd like to plant several different varieties together. Makes the management more complicated, but it's healthier than having a monoculture."

"So where do we get the other seedlings?"

"From the forestry people in São Paulo. We get seeds from them, and make our own seedlings. As for native species, we'll get them from that guy I met at the meeting, remember? Rosana's friend Gabetto."

Gabetto was a skinny young man from a large and quarrelsome family that owned land on the other side of Muriaé. His passion in life was his jeep. It dated from World War II, and he kept it in perfect running order, jumping at any excuse to take it out onto the back roads. He arrived to visit us in the pouring rain, swathed in an oversize waxed jacket salvaged from some military surplus store, carrying a plastic crate full of tree seedlings. His enthusiasm for the forest knew no bounds: He knew where to find the hardwoods, when they flowered and seeded, and how to collect the seeds. He could quote early scientific explorers and point us to rare books in the Muriaé library; he also could fix machinery and knew all about beekeeping.

Gabetto took us up onto Fazenda Graminha and pointed out the best area to turn into a forest reserve; he scrambled with us up the riverbed to look for orchids high in the canopy and tiny *palmito* seedlings on the forest floor. He explained why local farmers cleared an area of bare earth around their houses—to keep snakes and insects at bay—and why they cleared around the coffee trees (for the same reason). He knew the calls of birds and monkeys, showed us which plants were used by the Puri Indians to cure stomachaches and insect bites, and led us to a hidden spring of pure water to use in herbal remedies.

He was a treasure trove of information. He explained why Brazilian coffee used to be such poor quality—because the slaves were obliged to pick a certain weight of coffee berries per day, and stripped the trees of all their berries, whether or not they were ripe. He told us why people ran off into the forest when strangers appeared—a hangover from the days when country boys were press-ganged into the army, rounded up to build the roads, or forced to pay land tax. His passion was local history, and he kept us enthralled with stories of the early explorers and travelers, such as Guido Marlière, defender of the local Indian groups, who came to Itajuru in the 1820s, but hurried past, because of the ferocious wild animals, the bloodthirsty mosquitoes and the group of leprous Indians that was hiding in the caves.

Gabetto came from an old Portuguese family, but he had the soul of a forest Indian. A free spirit who came and went as he pleased, he had no sense of time and little sense of commitment. He'd promise to deliver a load of seedlings on a certain day, Albertinho would be hovering by ready to help unload, and Gabetto would forget to show up. He'd borrow his brother's truck and arrive late at night, after Albertinho was sound asleep. He'd wreak miracles on a temperamental engine, and leave Robin's tools scattered outside in the rain. When we tried to reason with him, he'd smile his engaging smile and change the subject. "I'd sooner do it myself," Robin muttered, scowling as he retrieved the missing parts.

Gabetto told us it was the right time to make eucalyptus seedlings and gave us the name of the store in Muriaé that sold the black plastic bags we'd need. Robin set his heart on ten thousand for the first planting, and João selected a shady spot on Fazenda Graminha for the eucalyptus nursery. He rode down on his mule one evening to discuss the forestry program.

"It's none of my business," he began, "but it seems a shame to be planting up that pasture. Where are we going to put the dry cows?"

Like most of his countrymen, João was deeply attached to cows, and considerably less interested in planting trees. Eucalyptus, perhaps, since it could be considered a crop, like coffee. But he couldn't see the sense of planting trees in the forest—particularly if you weren't allowed to cut them down.

"Those slopes are too steep for pasture," Robin told him. "And the law says they have to be planted in forest. But don't worry; I'm going to improve some of the existing pastures so they'll carry more stock."

João held his peace. "Oh, and another thing," he said, "I don't know how we're going to get all those seedlings made. I'm run off my feet as it is, what with setting up the nursery and digging ten thousand holes."

"I see the problem," Robin replied. "So what do you suggest?"

"*O senhor é que sabe*," said João. The *senhor* knows best.

"Oh no, he doesn't," Robin laughed. "You figure it out."

João grinned and scratched his head. "Ailton and I have been talking about it," he admitted, "and we thought maybe we could offer it out as contract work."

"That's a thought," said Robin. "Who would do it and how much do we pay?"

"Plenty of people could use the money, that's no problem. As to the payment, Ailton and I could sieve the soil, mix it with fertilizer, and see how many of those little bags we can fill in a day."

"Okay."

"Then we'll divide the daily wage by the number of bags, and that way we'll have an idea of what to pay."

"Fine," said Robin. "Let's do it."

The following week Robin wanted to check on the seedling project, but he was called away at the eleventh hour, so I volunteered to go in his place. It was a beautiful afternoon as I trotted through the *fazenda* with the sun hot on my back and Splittie running at my heels. We headed up the road and cut through the pasture onto Fazenda Graminha, dropping down past the farmhouse and around to the spot where João was setting up the nursery. As we rounded the corner, I could hear the laughter of children and the buzz of voices.

A small group of women was sitting on the ground, each one with a pile of sifted earth and a collection of plastic bags beside her. A couple of older girls were helping their mothers, several small children were playing tag, and a baby was sleeping peacefully in the shade. One of the women looked up, saw me, and stopped in midsentence. Everyone froze.

"Hey, ladies." I dismounted and tethered my horse. "How's it going?"

There was no reply, and one of the young girls stifled a giggle.

I searched for a familiar face and found João's wife, Neusa. "Well, Neusa?"

"Fine," she told me.

"Looks great to me," I commented. "And how many bags are you managing to fill?"

"It's a question of practice," she told me. "We've made coffee seedlings before, and it's not that different."

"Depends what time we get started," said an older woman. "I can't get here before ten myself, because I've got to make the lunch first, and it's a good half hour's walk from my house. But if I keep going till four o'clock I can do about five hundred."

"Is this the first time you've worked for a salary?" I asked her.

"Yes, it is. We usually trade days with one another, or work together in a group. But that doesn't give me any money and I want to buy a Singer."

"Singer?"

"So I can make clothes for the family. I've seen just the machine I want, and I'm saving up for a down payment."

"Great idea." I looked around the group. "And, talking of money, payday is on the fifteenth. And don't you send your husbands to collect your money. It's your money and you should get it yourselves."

Without planning anything, we had launched the first women's work front, and it soon became a hot topic of discussion down at the dairy. Of course women should work, but should they be paid for it? Was it right that they should earn the same as a man? Opinions were divided. Everyone agreed that the extra income would be a help to the family budget, but there were many men, and some women, who felt that it was going against the natural order of things.

Fia didn't care. She was already earning a regular salary, and was quick to point out that women didn't spend their money on *cachaça* or cigarettes, as the men did: Albertinho and Antonio both enjoyed a corn-leaf cigarette from time to time, and the other men occasionally took a drop of liquor (except for Valdeci—his family were Believers, and didn't approve of liquor, tobacco, or women working outside the house).

Payday arrived, and the Graminha women turned up all smiles, each one carrying a paper signed by João detailing how much she had earned. "What are you planning to spend your money on?" I asked as I handed them their payment.

"I'm saving up for the Singer." The older one smiled.

"A box of day-old chicks," said another.

"Paying off my pharmacy bill."

"Sandals for my son."

"Shall I tell you what I'm going to do?" put in a very young girl. "I'm going to buy a lipstick."

The ten thousand bags were quickly filled, and it wasn't long before the seedlings started to sprout. João reported that the women wanted more work, and Robin suggested they help with the planting when the time came. In the meantime, Maria plucked up her courage and asked if there was any work she could do, so Robin sent her to creosote timber with Fia, and Ailton's wife, Lucinha, took charge of our vegetable garden.

For the previous two years the onset of the rains had meant that construction on the new house was halted, the mud walls were swathed in plastic, and John the Baptist went off to work elsewhere. But this year he was determined to get the roofing complete so that work could continue. Robin was everywhere at once, calculating the angle of the beams, hauling timber and roofing

tiles, and supervising the placement of the chimneys. It was important to finish the tiling in the dry weather, because if the tiles got
wet they became extremely slippery and if anyone stepped on them
they would crack. It was hot up there on the roof, but John the
Baptist worked away doggedly and managed to complete the tiling
before the first storms.

The day the roof was finished, Robin showed me a letter he'd
received from an architect friend of his in the States. "I think it's
wonderful that you are building your own house," his friend had
written. "I can't wait to see it. I've never heard of rammed earth
walls four meters high, but there's no structural reason why they
shouldn't work, so long as they're sufficiently thick. The only way
you'll know for sure is when you put the roof on. If there's a fault in
the design of the walls they'll fall down." "I thought I'd wait and
see if he was right," Robin told me. "Looks like we'll be okay."

Despite the note of warning, the walls didn't fall down, and
suddenly it was beginning to look like a proper house. The carpenter came from Ervália to install the doors and windows, and
the glazier drove cautiously up from Muriaé with a truckload of
glass. The floors in the back wing were tiled with gray-green slate,
and terra-cotta tiles arrived for the kitchen. A visiting friend did
the lighting plan, Robin did the wiring, and John the Baptist
did the plumbing. Hardwood flooring was installed in the music
room, our bedroom, and the study; in the the courtyard cobbles
were laid, the gate was hung, and Robin planted flowers in the
tubs. It was the best house ever.

With so many things to be paid for, Robin couldn't stay
around for long, and his next trip came up just in time to
settle our debts. The rains were well advanced, and João had announced that he was ready to start planting the eucalyptus, with

the help of some of the women. Maria had undertaken to dig up some wild *palmito* seedlings and plant them near the house, Lucinha was working in the vegetable garden, and Fia was in charge of the calves in the dairy; the women's work front appeared to be functioning well.

One morning Maria turned up with a long face. "I don't like working in the forest," she told me.

"What's the problem?" I asked.

"It isn't safe," she said. "Because of the jaguars."

Later that day Lucinha complained that the work in the garden was too heavy and she needed a man to help her.

"Look here, Lucinha," I told her. "You know what the men round here feel about women earning the same wage. What are they going to say if I say you can't do the work and need one of them to help?"

Lucinha blushed. "I think I'm pregnant," she said.

"In that case you'd better stop," I told her shortly.

I told Luiza the whole story and asked her advice.

"No, honeychild," she smiled, "I don't think you've got it wrong. This business of getting women to work together, it's hard. Their husbands don't support them, so any little thing that goes astray is enough to put them off. That and the *mineiro* attitude that things are difficult anyway."

"So what do you recommend?" I asked her, remembering her experience with the Peace Corps.

"Well now, let me think. And while I'm thinking, how about one of my special cookies?"

Luiza's cookies were a secret concoction of condensed milk, butter, sugar, eggs, and chocolate that tasted delicious and were guaranteed to clog the arteries. Ignoring the warning bells in my head,

I took tiny bites and concentrated on the taste. "I've got it!" I announced. "How about making and selling Luiza's cookies?"

"No deal," laughed Luiza. "A family secret that will die with me. But in any case it's no good telling them what they want. You have to ask them. Talk to Julia about it. Vocational training is her specialty."

F ia volunteered to invite the women to a meeting with Julia, to be held the following week in my kitchen. Despite the steady rain, seventeen women showed up, and Julia managed to steer her small white Fiat around the holes in the road without getting bogged down.

"Well, ladies," she said, shaking the water off her umbrella. "It's good to see so many of you. Let's start by introducing ourselves, and then we'll talk about the really important thing—how we're going to make money. I'm sure everyone here could use a little extra at the end of the month?"

Everybody nodded.

"Fine," said Julia. "Now who is going to help me by getting a list of everyone's names?"

"I will," said Marinha, who had more schooling than anyone else in the room.

"There are two ways we can do this," Julia continued. "Either we make money by selling things, or we save money by making things we need. So here's what I can do for you. The extension agency can offer lessons in cooking, sewing, raising vegetables or chickens, growing and using medicinal herbs, and making jams, conserves, or liqueurs. Each of these can either save us money or earn us money. So let's talk about it and see what you'd like best."

I looked around the circle of faces, competent country women and their teenage daughters: Fia, Maria, Lucinha and Marinha from Iracambi; Neusa and her sister Carminha from Graminha; Orisa from next door; and some of the women who had worked with the seedlings.

The discussion wound slowly on, and I slipped out to answer the phone.

"We've decided on dressmaking," Marinha told me on my return. "And Julia says she can find us a teacher, no problem."

"The question is where to hold the classes," said Julia. "We'll need to set up tables for the machines, and there isn't room in this kitchen."

"How about the barn?" suggested Fia.

"Let's take a look," Julia answered, and we trooped up there. The front bit of the barn was open, and there was plenty of room to set up trestle tables so long as the inspection pit was covered.

"If they turn out to be any good," I said later to Julia, "maybe they could set up a small business. With a revolving loan fund."

"That's an idea." She smiled. "But let's not run before we can walk. We'll get them started first."

The sewing course began the very next week, and twenty-three candidates signed up. It was taught by a motherly woman who lived across the hills behind Zé Viricius's house. She asked if I'd like to join the class, but I had little interest and no skills, and politely declined. There were to be two classes a week for four weeks, culminating in the graduation ceremony, at which the clothes would be displayed and certificates awarded by the prefect's wife.

Robin returned from Mexico the week of the graduation and was reluctant to attend the ceremony. "It's not exactly my thing, you know," he told me. "Far better if you go."

"Of course I'm going, silly. But you absolutely have to attend. Noblesse oblige."

* * *

On graduation day, Julia and the teacher arrived early to set up the display and Fia laid out the refreshments: homemade lemonade and a large tin of Luiza's special cookies. One by one the women drifted in with their handwork and settled down to chat. Finally the prefect's wife arrived in a chiffon skirt and high heels, and Robin handed her out of the car and helped her into the barn while I ran back for my camera to register the scene. The barn had been transformed: Hay bales provided comfortable seating, brightly colored clothes were displayed on the tables, a patchwork sheet hung from one of the beams, and Marinha was presiding over the refreshment table. The ladies came up, smiling proudly, to collect their certificates and demonstrate their handwork. The prefect's wife made a short speech, the teacher thanked her students, and everyone thanked us.

"Good job," Robin commented later. "Some of their stuff wasn't bad. Although I don't know why anyone would want to make a cover for a gas cylinder."

"It's considered very chic to cook with gas," I told him. "The cover is a status symbol."

"Looks like the sewing course was a great success." He smiled. "Well done!"

"Well, it all came together at the end," I told him. "But there were some rough times along the way. I'm glad I stayed out of it."

"What do you mean?"

"I heard it from Cassandra—I mean Cassilda. She attended for the first couple of weeks but then she dropped out. Told me that there'd been a blood row between Marinha and Carmen. Somebody spilled oil on one of the benches, and Marinha got her skirt dirty. Yelled at Carmen and called her a nigger or something of the sort. And then Maria went after Fia and accused her of making eyes at Albertinho. For heaven's sake! Everyone took sides, and apparently the teacher had a hell of a job to keep the peace."

"Oh, dear," said Robin. "Well, that just proves it."

"Proves what?"

Robin gave me a seraphic smile. "A woman's place," he told me sweetly, "is in the home."

CHAPTER SEVENTEEN

Song of Limeira

The *fazenda* was bubbling with excitement. The Limeira referendum and the petition to the state government had been
successful, and the village was going to become a real town, seat of
a new county. There would be access to state funding, and there
was talk of road machines, school transport, a clinic, an ambulance,
piped water and drains, and maybe, just maybe, the road would
finally be paved. But first Limeira had to elect a prefect and a chamber of councilors.

Voting day was set for several months ahead, and there were
two main candidates for prefect. The first was Councilor Bertoni,
who lived in the house with the white sofas. His fortunes had recently undergone a dramatic change—after his wife had discovered him in bed with one of the schoolteachers. Sick and tired of
his infidelities, she had departed in style, taking her share of the
money and the family tractor, registered in her name. Nadia the
schoolteacher moved in the very next day, gave up her job, and
started to plan her future as First Lady of Limeira.

Bertoni was backed by the family of Armir Toko, to whom he

was distantly related by marriage. He'd been the councilor for Limeira for many years, without distinguishing himself in any way—except for once punching a fellow councilor during a particularly acrimonious meeting. She had whacked him with her stiletto heel, and the subsequent commotion had woken the town reporter from his afternoon nap in the back of the council chamber. The report he filed for the weekly paper made for some of the most stimulating reading in years.

The other candidate was our friend Edson from the extension service. It was his first venture into politics, but the country people knew and liked him and he had many promises of support. Unlike Bertoni, he didn't have the money to hand out T-shirts and bags of cement to the voters. And there was another complication: Armir Toko, who was financing Bertoni, was the patriarch of the Toko family; Edson was related to the Freitas. These were the two families engaged in the long-standing vendetta Lenin had warned us about.

O kay, guys, we've got to get out there and vote." Robin was holding a special meeting with the farm staff and was determined that everyone should understand the consequences of using their vote wisely. "It's no good sitting back and complaining that all politicians are corrupt. If we want things to change, we have to make sure they do. And we have to think very carefully about the person we vote for. We've got two candidates for prefect, right?"

"Right," said someone cautiously.

"Okay," he continued. "One of them is Bertoni. He's been our councilor for several years."

"Never did a damn thing," muttered somebody.

"Is that right?" I chipped in.

There was a chorus of agreement.

"Well, if that's the case we need to think about it," I continued.

"Remember one thing: He works for us. His salary comes out of our tax money. So if he never did a damn thing, why elect him prefect?"

"Prefects don't do anything anyway," said Valdeci. "Paulo Carvalho's twice been prefect and what did he ever do for us?"

"Nothing," Antonio answered.

"If he never did anything, how come people keep voting him in?" asked Robin.

There was a silence.

"Goes around buying votes," chuckled Albertinho.

"Exactly," said Robin. "And we don't want that to happen in Limeira."

"Edson can't buy votes," João pointed out. "Doesn't have the money."

"Well, here's a suggestion," said Robin. "How about we invite Edson over here to meet with us? Then he can tell us what he plans to do. We could invite Bertoni, too."

People were nodding in agreement.

"They won't come to the same meeting," said someone.

"No, let each man have his say."

"Why don't we ask the neighbors? I'm sure they'd like to attend."

"Good idea."

As the weeks rolled on toward the election, the level of excitement rose. Never before had so many cars been along our rutted roads. In addition to the post of prefect, there were nine vacancies for town councilors, and a total of twenty-six potential candidates. Soapy Sam, owner of the grocery store, dropped by to solicit our support. He was a fervent member of one of the Believer churches and sprinkled his conversation with biblical references, such as "The Lord loves a cheerful giver." Aparecida Braga appeared in tight purple Lycra and platform heels to request our vote. Geraldo Gudim, father of John the Baptist, decided to run for the Workers Party.

Limeira was transformed from a sleepy little one-horse town to a bustling center, and a couple of enterprising traders set up stalls in the main square, selling corn on the cob, hot dogs, and shots of *cachaça*. Bertoni's supporters handed out blue and red T-shirts—Edson's party distributed baseball caps. Bertoni threw a party on his farm—Edson hired a local band to play in the square. Banners were strung across the road, and every house sprouted a poster. The talk was all of politics, and people had never had so much fun.

Robin was called away to Mexico, and departed with the greatest reluctance. "Too bad I'll miss the action," he told me. "But I rely on you to make sure everyone gets out there to vote. And I'll do my damnedest to get back in time for the election."

Luiza called from Muriaé. "I'm coming up on the afternoon bus. Sounds like you're having the best time up there."

I drove into the square just as the bus was rounding the corner. People were seated at tables eating and drinking; there was a buzz of conversation and music was blaring out of Murilo's bar. "You've arrived at just the right moment." I gave Luiza a big hug. "On Wednesday we're having a meeting on the *fazenda* with Bertoni, and Edson will be coming over next week. John the Baptist reckons lots of people will come. People really want to hear what these guys are offering us."

"Grand!" said Luiza, lighting a cigarette.

"I must tell you something funny," I added. "Bertoni's people called the other day to ask whether they could count on the Iracambi vote. Told them I'd make sure everyone turned out to vote. Of course, I didn't say who they'd vote *for*."

"Perfectly wonderful," exclaimed Luiza. "I just love it!"

* * *

Bertoni's meeting attracted the largest crowd yet seen on the *fazenda*. The kitchen of the blue house was crammed to capacity; people were overflowing onto the back veranda and standing on tiptoe to peer through the windows. Horses were tethered along the fence, pony carts were parked along the road, and one young man roared up on a motorbike, frightening a donkey that galloped off into the darkness, braying loudly. There was an air of happy anticipation in the room, and everyone was chatting animatedly. Jair pushed his way to the front, followed by Cassilda. João Red Face pumped my hand vigorously and settled himself ponderously on the end of the bench. Adão and Orisa were leaning against the wall, chatting to Dona Maria, who had a smart new pair of glasses strung around her neck. John the Baptist had brought several of his children, and all the farm staff were present, complete with their families. A very young man came over and thrust a crumpled piece of paper into my hand. "I have a question for Bertoni," he said.

"That's great," I said, squinting to decipher the writing. "Remind me of your name."

"Admilson, son of Zé Mané."

"Okay, Admilson, do you want me to hand it to him?"

"No, I want you to ask it for me."

"It's better if you ask it yourself."

"I don't speak very well." He blushed.

"You just get up there and open your mouth," said Luiza, her eyes twinkling "You'll be fine, I promise you."

More and more people jammed into the room, and the noise level rose alarmingly. I checked my watch—twenty minutes late. What would happen if Bertoni didn't show up? I would have to improvise. I was just rehearsing what I would say when I heard the sound of music outside. It was Bertoni's campaign song, played at full volume from a loudspeaker. Blocking my ears, I pushed my way to the door to greet Bertoni and his entourage. He swept in, accompanied by his mistress Nadia, Armir Toko and his son Armir the Younger, Aparecida, and Soapy Sam. They made their way through the crowd, smiling and shaking hands.

When everyone was seated, I rose to my feet. "Welcome to Fazenda Iracambi," I started. "We are delighted to see you all, and really look forward to hearing your plans for Limeira. We'll be leaving plenty of time for questions, so that everyone here has the chance to speak as well as listen. A round of applause, please, for Senhor Bertoni."

Amid scattered applause, Bertoni stood and glanced around the room. "Ladies and gentlemen," he began, and I concentrated on noting down his main points. There weren't many. He started by exhorting us all to work hard and pay our taxes, announced that he would continue to serve us faithfully, and ended by inviting us to a barbecue the following weekend. No hint of any political program, no word about schools or health care or improving the roads.

He was followed by the blond schoolmistress. "You all know Bertoni," she announced. "Man of the people, son of the soil, well known for his hard work and honesty. Like most of you here, Bertoni was educated in the School of Life. He started work in the fields at age eight and now he owns a coffee business—living proof that hard work pays off. Deprived of the chance to study, he will devote his energy to seeing that every child has the opportunity to attend school, every family has access to proper health care, and that there are jobs for all."

"Jobs for all," echoed Young Armir, smiling broadly. "Health, education, transport, fair prices for farm produce and affordable housing. Working together, we can make Rosário da Limeira a byword for good government."

"Thank you," I said, as there was a ripple of applause. "May we please open the meeting to questions?"

Nobody stirred. The young man with the crumpled paper rose abruptly to his feet and turned to Bertoni. "Senhor Bertoni," he said respectfully, "I would like to ask you a question."

Bertoni looked up benignly.

"I would like to know," said Admilson, taking a deep breath and blushing scarlet, "why you gave my father three hundred bucks to vote for you?"

I held my breath. Bertoni said nothing. Nadia whispered urgently in his ear, and there was a buzz of comment in the room.

The situation was saved by Young Armir. "Senhor Bertoni is a charitable man." He looked around the room, narrowing his eyes. "But like all true Christians, he likes to do good in secret. In the words of Our Lord: 'Let not the right hand know what the left hand doeth.' I ask you, my friends, is this not the man we should elect as our leader?"

"Good save," hissed Luiza, and the meeting wound on.

"I can't think what we're going to find to talk about after this is all over," I remarked to Luiza later that evening.

"Well, there's always Edson's meeting," said Luiza.

Edson's meeting drew another full house, and he presented a development program that covered everything from health and education to improving the roads, installing a bulk refrigeration unit for the dairy farmers, and putting a community television antenna in the village. "I can't do this alone," he told the audience, after outlining his five-point plan, "so I'm counting on you to help me." He was given a standing ovation.

As the closing days of the campaign drew near, we were bombarded with calls from the potential councilors. Luiza amused herself by keeping a log of the calls. "I think it's Soapy Sam," she whispered as she handed me the phone. "I didn't know there were so many phones in the village."

"There aren't," I told her. "There's a public phone in the bar and another one at the gas station. Hello?"

But the voice that came down the line wasn't that of Soapy Sam. It was Edson. "Bianca, I want you to make a speech," he told me. "Something's come up and I need your support. I'll come over this evening and tell you about it."

"Okay," I shouted, over the hiss of static as the line went dead.

"It's like this," Edson explained that evening. "I think we've got Bertoni on the run. He thought he was going to win hands down, but the polls are showing that he's dropped behind. So he's adopted a new tactic. Started a rumor that people who don't vote for 'progress'—that means him—will be laid off. And guess who are the main employers in these parts? You've got it—the Tokos."

"He can't do that!" exclaimed Luiza hotly. "It's illegal. And anyway it's a secret vote."

"Of course it is," said Edson. "But here's the cunning part. He's let it be known that he can find out who people are voting for. Through the computer. Nobody really knows what a computer is or how it functions. Armir is the only person in Limeira who has one. Apart from you. So I need you to explain that it's a secret ballot, that all the computer can do is count the votes, and that anyway we're voting with pencil and paper."

"Hold on a minute," I protested. "I'm not a voter, remember?"

"That doesn't stop you from making a speech," said Edson. "This is a free country, you know. Anyone can say anything."

"All right, seeing it's for a good cause."

"Okay," said Edson. "Thursday is the last day of canvassing, and Armir Toko is really pushing the boat out. He's laying on a rodeo and free beer."

"Bread and circuses," muttered Luiza.

"We're having a party in the square. With an electric trio. All you need do is give a short speech. Just tell it like it is, okay?"

"Okay," I agreed, as Edson got into his car and drove away.

Honeychild," said Luiza sternly. "You and I are going to sit down and think this through very, very carefully. Emphasize the positive, and not a bad word about Bertoni. Not unless you want a bullet in the back."

Luiza and I wrote several drafts of the speech, and by the time Thursday came, we were satisfied with our efforts. As we drove into the village we could catch the smell of roasting meat drifting across from the Toko family's barbecue. Edson's supporters had set up a stage in the main square and a band was pounding out hard rock at full volume. A large crowd had assembled, many of whom had already stopped off at the barbecue.

Luiza settled herself on a bench in the square while I made my way through the throng of people to Edson's side. "Bianca!" he exclaimed. "There you are! Let me tell you what's happening. I'm going to deliver a short speech and then it's your turn, okay?"

"Okay," I said, suddenly remembering Lenin's warning about not getting involved in local politics.

I squeezed in beside Luiza and waited for the action to start. The band struck up at deafening pitch, the crowd roared out Edson's campaign song, and there was prolonged applause as the candidate took the microphone.

It was a short speech but a rousing one, and he ended by saying that there was something very important that they needed to know, and Bianca was going to tell them.

"Go for it, honeychild," said Luiza, and I heard the first shouts: "Bianca! Bianca!"

I made my way up onto the stage and looked out over a sea of intent faces. As the noise died down, I took a deep breath and stepped up to the microphone.

"You know me," I told them. "I'm Bianca, and I live on Fazenda Iracambi. I'm not voting in this election because I'm not Brazilian. I come from England, and my country is special for two reasons. First, because we invented *futebol*—"

There was a burst of applause.

"And second, because we've been choosing our leaders for eight hundred years. It hasn't been like that in Brazil. Some of your grandfathers were born into slavery, and you all remember the military dictatorship. Your forefathers didn't have the vote, your parents didn't have the vote, but you do. And a vote is something extremely precious."

The crowd had fallen silent and was listening attentively. "The vote is precious because it allows us to decide how we are going to spend our money," I continued. "We want better schools, better health care, better roads. And we want the best possible people to work for us.

"Some people think our votes are for sale. So they hand out T-shirts, or sacks of cement, or they promise us favors. Bribing us with candy bars like a bunch of kids. If that's how they want to spend their money, it's okay. It doesn't mean that we are going to sell our votes for a T-shirt, or a candy bar."

One or two people in the crowd were nodding in agreement as I took a deep breath and pressed on.

"Some people have been saying that if we vote for this candidate or that candidate something bad could happen. We might, for example, lose our jobs. They're saying that the computer will tell them who we voted for. Well, folks, that's a lie.

"Let me tell you why. The computer is just a machine. It's like a calculator. It does exactly what we tell it to do, and nothing more. It doesn't have ears, it doesn't have eyes, and it doesn't have a mouth. It can't see what you are doing, it can't hear what you are saying, and it can't tell on you. Your vote is secret and the only person who knows about it is you.

"And there's one more thing. In this election we are not going to use a computer. We'll be using paper and pencil. We are going to put a cross beside the names of the two people we are voting for—one person for prefect and one person for councilor. Take your pencil and vote for the two people that you think will do the best job for you, your family, and all the people of Limeira."

There was a roar of applause and I stepped down from the stage and made my way back to Luiza. "Good work, honeychild," she said. "You told it like it is. I'm proud of you."

The next morning I received two phone calls. The first was from Edson. "Bianca!" he shouted. "That was terrific. Thank you."

The second caller didn't identify himself. "Bianca?" he said.

"Yes?" I answered.

"Just a friendly warning," came the voice. "You'd better watch your step. You wouldn't want to meet with an accident."

I dropped the phone as if it were red hot and rushed into Luiza's room. She was sitting up in bed, tranquilly reading a detective story. "What's up?" she asked as she saw my face.

"An anonymous call," the words come tumbling out, "sounded like some sort of threat."

"Can't say I'm entirely surprised," said Luiza calmly. "This is Brazil, after all. We'll keep our heads down for a few days, until things cool off a bit. Don't worry, I'm sure it's all bluff."

But it wasn't. Two days later a group of unexpected visitors showed up on the *fazenda*. It was a beautiful Saturday afternoon, the last weekend before the election, and everyone was in Limeira doing their weekly shopping, visiting friends and family. Luiza wanted to do some sketching, and I had taken her up into the forest.

It was only the next day that we heard what had happened. Jair was wandering down the road outside the farm gate when he heard the sound of a car. During the weeks of electioneering it was a sound to which we had become accustomed. But now the campaigning was over—the election would be within two days. Jair looked up the road and saw a farm truck carrying a dozen or so young men.

The truck screeched to a halt. "Fazenda Iracambi, right?" shouted the driver.

Jair nodded.

The driver accelerated through the open gate without a word.

"That's funny," said Jair to himself, taking off his hat and scratching his head. "I wonder what they want."

The only people on the *fazenda* were the dairy staff, and they were in the middle of the afternoon milking. Jair squinted to see where the car had gone. He couldn't see very well without his glasses, but he was able to verify that it had stopped at the fishponds, and that the men had settled down to fish. "Well, look at that!" he said to himself. "I'm sure they're not supposed to be fishing. In any case the fish won't bite on a hot afternoon like this." After an hour or so they packed up their rods and drove away. Jair just happened to glance over and see them leave.

Luiza and I returned that evening, tired and happy from our excursion into the forest, unaware of the afternoon's events. It wasn't until the next day that we managed to piece together the story.

Something had been bothering Jair all morning, as he drove his pony cart on the morning milk round. He'd been trying to remember the identity of the man who'd driven the truck onto the *fazenda* the previous afternoon, and try as he might, he couldn't place him. He was trotting home for lunch when it suddenly came to him—it was Jorge the *pistoleiro*. He worked for the Tokos, and behind his back people called him Rattlesnake. Jair whipped his pony into a canter and headed for the blue house.

"Don't you worry about a thing," said Luiza robustly as she and I discussed the matter after Jair had left. "It's not as if they actually did anything. Tried to catch some fish, that's what Jair reckons. Bully tactics, that's all."

"How do we know they didn't come to the house?"

"I think it's very unlikely. The place was all shut up. And anyway, they wouldn't have known which house to go to."

"That's all very well," I said, feeling suddenly that I was standing on the edge of a precipice. "But we can't have *pistoleiros* running around the place. What the hell are we going to do now?"

"Now listen up." Luiza poured me a tumbler of brandy. "Here's what we'll do. We'll call a meeting and discuss it with the farm staff. I doubt if those guys will come back, but we'll keep that revolver handy just in case."

That night we called a *fazenda* meeting and invited Jair as a special guest. He wrung every inch of drama from the story, and had me sitting on the edge of my seat. "That Rattlesnake is a danger to us all," he declared. "We're none of us safe in our beds while he's around."

There was a momentary silence, then several people spoke at once.

"One at a time!" I protested. "You first, João."

"Well, Dona Bianca, it's like this," said João. "This place is backed up against the mountains, right?"

I nodded.

"We're at the end of the road, right?"

"Yes, we are."

"So nobody can come in here without being seen," he continued.

"Right."

"Well then," Antonio cut in, "it's really quite simple. If any *pistoleiro* comes here again . . ."

"Yes?"

Albertinho cleared his throat and spat. "If any *pistoleiro* tries to come in here again," he said firmly, looking me straight in the eye, "we'll break his fucking neck."

CHAPTER EIGHTEEN

Forest Angels

R obin had been determined to get back in time to vote in the
election. Several months earlier he had unexpectedly been
summoned before the judge in Muriaé for his naturalization ceremony. He had carefully read all 249 articles of the Brazilian consti-
tution together with the fifty-something amendments, memorized
the names of all thirty-two presidents, and could draw a passable
map of the twenty-six states. I had made a point of attending the
ceremony on the off chance he might have to sing the national
anthem—Robin was a man of many talents but he never could
hold a tune—but in the event the judge had taken him through
the oath of allegiance, shaken him warmly by the hand, and assured him that it was the first time in his thirty-year career that he
had had the pleasure of welcoming a brand-new citizen of Brazil.

In order to get back, Robin had some tight connections to make,
but luck was with him and he arrived home late on the eve of voting
day. Next morning he was up even earlier than usual, and I could
hear him humming the national anthem as he made the morning
coffee.

"I'm taking as many people as I can fit into the car," he told me as he bolted his breakfast. "Want to get there ahead of the crowds. See you. Bye."

Luiza was still sleeping; the farm staff had gone off with Robin to cast their votes, leaving Antonio to do the milking; and I had the place to myself. I settled on the front steps in the sunshine, as the mist curled off the fishponds and a flock of green parrots raced overhead chattering loudly. All was well with the world.

Meanwhile, Robin was driving the heavily laden Toyota into Limeira. Everyone was in a holiday mood, sporting Edson's campaign baseball caps—except for João, who was wearing a red Bertoni T-shirt and enduring some good-natured ragging from his fellow passengers. "I wasn't about to turn down a free gift," he protested. "Doesn't mean I'm voting for him."

The square was buzzing with activity: voting booths had been set up in the school, there was a long line waiting outside, and extra policemen had been drafted in to keep the peace. Bertoni and Nadia were standing by the school gate, and as Robin climbed out of the car Nadia pulled out her camera and took his picture. Nice to have my presence registered, Robin thought to himself, as he took his place in line behind Jair. Jair turned to Robin and grinned. "You know why she wanted your photo? She's going to denounce you for busing in voters. It's against the law, you know."

"Busing in voters?" Robin exclaimed. "Nonsense! Just giving a ride to some of the neighbors. And anyway," he raised his voice, "it's against the law for candidates to stand outside the polls. It's called harassment. Isn't that right, Sargento?"

"That's right." A smartly dressed policeman tapped Nadia on the shoulder and politely asked her to move away.

"You ought to take a look in her purse," a voice came from somewhere at the back of the line. "That woman always carries a gun."

"Move along please, *senhora*," said the policeman as Nadia walked off, head held high.

"So how did it go?" I demanded when Robin returned several hours later.

"Remarkably well," he said cheerfully. "Took a long time because there were a lot of old ladies who can't read and write and weren't sure what to do. But it's a small price to pay for seeing democracy in action."

"Did you get any feel for how things were going?" asked Luiza.

"There were a lot of Bertoni T-shirts," Robin told her. "I only hope they didn't all vote for him."

"That's one of the things I talked about in my speech," I said. "But it's a hard habit to break. By the way, what time are they expecting the results?"

"The polls close at seven, so I guess we can call around nine."

But when we called, the line was busy, and there was nothing to do but wait till the morning.

Morning dawned and Murilo's bar wasn't answering. "I expect they were up late," said Robin. "I'll run down to the dairy for some milk, and after breakfast I'll go into town to find out what happened."

"Town?" I laughed. "Do you mean Limeira?"

"It *is* the county capital," he told me as he swung off with the milk jug.

He was back in record time. "Great news!" he announced. "Just heard it on the dairy radio. Edson won by nearly three hundred votes."

"Wow! That's terrific!" I gave him a hug. "What happens next?"

"Nothing. He doesn't take office till the first of January, so we can all relax. And now I'm back there's a million things I want to do. Get the house finished, for a start. You wait till you see what I brought back from Oaxaca. Tiles for the courtyard, and woven blankets in the most gorgeous colors."

T he next few days passed in a whirl. While Robin and Luiza huddled together discussing color schemes, I was dispatched on a multitude of errands and a new surge of energy pervaded the building site.

I had run down to the kitchen to fix a new flask of coffee when the phone rang. "Bianca!" shouted an indistinct voice.

"*Alô?*"

"*É você*, Bianca?"

"*É, sim . . .*"

"*Aqui Rosana—*"

"Rosana! My favorite inseminator! Haven't seen you for months!"

The line went dead. I couldn't call back because I didn't know where she was calling from, but Rosana was extremely resourceful and would get back to me somehow.

I was filling the kettle when the phone rang again.

"Bianca!"

I could hear better this time.

"Bianca! I'm coming up to see you. On the afternoon bus."

"Right!" I shouted, and the line cut out again.

I took the Toyota into the village and parked outside Murilo's bar. It wasn't long before Our Lady's bus came wheezing up the road. Rosana jumped out and gave me a big hug.

"So this is the seat of the new county!" she exclaimed. "Still looks like a one-horse town to me. But I guess that'll change. Do we have time for a cheese pasty? I'm starving and I've got lots to tell you."

"Sure. So what's new?"

"I've got it!"

"Got what?"

"The visa, silly! My American visa!"

"Fantastic!" I said. "That's wonderful! Tell me all about it."

Rosana was about to fulfill her long-standing ambition: She was going to the States. "And you're the very first person to hear about it!" she said. "After all, I owe it all to you."

Several months earlier we'd had a visit from a friend of our son Gus. A tall, lanky American whose name was Mark, he'd been taking time out to figure out what to do with his life and had spent several weeks on the *fazenda*. He came from farming stock and was an easy guest who made himself extremely useful about the place.

He came down with us on the weekly trip to Muriaé and there he met Luiza, who took to him at once. "You know what we must do?" she said to me when Mark was out of the room. "We must introduce him to Rosana. Perhaps he can give her some tips on how to get to America."

Mark fell in happily with Luiza's plan. So happily, indeed, that he spent more time with Rosana than with us. Before leaving Brazil he confided that he was thinking of inviting her to pay him a visit in San Francisco.

Rosana's family was outraged. She couldn't possibly go. Who would look after the cows? Who would see to the insemination? And besides, how could she afford the ticket? Rosana paid no attention. She sold her car, she sold her cattle, she sent in her visa application, and she booked her ticket.

And now she was all set. "My mother is mad at me," she confided, as she bit into her cheese pasty. "Told me no decent girl would go off with a guy she scarcely knows. And I am a bit nervous, to tell you the truth. Suppose I get there and I don't like it?"

"You'll be fine," I said with certainty. "The important thing is to fix yourself up with a job. It's easy to find something if you don't mind babysitting or cleaning, and you absolutely must enroll in an

English course. After all, it's not as if you'll be on your own. Mark will be around."

Rosana blushed. "Well, I've got to make a go of it. I couldn't possibly face my family otherwise."

We climbed into the pickup and bumped our way over the road to the *fazenda*. "To tell you the truth, I am a bit sad." She smiled. "I'll miss my cows. And I'll miss you guys, too. But I'll write, and when you get e-mail we'll be able to keep in proper touch. Now tell me everything. How's it going with the women's work front?"

I frowned. "We've made a start. Trouble is, the men don't like the women to work. They might start having ideas of their own."

"That's exactly it." Rosana nodded. "Men like to be in control. Don't want their women working outside the house. And the middle class is just as bad. My uncle Roosevelt can't understand how I could possibly want to leave. Keeps telling me I'll regret it. And I'll never get a husband."

"*Machos,* the lot of them!" I laughed. "Brazil's got a long way to go in that respect."

"Right," said Rosana. "And it's partly our fault. We raise our daughters to be dependent and we spoil our sons. All that silly non-sense about 'A woman's place is in the home.'"

"You'll see some bumper stickers about that in the States," I told her. "They say A WOMAN'S PLACE IS IN THE HOUSE. They mean the House of Representatives."

"That's all very well in the States. But it won't wash in Rosário da Limeira. Now, I want to hear all your news. How's the new house coming on?"

"Fantastic! We're on the last lap. After lunch I'll take you up there and you can see for yourself. Oh, and Luiza's back. Says it's so much fun up here she's threatening to move in. She's painted the most beautiful hummingbird tiles for the kitchen wall—you never saw anything like them. And she's already planning the housewarming party! Says she just loves having something to prepare for because when you get older it's important to have something to look forward to."

We drew up in front of the blue house and Rosana climbed out of the car, stretched her long legs, and sighed happily. "Hey, Robin! Luiza! I'm back! Come tell me the news."

Luiza was delighted to see Rosana, and insisted on hearing every last detail. "I can't tell you how happy I am." She gave Rosana a big hug. "Although I'm not entirely surprised. Poor Mark, once he'd seen you he didn't have a chance."

"You matchmaker!" I laughed. "You planned this from the start."

Luisa opened her blue eyes wide. "I don't know why you'd think that! Now, let's take Rosana up to the new house. I want to see how the tiling looks."

John the Baptist and a young helper were finishing the kitchen counters. "Good job, João," Luiza told him. "Those blue and white tiles look wonderful as a border."

"Thank you." John the Baptist smiled.

Luiza looked critically at the white-tiled wall with its delicate tracery of hummingbirds. "Well, let me tell you something. I never want to paint another hummingbird as long as I live. You won't believe what a lot of work they were. But I must admit they look good. Real good."

"They're wonderful," I told her. "We can never thank you enough."

"Well, honeychild," Luiza announced, "we all have a lot to celebrate—the house nearly finished, Rosana off to the States, and now the new county. Julia was in Belo Horizonte last week and read something about it in the paper. The article said there were five hundred–something counties in Minas already, and now there's yet another. In a tiny little place called Rosário da Limeira that nobody's ever heard of."

John the Baptist grinned. "They may never have heard of us, but they will, you'll see. And the great thing is, we managed to elect Edson."

"Yes, I must congratulate you folks on that," said Luiza. "Just imagine if you'd got Bertoni."

"It was a close thing," said John the Baptist. "He went around buying a lot of votes."

"João Larino, for one," said the helper.

"Do I know him?" Luiza asked.

"João Red Face," I whispered. "The one who goes very odd when the moon is full."

"Oh, him!" Luiza said. "Wait a minute, I thought he was in the hospital?"

"He was. And it's quite a story. You remember he suffered from ill health?"

"Seasonal, wasn't it?" Luiza's eyes twinkled.

"Yes, well. He had a major breakdown and they sent him to the hospital in Itaperuna. Kept him doped up, and he got so bored he started smoking heavily. He'd always been on the heavy side, and the doctor told him he'd better cut it out, otherwise he'd have a heart attack. So he stopped, but then he got steadily worse. Finally he made up his mind he was dying, and one of the nurses took pity on him and sneaked him a pack of cigarettes. Thought he might as well die happy. And the most amazing thing happened. He made a complete recovery, and now he's home. Bertoni gave him some cement to build a new bathroom, so of course he voted for him. Went round telling everybody."

"That's funny!" laughed Luiza. "And is he still on the cigarettes?"

"Smokes like a chimney," said John the Baptist.

"There you are." Luiza pulled out a pack and lit up. "I always knew they were good for you."

* * *

I must say I think the new house is going to be fantastic," said Rosana as we sat around the table that evening over supper.

"I agree," said Luiza. "I just love Robin's design. It manages to be spacious and cozy at the same time. And the views are terrific."

"I'm not responsible for the views," Robin smiled, "but I'm glad you like the design."

"Now tell me your plans for the *fazenda*," Rosana said. "I shall want to know everything when I'm away. Particularly about the cows."

"We'll keep you in the loop, don't worry," Robin assured her. "After all, you taught us everything we know."

"Tell you what I think," said Rosana. "I think you should buy the piece of land between Iracambi and Graminha. Drain the swamp there and plant it up with maize and sorghum. Then you can produce your own feed."

"Funny you should say that. We have our eye on that piece of land already. It's a bit complicated because the owner just died and it's been inherited by her four kids. Naturally they're all squabbling over the inheritance."

"Who was the owner?"

"Silvério's wife. Remember how she kicked him out when he took up with another woman? Seems she changed her mind. Said she just couldn't get on without him. Said they'd been together almost fifty years, and invited him to move back in."

"And did he?"

"That's what I don't know. Next thing I heard she was dead."

"Murdered?" Luiza raised an eyebrow.

"Heart attack, I heard. But you know how complicated the inheritance laws are in Brazil. The estate will be divided among her kids, and the whole thing could take years."

"Oh, dear!" laughed Rosana. "And how is the forestry going?"

"The eucalyptus is going fine. Transport's a problem on those steep slopes and we've had to use the donkey to carry the seedlings. But all this rain is great for planting trees."

"I tell you who's been really helpful over the native species, and that's Gabetto." I turned to Rosana.

"Nice young man," commented Luiza. "Pity he speaks so fast. I can't understand what he's saying half the time."

"If it's any consolation, I can't either!" Rosana smiled. "But I do think your forestry work is important. Even though I'm a cattle person through and through."

"I entirely agree." Luiza lit a cigarette and pulled her chair up to the fire. "But the most important thing is your work with the people. You think you're planting trees and raising cows and fish and all that, but what you're really doing is raising people. And if you raise people, they'll raise the cattle and the trees."

Wow, I thought. She's right there.

I woke in the early hours with the moonlight shining full on my face. The frogs were singing in the pond, a barn owl was screeching somewhere nearby, and a little wind was rustling the leaves of the gourd tree. It was a warm night, but I felt a sudden chill and pulled the sheet around me. My head was whirling with thoughts about raising people. Robin and I had talked about it many a time. I remembered standing on the veranda three years earlier and wondering whether I was going to find myself on some crazy mission, and whether we were making a terrible mistake. Since then I'd seen for myself how hard it was to live with bad roads, bad schools, and bad health care, but I'd been exasperated by the fact that our neighbors did so little for themselves. If the bridge was washed away, they complained about it and waited for the prefect to repair it. If the schoolteacher was transferred, they kept their children home. If something went wrong, they left it for someone else to fix. It saved a lot of effort and provided plenty of opportunity for having a good grumble.

But things were beginning to change. We'd lobbied hard to create a new county and we'd succeeded. We'd elected an honest prefect. But we couldn't just sit back. It was up to us to make sure he delivered on his promises. I turned over and drifted back to sleep.

I raised the subject the next morning over breakfast, as we sat in the sunshine. Luiza, who refused to eat anything before lunch, was sitting in the rocking chair enjoying the first cigarette of the day.

"I've been thinking about this business of raising people," I began. "And I'm convinced that the fundamental problem is lack of self-confidence."

"I agree," Rosana said. "It's largely due to paternalism. Being treated like children."

"Slavery," added Luiza. "That attitude takes years to eradicate. You can see the exact same thing in the Deep South even today. A combination of fatalism and apathy."

"It's the same across the world." Robin poured himself another mug of coffee. "I've seen it in villages in Africa and Asia, and even southern Europe. It's almost like people don't expect things to get better. But I do see changes here. Take Albertinho. Nobody ever used to pay him any attention. They used to refer to him as 'that Indian.' Okay, he can be a little difficult sometimes. But he's come on a lot and he's a genius at fixing things."

"Valdeci has done well, too," said Rosana. "He used to be so shy he could hardly look you in the eye. And now he's been to a university!"

"Don't forget the women," Luiza added. "Employing women like you do, that's a real first."

Rosana smiled. "You guys are probably the only people within a hundred miles to treat your farm staff so well."

"We haven't got it quite right yet," I told her. "We pay a decent salary and all sorts of benefits, but people go on expecting us to solve their problems."

"Well, you're still learning," said Luiza. "And you probably can't see how things have changed—you're too close to it. But even in the short time I've known you I can see the difference you're making. Just being here and opening doors for them. Creating opportunities. And speaking of that, there's something I want to discuss tonight. Something important. I'll just get my thoughts together and we'll talk about it over supper, okay?"

After breakfast Robin disappeared down to the dairy with Rosana, Luiza set herself up at the kitchen table with several large sheets of paper, and I took myself off on a horse for some thinking time. There was something about the gentle rhythm of horseback riding that cleared my head and soothed my spirit. The group that assembled in the kitchen that evening was happily tired and sunburned—except for Luiza, who preserved her creamy white skin by never going out into the sunshine. I whipped up a Spanish omelet, Robin dressed the salad, Rosana mixed limes and sugar with *cachaça,* and we settled ourselves around the kitchen table.

"It's about raising people," Luiza began. "And I think we should seize the moment, now that there's a new county."

Looking at each of us to make sure she had our full attention, Luiza laid out her plans for our future. We had spent a lot of time and effort planting trees, she reminded us. And although *we* knew it was a good thing, our neighbors didn't. Furthermore, if we couldn't change people's attitudes, one day all those trees would be cut down. The question was: Where next?

We looked at her expectantly and Luiza smiled. "Well," she said, "I've jotted down a few thoughts to share with you." She produced a large sheet of paper covered in her neat handwriting. The title read:

Iracambi Forest Angels

SAVING FORESTS, CHANGING LIVES

"Good title!" I exclaimed.

"I'm glad you like it."

She proceeded to explain, starting with the headings.

The first heading was "Environment." It was vital that we work with the schoolkids, and here was one way we might do it. Why not take advantage of all the wonderful forest on Iracambi by making a nature trail and taking the kids out on adventures in the forest? Get them to look at the bromeliads, splash around in the river, learn how to call the birds, that sort of thing. Get them really fired up, and raise a new generation of conservationists.

Robin nodded, and Luiza smiled.

Her next heading was "The State Park." Now that the money had come through, people needed to understand what the park was all about. We had to show them that the forest was bringing them lots of benefits already, and could bring them still more. Eco-tourism, for example. The state park might seem awfully far away, but Itajuru was right in our backyard, and she'd bet that Edson was interested in setting up a conservation area in the county.

"You're right," said Robin. "He's already talking about it."

"Just as I thought."

Her third heading was "Education": the most important one of all. Of course the schools would improve with the new county funding. But education wasn't only for kids. We needed to reach the adults. And one of the best ways to do that was by heading number four: "Community Radio." We could start with a list of "Did You Know" facts, and get a thirty-second spot on the radio.

For example:

DID YOU KNOW THAT FLEAS JUMP 150 TIMES THEIR LENGTH? If you could do the same you would jump three hundred meters!

DID YOU KNOW THAT WHEN SNAKES FLICK THEIR TONGUES THEY ARE USING THEM TO SMELL? Can you smell with your tongue?

DID YOU KNOW THAT *EMBAUBA* TREES PRODUCE A SWEET NECTAR THAT ATTRACTS ANTS, WHICH THEN ATTACK ANYTHING THAT COMES NEAR THE TREE?

"I've got one," said Rosana. "Did you know that some plants heat up their leaves at night to release the scent that attracts night pollinators like bats?"

"No, I didn't, but that's the sort of thing I mean." Luiza paused and lit a cigarette.

"Go on, Luiza. This is interesting."

"The next heading is more like a question. It's 'Where?' And I'm thinking of a place. Sort of like a clubhouse. Needs to have enough space for the kids to fit inside, and it needs to be near the forest."

"How about this house?" I suggested. "After we move out, I mean."

"I've got a better idea," said Robin. "The old farmhouse on Fazenda Graminha."

I'd always liked that house. It was solidly built with wonderful hardwood beams, and I'd once suggested to Robin that we move in ourselves, but he said it was too far away.

"Perfect!" said Luiza. "We could fix it up and turn it into an environmental center. Make a little classroom and cut a nature trail through the forest just behind it, invite the kids over and give them the time of their lives."

"Would their parents let them come?" asked Robin, ever practical.

"We'd have to work through the schools. But the first thing is to find a student to help out. There are plenty of young people burning to help save the rainforest—high school kids, university students, that sort of thing."

Rosana had been sitting quietly listening. "We could get students from the University of Viçosa," she offered. "Everyone there has to do an internship."

"Exactly." Luiza nodded. "And I just met an exchange student in Muriaé. She comes from Canada and told me she wants to teach school later on. I'm sure she'd be interested."

I had a flashback to Dorothee sitting under the gourd tree three years earlier. What was it she'd said? Something about people beating a path to our door.

"It's exactly the sort of thing that's missing round here," Robin said. "I worked once with a theater group in Malawi that went round the villages putting on sketches about water or trees, or burning the garbage. People loved it and it was a great way to spread the message."

"Remember that band of clowns from the Amazon that was performing at the Earth Summit?" I turned to him. "I think they were called Health and Happiness. They used to go round by boat doing circus performances in the villages along the river. Got everyone to join in and then the clowns acted out giving vaccinations.

People had such a good time they didn't mind when they started the vaccination campaign for real."

Robin nodded. "One of the things that I always remember was our friend Rudy from Sri Lanka," he said. "Rudy's a big shot in the Smithsonian these days, but when he was a student he founded a small environmental club in one of the schools. Years later, when he was back in Colombo, he saw a big demonstration of schoolkids protesting against a hydroelectric dam that was going to flood a large area of forest. He was so impressed that he started talking to them, and then he realized it was a national movement that had grown out of the club he'd founded all those years before."

"That's exactly what I mean," Luiza told him. "Start small and who knows where it will lead? The first step is to fix up the house. That won't take much."

"It doesn't have a bathroom," Robin pointed out.

"Most houses don't," laughed Luiza. "I didn't have one myself when I was a child in Arkansas. But that's easily solved. Let me tell you, if I was ten years younger I'd move up there myself. And if I was twenty years younger I'd paint up a sign saying IRACAMBI FOREST ANGELS and run it myself."

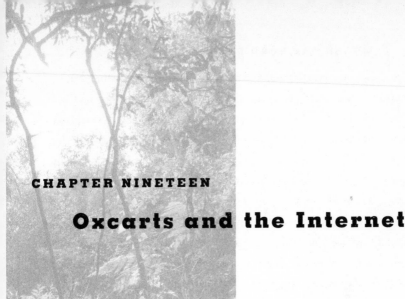

CHAPTER NINETEEN

Oxcarts and the Internet

Six months later the new house was finally ready. Luiza joined us for the opening ceremony, cutting a scarlet ribbon and opening a bottle of champagne, and afterward we sat contentedly on the front veranda looking out over the valley.

"Here's to the pair of you." Luiza raised her glass. "I know you'll be very happy here. It's the most wonderful house."

We'd started our married life in a tiny wooden cabin on a tea estate in Kenya. Robin's boss had installed a covered walkway from the outside kitchen in my honor, but we weren't there long before we discovered that one of the walls had been completely eaten by termites, and we had to move out. Since then we'd lived in a small apartment in London owned by a family from Bangladesh and always smelling of curry, a Quonset hut in the American Midwest where we'd shivered through the frigid winters and broiled through the torrid summers, and a large empty house in the Jakarta suburbs where the elaborate marble guest wing had collapsed. We'd spent a few months in a damp cottage in the south of England with a temperamental washing machine that refused to wash the children's diapers, and several years in a five-story house in central London, filled with a strange assortment of lodgers. One of our favorites had been a converted farmhouse in the Virginia woods, where we'd woken up one Christmas Day to find all the pipes frozen hard, and had taken an ax to the ice on the creek in order to get water. Another had been our beachfront house in Recife, where something had gone drastically wrong with the electrical wiring and we discovered that all the walls were live.

And now we were three and a half years into the Brazilian adventure, and Robin had built his dream house. I remembered Jair asking us if we were going to stay long—and I still didn't know the answer. But somehow it didn't matter.

In some ways these past years had been the most challenging of my life. But they certainly hadn't been dull, and the pace of change had been astonishing, particularly over the previous year. There was a new spirit abroad in Limeira as Edson set out to install drains and piped water, place shiny new garbage bins on every corner, and refurbish the schools. A bevy of smartly uniformed health agents, headed by a sister of John the Baptist, visited every house in the county, taking the first-ever family-health survey. They arrived at the *fazenda* by motorbike and took us through a long checklist, which looked like this:

NAME

AGE

PROFESSION

SCHOOLING

HEALTH HISTORY

A special section for people over fifty detailed a variety of potential health problems ranging from uterine prolapse to high blood pressure, from varicose veins to gallbladder problems, various cancers, heart trouble, and senility, and our teenage health agents were clearly disappointed when we told them that we suffered from none of the above.

Another dramatic improvement was in the schools. Previously, the farm children had walked two or three miles over the mountain roads, to either São Pedro or Graminha. The teachers, known as aunties, had done their best despite the lack of the most basic equipment, and the main attraction for the poorer families had been the school lunches—if there was money in the budget for food. Since the founding of the new county, the children were collected in a Toyota pickup with a bright orange tarpaulin rigged over the back. They were taken to Limeira, where they had access to grades five through twelve and got free meals every day.

The newly privatized phone company improved its service beyond recognition, and installed four additional public phones. A series of local committees were formed to discuss the needs of each community, and Robin volunteered to accompany county staff as they visited even the most remote farms to draw up a list of their needs. Meanwhile, in the village, several new stores opened for business, a forest of television antennae bore witness to growing prosperity, and people started buying washing machines and motorbikes. The town even posted a notice forbidding horses from being tied in the main square.

"That's because of the dung," Robin explained. "They're talking of paving the streets, and they want to keep them clean. They've made a horse park round the back near the butcher's."

"Paving the streets?" I exclaimed in surprise. "What they ought to do is pave the road."

"Well, I have news for you," said Robin. "They're going to do that, too."

"You don't say?" Luiza said incredulously when she heard. "They've been talking about that as long as I've been here. Election promises that never come to anything."

"Edson's been to Belo Horizonte to meet with the governor," Robin told her, "and he promised to do the little road off the highway as well. Something to do with a federal law that guarantees access to every county capital."

"All the way to Limeira?" Luiza laughed. "This is beginning to sound positively suburban."

T he sun was setting behind Graminha peak that evening when we heard the sound of a car. It wasn't a VW Beetle, and it wasn't a Toyota, so we figured it must be one of fleet of small cars belonging to the county. Leaving Luiza to tend to the woodburner, I headed out onto the back veranda just as Edson drew up.

"Hey, Edson, how are you? Come on in."

Edson carefully wiped his shoes on the mat and stepped into the kitchen.

"Good evening, Edson, and what can we do for you?" Robin swung in from the courtyard.

"A couple of quick things. The first is about environmental education."

We looked at one another and laughed.

"What's so funny?"

"Nothing, nothing at all. It's just a coincidence. It's something we've been thinking about ourselves. We're planning to cut a trail through the forest and invite some of the schoolchildren over for an adventure. We've got a couple of high school kids from Muriaé who are willing to help out."

"I was just thinking of something in the classroom," Edson admitted. "But this sounds far better. And I could make the school bus available to bring them out. We might have to fix up the road a bit, but that's easily done. What I want to do is make them excited about nature instead of scared of it."

"Create a little club for the kids that are interested, something like the Boy Scouts," Luiza told him. "We could do a couple of trial visits now, and then something a bit more permanent when school starts in February."

"Okay, let's do it. Oh, and there's one other thing. I need some technical advice. About e-mail."

"How very up-to-date you are." Luiza smiled. "I didn't know you knew about such things, Edson."

"I don't. But I'm willing to learn."

"Good for you. I'm too old myself."

"Never, Luiza!" I said loyally.

"You can't believe what a lot of correspondence I have to look at," Edson told us. "And I haven't been able to find a very good secretary. I thought it would be quicker and easier with e-mail. And farther down the line we might even set up a Web site. That would be cool, wouldn't it?"

"Well, if you're going to take the plunge, you've chosen exactly the right time," Robin told him. "There's an e-mail provider just set up in Muriaé. We've been using one in Rio, but it was very expensive and we had to send our messages late at night when the calls were cheap. With a provider in Muriaé it's just a local call. I'll be happy to explain it to you anytime you like."

"Thanks so much." Edson smiled. "And now I'd better be off. I'm late already."

"Don't forget the barbecue on Saturday," I reminded him.

That evening we held a farm meeting in the kitchen. There was a lively discussion about new developments in the county.

"I didn't really follow what was going on," said Luiza after the meeting, during which she had sat in the rocker placidly reading a murder mystery. "But it sounded like a good meeting."

"Remember how it used to be?" I laughed. "Nobody opened their mouths. Now they never stop talking."

"It's to do with people raising." Luiza smiled.

"It's partly to do with the county," Robin said. "People saw they could actually do something instead of sitting back and complaining. There's more employment and more money, and now the currency has stabilized, the standard of living has improved noticeably. People are eating better and they're better dressed."

"I've noticed that." Luiza replied. "That girl, what's her name, the wife of João up on Graminha?"

"You mean Neusa?"

"That's right, Neusa. The one that used to go around dressed in rags. She's looking very neat and tidy these days."

"That's thanks to Julia and the sewing class," I told her. "People are looking after themselves more. Remember what terrible teeth they used to have? All that sugarcane, I suppose. Well, these days they're getting toothbrushes and they're even getting false teeth. They've got more self-respect."

"Horizons are getting wider," said Robin. "One of Adão's sons has bought a motorbike and he's courting a girl who lives on the other side of the mountain. Until recently you couldn't get to the other side of the mountain. Nowadays they can even talk to each other on the public phone."

"Murilo's bar is selling telephone cards," I added. "And of course the big revolution is our connection to the Internet."

"I don't really understand what the Internet is," said Luiza plaintively.

"Well, Luiza," said Robin. "Think of it as some great big library. Like the Library of Congress, for example. Anyone with a computer and a connection can access it, and find any sort of information they want."

"I can understand that bit. But what I can't understand is, where *is* it?"

"It's everywhere. It's a way of linking all the computers in the world. So everyone can have access to everyone else."

Luiza closed her eyes and tried to picture it. "I'm still not very clear about it. But it sounds like a perfectly marvelous idea. I think, though, that I'm going to have to leave it to you children. I'm still stuck in the horse-and-buggy age myself."

"That's the beauty of it," I told her. "Here we are in the horse-and-buggy age, and we've got access to all the information in the world. We haven't got a paved road but we're on the information superhighway. We've got no tractor and we still use oxen. But hey, we're on the Net. Oxcarts and the Internet."

Under Luiza's direction, we had chosen the date for the housewarming party, and there was no lack of volunteers to help with the preparations. Valdeci had selected a steer for slaughter, and one of João Red Face's sons had been drafted to prepare the barbecue. Several of the women had offered to help with the cooking: mountains of rice, beans, vinaigrette salad, and roasted manioc flour, with lemonade and Coca-Cola to drink. Fia had borrowed the cooking pots from the Graminha school, and Marinha had volunteered to round up plates, glasses, and cutlery. Luiza had gone home for a few days and promised to return with a large batch of her famous cookies. Lenin's wife was bringing cheese bread, and both Gabetto and Julia had offered us some of their home-brewed *cachaça*. I filled the house with flowers, enlisted some of the children to blow up balloons, cleared a space along the fence for tethering horses, and found some tapes of Brazilian country music.

Albertinho had dug a barbecue pit and run a light outside so the cooks could see what they were doing. The evening star was rising and the smell of roasting meat was wafting through the air as the first guests arrived. A pony cart trotted up the hill and out lumbered João Red Face, looking none the worse for his adventures. Adão and Orisa walked over from next door, together with Zé Viricius and his brother. Jair cantered up on his mule, and Cassilda came on her feet. Albertinho swung up the drive whistling, with Doggie at his heels, followed by Sandra—looking suddenly a young lady in a short skirt and a tight blouse. Valdeci's little girls shepherded their younger brother up the hill, three-year-old Viviane came in the arms of Grandfather Olavo, and John the Baptist brought his pretty wife on the back of a brand-new motorbike.

Inside the house, Fia was presiding over the food, with the help of several family members, notably Dona Maria, who was wearing a new pair of glasses with pink plastic frames. Ailton was handing around the soft drinks, while Gabetto was focusing on his home brew. At first sip it felt raw on the throat, but was followed by an agreeable sensation of well-being, which insulated one from the cares of the world.

Lenin and Ircema were ensconced on one of the sofas, chatting to Edson and his girlish wife.

"Any news of Rosana?" I asked as I passed.

"She wrote from San Francisco," Ircema told me. "Seems to be doing fine, despite everything."

"I wasn't opposed to it." Lenin shook his head. "After all, I've worked in the airlines myself. Does you good to have a change of scene, and she's not afraid of hard work, that one. Earning good money babysitting, so she says."

Luiza swept into the room wearing a brilliantly painted caftan, accompanied by a young girl with long blond hair. "Are you talking about Rosana? I always knew she'd be fine. She'll go far, that girl. And, speaking of going far, let me introduce you to Tara. She's here from Canada on a high school exchange program, and I'm trying to talk her into helping us with the schoolkids."

"You are welcome in my country," said Lenin in impeccable English. "It is a pleasure for us to have you. And now," he switched to Portuguese, "I would like to propose a toast to our hosts, Robin and Binka. In honor of the occasion I have written a short poem."

Lenin positioned himself in front of the grand piano, pulled out his glasses, retrieved a sheet of paper from his pocket, and began to declaim. It was a lengthy poem in flowery Portuguese with frequent references to the gallant people of Brazil who had braved the perils of the ocean to found their great country. He spoke of the mighty forests, the sparkling waters, the Southern Cross in the night sky, and the land blessed by God. It was written in a high literary style unfamiliar to most of our guests, but they listened respectfully and there was a ripple of applause when he finished.

"Thank you very much, that was beautiful." Robin bowed in Lenin's direction. "And now I'd like to welcome you all to the new house, and thank you for coming. We have some very special people here this evening. First, John the Baptist, who worked on this house over a period of three years. Without him none of us would be standing here tonight. Congratulations, João, you've built a masterpiece. Thank you to Albertinho, Antonio, João, and all the people who dug foundations, mixed cement, and moved hundreds of tons of earth. Thank you, Luiza, for painting the hummingbird tiles on the walls. And, last, thank you, Bianca, for putting up with all of this and for running the *fazenda* when I was away. Thank you all for your part in making this house a reality. And now, if you'll take your plates, dinner is ready."

I put on the music, a nostalgic song about white wings over the drylands that was soon drowned out by the rattle of cutlery and the buzz of conversation. Jair edged his way over to Robin. "Took you long enough to get this house finished, didn't it?" He grinned.

"Good things take time," Robin answered, unruffled.

"Yes, well, it's very large," Jair continued. "Going to be quite a job keeping it warm in winter, I'd say."

"It'll be very windy up here," Cassilda darted up to join him.

"That's right," I told her. "We get lots of wind and lots of sunshine. We love it."

The party wound on, and when every scrap of food was gone, and everyone had walked through the house, our guests started to take their leave. Ircema pressed a small package into my hands. "A little housewarming present," she said. "I hope you'll be very happy here, and I only wish you lived a little closer."

Lenin enfolded me in his arms. "Seems like yesterday that you brought the family down from Recife," he said. "And we never dreamed you'd actually come here to live. I remember saying to Ircema—"

"Never mind," Ircema interrupted. "The important thing is that you stuck it out. You've built up the farm, you've got this wonderful house, and you've put Limeira on the map. I can't wait to see what you do next. Come on, Lenin, it's time to go."

One by one our guests harnessed up their horses and trotted off into the starry night. Old Olavo departed with a large bunch of balloons, Orisa wrapped her youngest grandchild securely against the evening chill, and João Red Face made his way unsteadily down the steps to his pony cart. "G-good night," said Zé Viricius as he set off briskly up the hill. "G-good party, thank you."

"I'll be off now, honeychild." Luiza hugged us both, one after the other. "After all this excitement it's time for a little rest. See you soon."

Albertinho dismantled the light by the barbecue and swung off whistling down the drive. Valdeci's little girls helped Fia stack the dishes and glasses and mop the floor. "Thanks so much," I told them, handing them Luiza's last few cookies. "Thank *you*," they said with shining eyes, as they hurried off home.

"That was great," I said to Robin as we sank down on the swing chair with glasses of Scotch. The field below the house was alive with fireflies, and the mountains were sharply defined against the starry sky. "I can't believe this is our sixth year! Do you realize we've been here longer than any other place in the whole of our married life?"

"That's right." Robin nodded.

"Remember our first night in the blue house, and how cold it was? You insisted on sleeping with the shutters open and I woke up with my sleeping bag all wet."

"That was nothing to do with the shutters, silly, it was the roof leaking."

"It never got properly fixed, either. Those tiles are all very well but they don't keep the rain out. And talking about rain, I never realized just how much it rains in rainforests. All that mildew in the bathroom. Ugh!"

"What's a little mildew among friends? There's a lot worse than that."

"You can say that again! The time you got hit by the cow and they were talking about brain surgery. The time you got shot, for God's sake. It's just as well I wasn't there at the time. I'd have freaked out completely."

"Let me tell you one thing," said Robin. "If we'd stayed in Washington you'd never have learned how to run a farm. Or inseminate a cow."

"I'd never have had gunmen running round the place, either. And you'd never have got to build a house out of mud."

"Or plant a hundred thousand trees."

We smiled at one another. "So now," Robin turned to me, "do you reckon you'll stay?"

"I might," I told him. "If you make it worth my while."

We sat in silence looking out over the valley. The moon slipped up from behind the mountain and lit the fishponds, and for a moment there was no sound except the creaking of the swing seat.

"What's that?" said Robin, a moment later. "Sounds like a horse. It is a horse! Looks like it's Jair. What do you suppose he's forgotten?"

Jair came galloping up the drive, vaulted off his mule, and ran up the steps. "I thought you ought to know," he announced breathlessly. "The milk truck has just fallen through the bridge."

"The milk truck? What's it doing here at this time of night?"

"Coming to the party," Jair explained. "Gone right through the planks and I've no idea how you're going to get him out."

"Oh my Lord, is the driver okay?"

"He's fine," said Jair. "But it's going to be the devil of a job to get the truck out. I reckon you'll need a tractor, and that'll cost you a pretty penny."

"Okay, Jair," sighed Robin. "We'll come down and see. Although there's probably not much we can do about it at this time of night."

Jair mounted his mule and trotted briskly off, and Robin took his flashlight and disappeared into the shed in search of a heavy chain. I was just reflecting that if I'd stayed in Washington I wouldn't be pulling trucks out of the river in the middle of the night when Albertinho came up the drive, whistling.

"So, Albertinho, what's the story?" I asked. "Do you reckon we can get him out?"

Albertinho stroked his mustache. "Maybe," he said. "But we're going to need the oxen, and the problem is that one of them has hurt its foot. I don't like to leave the truck there all night. Nobody can get past."

"The driver's going to need someplace to sleep," I was thinking aloud.

"That's no problem, but what about that darned truck?"

"We'll leave it till morning." Robin reappeared carrying the chain. "Nobody will be coming through at this time of night."

"Right." I nodded. "They'll all be in bed by now. After all, Iracambi is where the road ends."

Albertinho stared at me, and then his shoulders started to shake.

"Where the road ends?" he spluttered.

"That's right."

"That's a good one!" he told us.

"God's truth," I assured him.

There was a pause, and then Albertinho burst into a glorious laugh. "You're right," he said, the tears streaming down his cheeks. "Where the road ends. *Ah eh.*"